WORKS ISSUED BY
THE HAKLUYT SOCIETY

Series Editors
Gloria Clifton
Joyce Lorimer

SPANISH AND PORTUGUESE CONFLICT
IN THE SPICE ISLANDS
THE LOAYSA EXPEDITION TO THE MOLUCCAS 1525–1535.
FROM BOOK XX OF
THE GENERAL AND NATURAL HISTORY OF THE INDIES
BY
GONZALO FERNÁNDEZ DE OVIEDO Y VALDÉS

THIRD SERIES
NO. 38

INTERNATIONAL REPRESENTATIVES OF THE HAKLUYT SOCIETY

SPANISH AND PORTUGUESE CONFLICT IN THE SPICE ISLANDS

THE LOAYSA EXPEDITION
TO THE MOLUCCAS 1525–1535.

FROM BOOK XX OF

THE GENERAL AND NATURAL HISTORY

OF THE INDIES

BY

GONZALO FERNÁNDEZ DE OVIEDO Y VALDÉS

Edited by
GLEN F. DILLE

Published by
Routledge
for
THE HAKLUYT SOCIETY
LONDON
2021

First published 2021 for the Hakluyt Society by
Routledge
2 Park Square, Milton Park, Abingdon, Oxon OX14 4RN

and by Routledge
711 Third Avenue, New York, NY 10017
Routledge is an imprint of the Taylor & Francis Group, an Informa business

British Library Cataloguing in Publication Data
A catalogue record for this book is available from the British Library

Library of Congress Cataloguing in Publication Data
Names: Fernandez de Oviedo y Valdés, Gonzalo, 1478–1557, author. | Dille, Glen F., 1940– editor. | Hakluyt Society, issuing body.
Title: Spanish and Portuguese conflict in the Spice Islands : the Loaysa Expedition to the Moluccas 1525–1535 : from Book XX of the general and natural history of the Indies / by Gonzalo Fernández de Oviedo y Valdés ; editor, Glenn F. Dille.
Other titles: Historia general y natural de las Indias. Libro 20. Selections. English. | Loaysa Expedition to the Moluccas 1525–1535
Description: Abingdon, Oxon ; New York, NY : Routledge, [2021] | Series: Hakluyt Society, third series ; No. 30 | Includes bibliographical references and index.
Identifiers: LCCN 2020045783 (print) | LCCN 2020045784 (ebook)
Subjects: LCSH: Jofre de Loaisa, Garcia, –1526—Voyages and travels. | Maluku (Indonesia)—Discovery and exploration—Spanish. | Loaisa Expedition (1525)
Classification: LCC DS646.6 .F47 2021 (print) | LCC DS646.6 (ebook) | DDC 959.8/5015—dc23
LC record available at https://lccn.loc.gov/2020045783
LC ebook record available at https://lccn.loc.gov/2020045784

ISBN: 978-0-367-70075-1 (hbk)
ISBN: 978-1-003-14447-2 (ebk)

Typeset in Garamond Premier Pro
by Waveney Typesetters, Wymondham, Norfolk

Routledge website: www.routledge.com
Hakuyt Society website: www.hakluyt.com

CONTENTS

MAPS

PREFACE AND ACKNOWLEDGEMENTS

This volume has been brought to publication in unusual circumstances. Professor Glen Dille submitted a proposal to the Hakluyt Society in 2018 for an English translation and edition of Gonzalo Fernández de Oviedo y Valdés's account of Garciá Jofre de Loaisa's expedition to the Moluccas, 1525–35. This went through the regular process of assessment and consideration, which involves the submission of specimen sections and consultation with specialist readers. The process can be fairly prolonged, as we await reports from busy scholars, responses from the intending editor, and discussions at meetings of the Society's Council. The outcome was that Council agreed that Professor Dille's proposal should be accepted and several communications were sent to him to that effect, which elicited no reply. On further inquiries I discovered the sad news that Professor Dille had passed away in March 2019.

At this stage Professor Dille had been asked to submit only specimens of the work, as well as the usual requirements of an outline of the whole and an account of the significance of the primary text. The reports had been favourable and the Society wanted to proceed. There was no doubt that Professor Dille's ambition had been to publish his translation with the Society, which in turn was keen to move forward but did not have a full manuscript, and nothing had been confirmed by contract.

With help from Professor's Dille's former department at Bradley University in Peoria, Illinois, we were able to make contact with his family. Professor Dille's daughter, Margaret Mazzullo, was pleased to hear from us and gratified by the thought that her father's work might yet be published as a fitting memorial. She has been exceptionally helpful in searching his papers and computer files. She was able to provide us with the complete manuscript that her father had produced. We received the Introduction to and translation of Oviedo's text, with references and a bibliography. She also generously answered all our enquiries, and deserves our warmest thanks. Thanks are due also to Professor Dille's executor for granting the Society the publication rights and transfer of copyright that has allowed us to proceed. Every effort has been made to trace and contact any other copyright holders prior to publication. If notified, all reasonable efforts will be made to rectify any errors or omissions.

We placed all the material in the hands of one of our Series Editors, Professor Joyce Lorimer, who herself works with Spanish and Portuguese materials of that period. Professor Dille had modestly acknowledged in his proposal that his experience had been more that of a linguist than a historian, and that his footnotes could be expanded. Professor Lorimer has edited and in places augmented the historical information in the Introduction and footnotes and Bibliography to update them in line with recent historical and anthropological studies, and produced draft maps for production by the Hakluyt Society's usual cartographer. This kind of task is customary for Hakluyt Society Series Editors, but it is a more demanding one when the volume editor cannot be consulted for an opinion or asked to augment or extend the work as needed. We owe Professor Lorimer a debt of gratitude for a volume that sits comfortably in the editorial traditions of the Hakluyt Society.

It is a source of satisfaction to everyone involved to have helped bring to publication a distinguished scholarly translation and edition that could easily have been lost, and to have brought to fruition a worthy ambition of the late Glen Dille.

This volume is published with the assistance of the American Friends of the Hakluyt Society.

JIM BENNETT

ABBREVIATIONS

AGI	Archivo General de las Indias, Sevilla
BAE	*Biblioteca de Autores Españoles*
F.	Folio
L.	*Legajo*
lib.	*libro*
N.	*Número*
NOED	*New Oxford English Dictionary*
R.	*Ramo*

NOTE ON SHIPS AND SHIPPING, MEASURES, WEIGHTS, AND CAPACITY

Ships and Shipping

Naturally, in Oviedo's narrative there is a good deal of vocabulary concerning various types of ships in use in European explorations and those found in South East Asian waters. The ships' characteristics varied widely from time to time and from country to country. 'Spanish Shipbuilding and the Contract of Martín de Arana', in Carla Rahn Phillips's *Six Galleons for the King of Spain*, is an indispensable source as is the bibliography.[1] Phillips's translation also makes available Pablo E. Pérez-Mallaína's important study, *Spain's Men of the Sea: Daily Life on the Indies Fleets in the Sixteenth Century*. In the several appendices to his work, Tim Joyner's *Magellan* provides important details on ships of the time with useful illustrations, shipboard routines, details about participants, and other information. Two other useful reference works are *The Oxford Companion to Ships and the Sea* and Julián Amich's *Diccionario Marítimo*. Although available only in Spanish, see the exhaustively researched work on ships and shipping of the time, *Sevilla y las flotas de Indias: La Gran Armada de Castilla del Oro (1513–1514)*, by María del Carmen Mena García.

batel A skiff, longboat or ship's boat propelled by oars. The skiff was either stored aboard a larger ship or else frequently towed. For the Loaysa armada, the loss of their skiffs during the stormy passage through the Strait and in the Pacific was cause for considerable concern as they were vital to ferry men and goods back and forth from a ship at anchor to the shore.

carabela A caravel. A ship with a lower forecastle than the aftcastle, described as being 'generally a long, narrow, and agile ship, useful for coastal exploration and liaison duty'.[2] Early versions were rather small but later designs were full-rigged with an increased capacity. Columbus preferred the caravel which, though smaller than the *nao*, was easier to handle.

fusta A quarter galley and an armed vessel similar to the pinnace and the caravel ships used by the Spanish and the Portuguese in the narrative of the Loaysa expedition with sail and oars.[3] Morison calls these ships triremes or galiots.[4] This is one of the most frequently mentioned types of vessel used by the Spanish and the Portuguese in the narrative of the Loaysa expedition.

[1] Phillips, *Six Galleons*, pp. 19–46.
[2] Ibid., p. 36.
[3] Amich, *Diccionario Marítimo*, p. 216.
[4] Morison, *European Discovery of America*: *Southern Voyages*, p. 488 (hereafter *Southern Voyages*).

galeón   A galleon. Phillips notes that the Spanish galleon of the earlier sixteenth century was a smaller ship, averaging 90 to 120 tons, and often carried oars as well as sails. By the time it had become 'the characteristic vessel of the Indies route' in the late sixteenth century, a typical galleon was 550 tons.[1] Confusingly, at the beginning of his history, Oviedo describes the *Santiago* as a galleon of fifty tons, but throughout the rest of the text, he refers to it as a 'pinnace'. Later, in at least one passage, he refers to the *Santiago* as a caravel.

junco   A junk. In the Celebes and Moluccas at the time of the Portuguese-Spanish presence the native islanders did not build large merchant vessels. The commerce in spices and other goods was carried by Chinese or Javanese junks to Malacca or to India. These junks could be very large indeed, dwarfing the European ships. During the period of the Chinese imperial treasure fleets (1405–33) under Admiral Zheng He, the largest junks reached about 400 feet long and 160 feet wide with ten masts. 'There were grand cabins for the imperial envoys and the windowed halls and ante-chambers were festooned with balconies and railings.'[2] By way of contrast Columbus's *Santa María* was 85 feet long. Later, by the time the Portuguese appeared on the scene the commercial junks were considerably smaller and no match for the European warships.

kora-kora (cora-cora)   A traditional Moluccan canoe, adapted by the Portuguese and Spanish and referred to as *coracora*. Low and narrow and usually about 10 metres long, it was flanked by bamboo outriggers which supported an upper bamboo platform which extended above the entire length.[3]

nao   Ship. Sometimes translated as cog or carrack, but also applied to other types of ocean-going vessels. As Jose Luis Casaban notes,[4] the term is often 'generically' applied to all the ocean-going vessels which were used in the two expeditions. This is a full-rigged (having both square and lateen sails), three-masted vessel with a high protruding forecastle, a high aft castle and a large cargo capacity. According to Oviedo, the *naos* of the Loaysa fleet were the *Santa María de la Victoria, Sancti Spiritus, Anunciada, San Gabriel, Santa María del Parral*, and the *San Lesmes*. However, Morison[5] classifies the *Parral* and the *Lesmes* as caravels, probably because they were both only rated at 80 tons.

nave   Ship. A generic name for ship, no longer in general use.

navío   A warship. Originally a general term applied to any vessel, but from the sixteenth to nineteenth century the term designated warships of 500 tons or more.

parao, prao, prau, proa   A local Moluccan boat, adapted by the Portuguese and Spanish and referred to as *paroles*. These were lateen-rigged canoes with outriggers. Oviedo describes them as light and fast vessels noting that the largest could be propelled by up to one hundred oarsmen with fighting men on a platform above them, and were also capable of carrying light armament.[6]

pataje, patax, pataxe   A pinnace or tender. Defined in The *Oxford Companion to Ships and the Sea*[7] as a small two-masted vessel of limited tonnage, normally square-rigged,

---

[1] Phillips, *Six Galleons*, pp. 19–46.
[2] Levathes, *When China Ruled the Seas*, pp. 77–81.
[3] Haddon, 'Outriggers of Indonesian Canoes', p. 117.
[4] Casaban, 'Outfitting and Sailing', p. 2.
[5] Morison, *Southern Voyages*, p. 478.
[6] Haddon, 'Outriggers of Indonesian canoes', p. 117; Casaban, 'Outfitting and Sailing', p. 3; see below, p. 3.
[7] *Oxford Companion to Ships*, p. 428.

carrying oars and sails. They were frequently used to carry messages between ships of the fleet, and often used to accompany early voyages of exploration because of their ability to navigate in shallow waters.

Measures

The measures of distance, weight and capacity found in Oviedo's text vary according to different sources. Not all have English equivalents.

legua League. This is the term Oviedo generally employs for distance and is generally understood as the equivalent of 3.5 miles. On a few occasions Oviedo uses the term *legua grande* (long or great league) which may be a *legua marítima* or sea league which the *Oxford Companion* reckons as 3.18 nautical miles of 6,080 feet, or 1,825 metres.[1]

braza Fathom. Slightly smaller than the English measure of 6 feet, the Spanish fathom is approximately 5.5 feet or 1.67 metres.

estadoa Measure based on a man's height; taken as about 7 feet.

vara Yard. About 33 inches. According to Phillips, the vara of 835 millimetres was equivalent to 3 *pies* or 4 *palmos* or 48 *dedos* or 40 *pulgadas*.[2]

codo Cubit. 22 inches or 565 millimetres, equivalent to 33 *dedos* or 27.5 *pulgadas*.[3]

pie Foot. 11 inches or 278 millimetres; divisible into 16 *dedos* or 12 *pulgadas*.[4]

palmo Palm span or hand. 8.2 inches or 209 millimetres; ¼ of a *vara*. equal to 9 *pulgadas*.[5]

pulgada 0.8 inches or 20.4 millimetres.[6]

dedo Finger's breadth. $\frac{1}{16}$ of a *pie*, 0.67 inches or 17 millimetres.[7]

Weights and Capacity

arroba A weight of approximately 25 pounds or 11.5 kilograms. As a liquid measure, the *arroba* varied from place to place but Phillips has it as the equivalent of 8 *azumbres*.[8]

azumbre 2.016 litres, approximately 4 pints.

bahar Oviedo has it at 203 *catiles*; Crofton at 200 *catties* or 662 pounds 8 ounces avoirdupois. Navarrete has it equal to 4 quintals or 400 pounds.[9] Villiers states that the *bahar* varied – in Banda 550 pounds, in the Moluccas 600 pounds, and in Malacca 530–40 pounds – and reports that the Portuguese generally

---

[1] Ibid., p. 313.
[2] Phillips, *Six Galleons*, p. 228.
[3] Ibid.
[4] Ibid.
[5] Ibid.
[6] Ibid.
[7] Ibid.
[8] Ibid.
[9] Crofton, *Pageant*, p. 64; Navarrete, *Colección de los Viajes,* vol. V, p. 474.

used 32 pounds of 16 ounces to the *arroba*, 4 *arrobas* to the *quintal* and 4 *quintales* to the *bahar*

cántara   16.33 litres, 8 *azumbres*.[1]

fanega   A dry measure of 55.5 litres, equivalent to about 1.5 bushels.

libra   Pound. 16 ounces, approximately 460.1 grams.

pipa   Pipe, cask, hogshead. A liquid measure of 27.5–30 *arrobas*.

quintal   100 pounds, 1 hundredweight.

tonel   Tun or ton, A measure of a ship's capacity. According to Phillips, the *tonel* was a measure more in use in Vizcaya, the space occupied by two containers of 30 *cántaras* each or 15 large quintals of 150 pounds.[2] The *tonel* was 1.2 times larger than the *tonelada*. Oviedo generally uses *tonel* to describe capacity in the Loaysa fleet, which was Vizcayan in origin.

tonelada   Tun or ton. Also a measure indicating ship's capacity more in use in Andalusia and the Indies trade; the space occupied by 2 *pipas* of 27.5 *arrobas* each.[3] Joyner holds that the proper capacity measure was the *tonelada* and was about 1 cubic metre.[4]

[1] Phillips, *Six Galleons*, p. 228.

[2] Ibid.

[3] Ibid.

[4] Joyner, Magellan, p. 319.

INTRODUCTION

Now part of the Republic of Indonesia, the Moluccas[1] form an island group in the Malay Archipelago north-east of Indonesia, lying between New Guinea and the Celebes. In the fifteenth and sixteenth centuries, the name Moluccas, or Maluco (as Oviedo referred to them), Spice Islands or Spicelands was generally applied by the Portuguese and Spaniards to Ternate, Tidore, Moti, Makian, Bachan and larger Gilolo.[2] D. F. Lach and E. J. Van Kley note that in order to 'avoid doing violence either to geography or history' it is important to recognize that other islands were 'intimately related economically, geographically, politically, or strategically to the trade and related ... [in] an interdependent economic complex' which included the Banda and Celebes groups and larger Sunda islands.[3] Clove (*Syzygium aromaticum*), was a commodity worth more than gold. The Banda Islands, were the sole source of mace and nutmeg (*Myristica fragrans*), spices even more valuable than clove. In the late fifteenth and early sixteenth centuries, the enormous profits to be made from these spices – together with pepper from Sumatra and the Malabar Coast of India, sandalwood and camphor from Borneo, cinnamon from India and Sri Lanka, and numerous other luxury products – lured the Portuguese and then the Spanish to hazard perilously long voyages.

1. The Spice Trade

a. Overview
The history of the spice trade is very long and complex. Spices imported from the Far East are well documented in the Old Testament, in Greek and Roman times, and in medieval texts. They were valued for enhancing flavour and preserving food, for cosmetic use, and particularly for their curative properties. The first authenticated reference to clove appears in Chinese Han dynasty records in the second half of the first millennium BC, where it is described as a spice obtained from the Philippines much prized for its aromatic and medicinal usages and as a condiment. In its westward journey, clove apparently came to Ceylon and India through the Malay Peninsula and is mentioned in the *Ramayana* (*c.*200 BCE). In Europe, the first description of clove is probably that of

---

[1] Now Maluku.

[2] Variants, Djailolo, Gilolo, Jilolo, and also called Batochino de Moro; now Halmahera. Spelled Gilolo by Oviedo which has been adopted here. Oviedo also noted that the indigenous name for the island was Aliora; see below, p. 131.

[3] Lach and Van Kley, *Asia in the Making*, III, p. 1300; Andaya, 'Los primeros contactos', pp. 63–6.

1

Pliny the Elder in his *Naturalis Historia* where he reports that clove was imported (in about 70 CE) because of its fragrance.[1]

The Moluccans themselves were not long-distance seafarers. Before the arrival of European traders their spices were transported by Persian, Malay or Gujarati traders to Malacca,[2] and thence on to Indian ports. Malacca was established as a city-state *c*.1400 by Prince Parameswara, who had been driven out of Palembang, Sumatra by the Javanese. Because of its strategic location – centred two thousand miles from India and two thousand miles from the Moluccas – and because it was under Chinese protection, Malacca quickly grew in importance.[3] From there, spices were sent on to eastern Mediterranean markets where the trade was controlled by Jewish and Levantine merchants, particularly those in Constantinople and Alexandria. Finally, clove as well as other exotic products were then dispersed throughout Europe, primarily through a Venetian monopoly. Naturally, all along the journey from the Spice Islands the prices of these commodities increased tremendously at each trans-shipment point. Charles Corn writes that 'The produce [spices] arrived … at exorbitant prices; a conservative estimate is that they rose in value 100 percent each time they changed hands, and this route required that they change hands hundreds of times'.[4] Although Venice's rival Genoa initially shared some of the trade, in time the Venetians came to control distribution in Europe and reaped huge profits that incited envy especially in the western maritime nations.

b.   Muslim Traders and the Spice Trade

After the birth of Islam in mid-seventh century Arabia, the religion spread rapidly throughout the eastern and southern Mediterranean lands and into the Iberian Peninsula in 711 CE. At about the same time, there was a similar wave of Muslim penetration along the eastern coast of Africa supplanting the earlier traders and creating powerful Islamic city-states such as Kilwa, Zanzibar, Mombassa, and Mogadishu that were actively involved in maritime commerce of the Indian Ocean. In the Arabian Peninsula, other important commercial ports such as Aden, Muscar, and Hormuz became Islamicized.

G. F. Hourani's work is an indispensable guide to the history of the seaborne commerce connecting Arabia with India and later with China. Hourani notes that, from the ninth century to the end of the fifteenth (when the Portuguese arrived), the Arabs remained the leading traders and mariners of the Indian Ocean, but that from 'Calicut and other

---

[1] Miller, *Spice Trade of the Roman Empire*, pp. 47–51, 58–60, includes an informative section on clove and nutmegs and notes that 'The Romans themselves were neither explorers nor traders', p. 277. Pliny uses a Greek word '*Caryophyllon*' (or *garyphyllon*) which some believe may refer to clove, Pliny, *Naturalis Historia*, Bk XII. Levathes, *When China Ruled the Seas*, is an informative source for China and the spice trade, particularly during the period 1405–33; see also Keay, *Spice Route*.

[2] Now Melaka.

[3] See Donkin, *Between East and West* for the spice trade before the arrival of Europeans. On Gujarati merchant seamen see Fernández-Armesto, *Civilization*, pp. 339–42. Recognizing Malacca's commercial value, the Portuguese, took control there in 1511, Levathes, *When China ruled the Seas*, pp. 107–11. Hall, 'Local and International Trade', pp. 252–3, notes that, although Melaka was the leading centre of Asian trade, it was merely an agreed upon 'market place' and that previous traders merely shifted to other ports in the Indian Ocean and South Asia.

[4] Corn, *Scents of Eden*, p. xxi; Keay, *Spice Route*, p. 201, notes a 35,000 per cent appreciation in the price of clove.

Malabar ports to China [the commerce] was made only in Chinese junks'.[1] By the early fifteenth century, Islam spread through the merchant and ruling classes along western coastal areas of India and the Malabar and Coromandel coasts. Calicut especially became a powerful and wealthy trade centre. Eastward beyond the Indian Ocean, Gujarati Muslim traders slowly began to make their way throughout the Indonesian area to become an important presence with regard to the spice trade. Nevertheless, Sanjay Subrahmanyam strongly opposes the concept of the Indian Ocean as a 'Muslim Lake'. He observes that the history of commercial activities in the Indian Ocean is complicated in the extreme, noting that, after 750 CE: 'We are dealing with a political and commercial network that was poly-centric in its organization; and there was no single epicentre that generated a pulse to which the entire "system" responded – even in the western Indian Ocean.'[2]

The Muslim political and commercial control of the eastern end of the Mediterranean came about due to the collapse of the Byzantine Empire and the fall of Constantinople to the Ottoman Turks in 1435. Christian Europe was then menaced by a militant Islamic presence on its southern (African) and eastern flanks. The devastating loss of the Holy Land and Jerusalem resulted in the Muslim monopoly of the lucrative spice trade so that both religious and economic interests combined to stimulate Iberian efforts to counter the threat.

2.   The Moluccas at the Time of the Arrival of the Europeans

Islam was fairly well established in the various small kingdoms and states that constituted the eastern part of the region around the important commercial city-state of Malacca, introduced by Muslim traders in the early fourteenth-century, who converted Gujarati merchants by preaching, and by force.[3] It took somewhat longer for Islam to be established as a commanding presence in the eastern area including the Moluccas, probably not until the early fifteenth century. However, as Subrahmanyam observes, 'We should bear in mind that this [early] Islam was as often heterodox as orthodox' much influenced by pre-Islamic native religion.[4] Influenced by their position in the trading network of Malaccan port-polities the Moluccas had adopted Malaccan political forms of governance and the use of the Malay language. The islands were organized into the four sultanates of Ternate, Tidore, Bacan, and Gilolo and troubled by constant conflict between the sultans of Ternate and Tidore, the two major polities of the island group. Monopoly control and cultivation of the cash-crop of clove, and of sagú trees, whose trunks provided the staple of Moluccan diet, was key to the success of the ruling houses.[5] Bacan was the least powerful of the four clove-producing sultanates of the northern

---

[1] Hourani and Carswell, *Arab Seafaring*, p. 85.

[2] Subrahmanyam, *Career and Legend*, pp. 95, 105–7, describes the great variety of traders of different religions in the Indian Ocean, which he compares with a similar situation in the Mediterranean world.

[3] *Cambridge History of Islam*: 2A, pp. 123–54. For an overview of the commerce of that area, see also Fernández-Armesto, *Civilization*, pp. 323–46.

[4] Subrahmanyam, *Career and Legend*, pp. 95–6, 105–7. The first Muslim ruler of Ternate is identified as Zayn al-Abidin (1486–1500) in *Cambridge History of Islam*, p. 135.

[5] Kathirithamby-Wells and Villiers, *Southeast Asian Port and Polity*, pp. 83–106.

Moluccas. When Europeans first arrived in the eastern archipelago, local rulers were often described to them by their hosts, interpreters, and guides by the Malayan title *raja, raje,* or *radja.* The islands of Makian and Moti had powerful chiefs named *sengaji*, but were subject to the sultans of Ternate and Tidore. R. F. Ellen notes that the term '*orang kaya*', also a Malayan title, 'is used variously to refer to indigenous ascribed leaders (chiefs), traditional leaders of the "big man" variety who had attained authority by the manipulation of resources in indigenously approved ways, local persons who acquired influence by virtue of being middlemen in the commodity trade'. The term was additionally applied to the very different political leadership of the Banda islands, with its 'oligarchy of elders'. Here, each village had an accepted leader whose power at the time of Portuguese contact appeared to derive from his monopoly of the export of spices.[1] Leonard V. Andaya explains that, despite the differences in wealth and political influence and the rivalries and conflicts between ruling families across the archipelago, the society of islands as a whole was unified by a shared cultural myth of their creation which produced an encompassing sense of communal familial belonging. At the same time, additional native ascriptions of names to the islands of Loloda, Gilolo, Bachan, Ternate, and Tidore established their position in a cosmology believed to be sustained by the dualities of an upper and lower world, and earth, sea and sky, and which worked, by opposition, to maintain a balance critical to the 'well-being' of their world. Oviedo noted instances of native religious belief which he referred to as held by pagans or gentiles.[2]

3.   Portugal Challenges the Muslim Monopoly

Other European explorers preceded Portugal's foray into the South China Sea. The Italian traveller Ludovico di Varthema (or Barthema) may have visited Ternate in the Moluccas in about 1505, and his *Itinerario* (Rome, 1510) includes the first description of the Spice Islands to circulate in Europe. As the precise location of the Moluccas was as yet unknown to the Europeans, once Malacca was taken, an expedition of three ships under the Spanish explorer Antonio de Abreu was sent out from Spain to find them. A member of this fleet, Captain Francisco Serrao, was, in all probability, the first European to come to the Spice Islands, arriving in Ternate around 1513. There he married a native woman, became the local sultan's advisor and died in 1521, supposedly poisoned, a victim of the seemingly constant regional warfare.[3]

Portugal was the first European state to respond to the Muslim monopoly. As Subrahmanyam describes it: 'Perched at one extremity of the Eurasian landmass, a *finisterra* looking out on to Africa and the still unknown Atlantic, [Portugal] in about 1450 was uniquely placed to create a model for a seaborne empire that would be imitated time and again in later centuries.' Although small in area and population in comparison with its neighbouring Spanish and Moorish kingdoms, Portugal was a unified and cohesive monarchy as early as 1250 'more or less defined in its entirety,' whereas Spain's

---

[1] Ellen, 'Conundrums about Panjandrums', pp. 48–50.

[2] Andaya, 'Los primeros contactos', pp. 63–8.

[3] Lach and Von Kley, *Asia in the Making*, III, p. 1406. For more on Serrao's adventurous life, see Parr, *So Noble a Captain*; Bergreen, *Over the Edge of the World*, p. 46. Parr identifies Serrao as a cousin of Magellan.

unification would take two centuries more.[1] Portugal also benefited from a long maritime tradition. Early on Portuguese voyages in the Atlantic began to lengthen their reach down the western coast of Africa. In the opinion of C. R. Boxer, 'the first stage of the overseas expansion of Europe can be regarded as beginning with the capture of Ceuta by the Portuguese in 1415 and culminating in the circumnavigation of the world by the Spanish ship *Victoria* in 1519–22'.[2]

The expedition against Ceuta, situated on the North African coast across the strait from Gibraltar, was represented by the Portuguese as a crusade against the Islamic presence in a strategic location menacingly close to the Christian sphere. But there was also a powerful economic motive. Ceuta was the northern terminus of the Muslim trans-Saharan trade in slaves, ivory, and other luxury goods (as well as gold from the then secret mines of the African interior). With the occupation of Ceuta, the Portuguese came to suspect that, by exploring the western coast of Africa, they might be able to discover and take over these gold mines and so cut out the Muslim middlemen of Barbary.[3] Phillips notes that, by 1440, Portugal's profits from gold, slaves, pepper, and ivory were enormous and could finance further African exploration.[4] African profits aside, there was always the ultimate goal that a way could be found through or around the landmass to the Indian Ocean, the fabled ports of India, and beyond.

Historians have long associated the Portuguese national project of explorations south along the western coast of Africa with Prince Henry (1394–1460). Given the sobriquet 'The Navigator' (despite the fact that he himself rarely navigated), he was the initiator and guiding force behind these expeditions. Traditional biographies report that he established a naval arsenal at Sagres to collect information and teach navigation, astronomy, and cartography.[5] The first obstacle to this programme of exploration was removed in 1434 by the rounding of the legendary Cape Bojador (26°7′ N). European mariners had previously considered this to be the limit of safe navigation along the coast. After that, year after year ships sent out by Prince Henry progressed down the African coast to reconnoitre and establish trading factories. To legitimize the Portuguese ventures and to monopolize the African coast against other potential rival nations, Prince Henry obtained from Pope Nicholas V the bull *Romanus Pontifex* of 8 June 1455 which 'recognized the twin motivations of crusading spirit [against Muslims] and commercial advantage'.[6] By this bull, the Portuguese were authorized to exploit the new

---

[1] Subrahmanyam, *Portuguese Empire*, pp. 30, 32.

[2] Boxer, *Four Centuries*, p. 5. For a detailed account of the crusade undertaken against Ceuta, see Russell, *Prince Henry*, pp. 29–58.

[3] Boxer, op. cit., p. 6. Eventually it became known that the source of the gold was the area of the Upper Niger and Senegal rivers

[4] Phillips, 'The Growth and Composition of Trade', p. 48.

[5] Subrahmanyam, *Portuguese Empire*, pp. 38–40, is less impressed with the prince's accomplishments, writing of him as 'perhaps the most mythologized figure in the history of Portuguese expansion ... There is no evidence of such scientific activities as ... eulogists would have us believe, or indeed even of the existence of a School of Sagres.' Russell, *Prince Henry*, pp. 6–9, likewise downplays his contributions as a 'romantic canard'.

[6] Boxer, *Four Centuries*, p. 7. Antedating *Romanus Pontifex* was a previous bull of Crusade, *Gaudemus et Exultamos* (1340), requested by King Alfonso IV 'apparently designed to permit the Portuguese to open up a front against Islam in North Africa at any time'. This bull was renewed in 1345, 1355, 1375, and 1377 by successive popes; see Subrahmanyam, *Career and Legend*, p. 33. Subrahmanyam explores the intertwining of religion and trade in *Portuguese Empire*, pp. 45–51.

lands in return for combating Islam by Catholic evangelization of the natives and by establishing contact with the legendary Christian ruler Prester John whose fabulous kingdom was thought to be in Africa as well as in other places. The hope was to establish contact with this shadowy figure and, consequently, to gain an important ally against the Muslims.[1]

Prince Henry died in 1460, but the explorations he began continued down the African coast year after year until Bartholomeu Dias rounded the Cape of Good Hope in 1488, proving that a sea route to the Indies was possible. Despite this, it took another decade before Vasco da Gama returned from India in 1499.[2] His cargo of spices earned an astronomical profit of 600 per cent for the investors. Profit aside, Nigel Cliff observes that da Gama's voyage was 'a mission not merely to reach India [but to] win allies and wealth there that would enable the Portuguese to invade the Arab heartlands and push on to Jerusalem itself'.[3] The Portuguese strategy would then be to attack Islam from behind by controlling the Indian Ocean and adjacent lands. In addition, they would attack Islam economically by wresting the very lucrative spice trade from Muslim hands.

On his first voyage into the Indian Ocean, Vasco da Gama visited and took the measure of the prosperous Muslim city-states up the Western coast of Africa to Malindi. There he picked up a pilot, long thought to be the famous Arabian navigator Ahmad-Ibn-Madjid, who guided the Portuguese to the great port of Calicut on the Indian Malabar coast, arriving there on 21 May 1498.[4] A second expedition to Calicut was led by Pedro Cabral. After Cabral reached India, he was followed by Alonso de Albuquerque and, after him, Da Gama returned to command. Despite vigorous Arab opposition to this intrusion into their trading territory, the Portuguese soon established maritime dominance of the Indian Ocean. Two years after their arrival, trading stations (known as 'factories') were established at Calicut and Cochín. Over the next twenty years, other factories and fortified settlements were established from 'Sofala in South East Africa to Ternate in the Moluccas', including such important cities as Hormuz, Aden, Goa, and Malacca.[5] Albuquerque's capture of the strategically located city-state of Malacca in 1511 gave Portugal control of the gateway to the East as far as China. In doing so, the Portuguese established a base from which to locate and exploit the mysterious Spice Islands.

C. R. Boxer[6] estimated the population of sixteenth-century Portugal at about a million. Of that number, he writes, it is 'unlikely that there were ever more than ten thousand able-bodied Portuguese men overseas in an empire which extended from South America to the Spice Islands ...' It seems incredible that by 1510 a country as small as Portugal

---

[1] For Prester John, see Russell, *Prince Henry*, pp. 121–2; Wey Gómez, *Tropics of Empire*, pp. 296, 374–80.

[2] Subrahmanyam, *Portuguese Empire*, p. 57, explains the lengthy wait before a paltry expedition of only three ships was sent to follow up on the entry into the Indian Ocean as due to: a lack of knowledge about those waters; the opposition from those groups more interested in African trade than Asian; and confusion with Columbus's discovery of what he reported as being China in 1492.

[3] Cliff, *Holy War*, p. 168.

[4] Only a Gujarati pilot is mentioned in *Oxford Companion to Ships and the Sea*, p. 234. Subrahmanyam, *Career and Legend*, pp. 22–8, does not accept that Ibn-Madjid participated in guiding the Portuguese to India.

[5] Boxer, *Four Centuries*, p. 14.

[6] Boxer, ibid., p. 20. In his *Seaborne Empire*, p. 52, Boxer estimates that 2,400 young men annually left for the Indies, most of them not to return. This figure was much greater than even that of Spaniards leaving for the New World.

could come to dominate the commerce and politics of such an extensive and populous area stretching from Brazil to Africa, the Malabar and Coromandel coasts of India, and then two thousand more miles to the Moluccas. Boxer discusses a variety of factors for Portuguese success: advanced naval design, ships' armaments, and superior maritime warfare tactics – coupled with the exploitation of territorial conflicts among the dozens of city-states that composed the eastern lands.[1]

Given the vast expansion of the colonial empire versus Portuguese national resources, it is no wonder that, eventually, manning and maintaining such an over-extended empire became untenable. Moreover, the great wealth that Portugal initially derived from the monopoly of Asian trade began to provoke envy among its European neighbours.

4.   Spain Challenges the Portuguese Spice Monopoly

Not surprisingly, the first challenge to Portuguese Asian hegemony came from neighbouring Spain. Spanish efforts to share in the lucrative Asian trade via a western route started with Columbus, continued with Magellan and then, by sporadic expeditions to the end of the sixteenth century, culminating with the establishment of a colony in the Philippines. By that time, the Dutch East India Company had overtaken the bulk of the South East Asian Portuguese trade. While the Portuguese were searching for a route to Asia by sailing south then east, it was an Italian mariner/adventurer who proposed an alternative by sailing west directly to Cipango (Japan), China, and the Spicelands. He imagined this path would be much shorter than rounding the immense African continent and then crossing the Indian Ocean. Christopher Columbus (born Cristoforo Colombo in Genoa, known in Spain as Cristóbal Colón) first tried to sell his plan to the Portuguese because of that nation's ongoing maritime programme of exploration. However, by 1488, with news of Bartholomeu Dias's rounding of the Cape of Good Hope, they were no longer interested in Columbus's untested proposition.

It was left to another foreigner in Spanish service to solve the problem of the westward passage to Asia. Ferdinand Magellan was a Portuguese navigator who previously sailed the *Carreira da India* around Africa and spent eight years in India and the Indonesian islands.[2] When he returned to Portugal, Magellan fell into disfavour at the court of Manuel I who developed a personal dislike of him. As the Portuguese had already reached the Moluccas, Manuel I was certainly not interested in Magellan's proposal to approach the islands from the Pacific Ocean.

With his career stalled in Portugal, Magellan left for Spain in 1517. There he offered to lead an expedition to discover a route around the New World to the East Indies via

---

[1] Boxer, *Seaborne Empire*, pp. 49–51. Subrahmanyam, *Career and Legend*, p. 109, states that 'the systematic use of violence on the sea' by the Portuguese, in the Indian Ocean, was not generally practised in those waters. Violence was 'confined to the land, where large armies were mobilized and brought to battle'.

[2] Fernão de Magalhães (*c.*1480–1521) was known in Spain as Fernando de Magallanes. Morison devoted considerable space to Magellan in *Southern Voyages*, chs XIII–XIX, and himself retraced Magellan's famous voyage as he had Columbus's first. His work is valuable for the maps and details of the expedition. For other works on Magellan, see Parr, *So Noble a Captain*; Joyner, *Magellan*; Bergreen, *Over the Edge of the World*.

an unknown strait he claimed he knew from cartographic secrets held by the Portuguese. Magellan's years of service with the Portuguese in India had taken him perhaps as far east as Malacca. While there, he had received glowing descriptions of the mysterious Spice Islands in letters from his friend and cousin Francisco Serrano who arrived there in 1513. On the basis of this information and the testimony of the well-regarded Portuguese cosmographer Rui Faleiro, who went to Spain with him, Magellan found a supporter in Bishop Juan Rodríguez de Fonseca, the all-powerful president of the Council of the Indies. Cristóbal de Haro, the agent of the Fugger banking company in Augsburg; and members of Charles's Flemish inner circle also lent their support and were able to convince King Charles I that the islands were within the Spanish sphere of interest.[1] The king needed a great sum of money to finance his candidacy to be elected Holy Roman Emperor (and hoped that Magellan's voyage would yield profitable spices). On 22 March 1518, he signed a contract authorizing the Magellan expedition to the Moluccas.

A point of contention concerning the expedition was the Treaty of Tordesillas. Shortly after Columbus returned from his first voyage of 1492, the Spanish Crown obtained from Pope Alexander VI in 1493 a series of papal bulls. These bulls established a north–south meridian 370 leagues west of Cape Verde (at 46°37′W) by a treaty signed at Tordesillas, Spain, on 7 June 1494.[2] Henceforth, north-east Brazil, all of Africa, the Indian Ocean including India, Ceylon, Malacca and points east would be in the Portuguese sphere of dominion while the West Indies, North, Central and the bulk of South America would be Spain's.

This division worked well for a time, but Magellan's proposed voyage to the Spice Islands raised a question – if the demarcation line, or meridian, were continued around the opposite side of the globe (the anti-meridian), on whose side would those fabled islands fall? As measure of its immense expanse was unknown, and just as Columbus had greatly underestimated the circumference of the globe, so also had Magellan underestimated the vastness of the Pacific.

In 1511, the Portuguese had approached the Spice Islands and China sailing east after their conquest of Malacca in 1511, but they also had no experience of the Pacific region. There was also the crucial question of the determination of longitude in those times. While the fixing of latitude was a matter of simply observing the meridional altitude of the sun by day and less accurately the altitude of the Pole Star at night, determining longitude was much more complicated. In the absence of accurate cartographic information, the assignment of the Spice Islands to one or the other dominion was entirely conjectural and both Spain and Portugal claimed them. Quite naturally, faced with this threat to their monopoly in a voyage captained by a man they considered a traitor, the Portuguese vigorously protested against the proposed Magellan voyage,

---

[1] Whereas Morison's work concentrates on the voyage of the *Victoria*, Parr, *So Noble a Captain*, pp. 131–262, includes an extensive account of Magellan's days in Spain in search of backers for his voyage to the East. Parr offers detailed background information on the principal players in this drama – Faleiro, Fonseca, Haro, the Fuggers, and King Charles I – based on documents of the time.

[2] Initially set at 100 leagues west of the Cape Verde Islands (38°W), and adjusted after strong Portuguese objections. For an English translation of the Treaty of Tordesillas, see http://avalon.law.yale.edu. This site also offers translations of Columbus's privileges and prerogatives (1492), and the earlier treaty of Alcaçovas (1479), by which Spain promised not to meddle in Portuguese affairs in Guinea.

insisting that the islands lay within their demarcation.[1] Nevertheless, despite Portuguese protests, on 10 August 1519, a fleet of five ships set out from Seville with about 270 men aboard. That the fleet sailed at all was a tribute to Magellan's characteristic determination and tenacity and to King Charles's firm desire that it happen.

The contract Magellan received from Charles I expressly ordered that the captain not enter and explore in the Portuguese dominion.[2] This provision assumed that the armada would return from its mission the way it came and that there was no intention to circumnavigate the globe as circumstances later dictated. Of the five ships, three years later on 8 September 1522, only one (the *Victoria*) survived to return to Seville. The rest of the fleet deserted, was scuttled, or wrecked. Ultimately, the credit for the first circumnavigation of the globe went to Juan Sebastián Elcano,[3] who eventually took command after Magellan's death in the Philippines and heroically brought the *Victoria* back to Spain with fourteen survivors. Like Columbus's reputation, Magellan's suffered in the years following his death. In Portugal, Magellan was remembered as a traitor; and in Spain, the expedition survivors blackened his memory to excuse their misdeeds. The payments due to Magellan's family under the terms of his contract were ignored by the Crown. Today, however, Magellan's name is generally associated with this first circumnavigation of the globe in spite of the fact that he did not complete that voyage.[4]

The horrendous loss of lives of the Magellan expedition was not at all an uncommon result of the lengthy voyages to Asia or, for that matter, those to the New World. The mortality rates for Portuguese fleets to and from India often reached 50 per cent and accounts of Portuguese shipwrecks came to form a literary narrative genre of its own.[5] Despite being by any measure a disaster in terms of human casualties, the Magellan expedition was a resounding financial success. The cargo of spices brought back on the *Victoria* yielded a profit of 45,000 ducats,[6] which more than covered the cost of ships and cargo. The quantity of clove one ducat would buy in the Moluccas would cost 100 in Europe.

5. Gonzalo Fernández de Oviedo y Valdés's *General and Natural History*

Gonzalo Fernández de Oviedo y Valdés (1478–1557) is now generally acknowledged as the most important historian-chronicler of the first half-century of the Spanish presence in the New World. His monumental *General y Natural Historia de las Indias* is still a

---

[1] Morison calculates the meridian at 45°30′W longitude, giving an anti-meridian of 134½ E longitude, placing the Philippines, the Moluccas, and most of Indonesia within the Portuguese demarcation; *Southern Voyages*, p. 477.

[2] Magellan's contract and instructions are reproduced in Navarrete, *Colección de los Viajes*, vol. 5, p. 474. For an English translation of Magellan's will as well as an expedition proposal Magellan and Faleiro presented to the Crown in 1518, see, Joyner, *Magellan*, pp. 299–302.

[3] The Basque navigator. Secondary works give variant spellings of his family name as, de Elcano, del Cano, Delcano, Elcano. Elcano is now commonly used in historical studies.

[4] Morison held that Magellan did circumnavigate the Earth, if his westerly travels are added to those of his earlier Portuguese service when he sailed east as far as the Celebes Islands. The same case could be made for Magellan's East Asian slave, Enrique.

[5] See Blackmore, *Manifest Perdition: Shipwreck Narrative and the Disruption of Empire*.

[6] Parr, *So Noble a Captain*, p. 371.

major primary source for researchers of the period 1492–1548. From the first, Oviedo's work had its fierce detractors, chief among them Bartolomé de las Casas and Ferdinand Columbus, but it subsequently enjoyed renewed interest and more favourable re-evaluation. At the beginning of his introduction to his 1959 edition of Oviedo's work, the eminent Spanish historian Juan Pérez de Tudela y Bueso wrote 'if I were obliged to select a figure through whose biography one ought to be able to define the moment of the flowering of imperial Spain, I would prefer that of Gonzalo Fernández de Oviedo'.[1] More recently, Kathleen Ann Myers described this work as 'The most comprehensive history of the discovery, conquest and colonization of the Americas from 1492 to 1547. ... The most authoritative text on the Americas', adding that 'Oviedo's text itself served as a catalyst for European historiographical change'.[2]

Born in Madrid in 1478, of a hidalgo family with origins in Asturias, Oviedo's early life was spent in service to households of family members of King Ferdinand of Aragon, and in royal and aristocratic household service in Italy. Myers notes that, in the years after he returned to Spain in 1502, 'he held a variety of important positions that required good writing skills', in the service of the Inquisition, the city of Madrid, of the Duke of Calabria and began his career as a chronicler about 1505 when King Ferdinand asked him to write the history of the monarchy of Castile. His career in the administration of the Spanish Indies and as its future first chronicler began in 1514, when he in sailed to the New World on the great 1514 fleet taking Governor Pedrarias Dávila to Santa María de la Antigua (now Panama). Santa María was the first viable mainland settlement on what was then the very edge of the known western world. With the exception of various periods when he returned to Spain on his own or official business, Oviedo spent the remainder of his life in the Indies occupying various governmental positions until his death in Santo Domingo on 25 June 1557.[3]

Despite his multiple official duties and personal affairs, and without a university education (for which he was denigrated by his fellow historians), Oviedo was an astonishingly prolific author. On the strength of his experience of the Indies, in 1526, he published a short descriptive work *De la Natural Historia de las Indias*, or *Sumario de La Natural y General Istoria de las Indias* at the request of the Holy Roman Emperor Charles V, who wished to learn something about his new overseas possessions. The surprising popularity of this initial work, often referred to as the *Summary*, is attested to by its numerous translations during Oviedo's lifetime. This work is still in print today in an English edition and is a foundation text of Latin-American colonial history. Buoyed by the astounding success of this small work, Oviedo assiduously worked to establish himself in Spain and beyond as the definitive authority on the Indies. In 1532, his efforts were rewarded when he received an imperial appointment as Official

---

[1] Published as vols. 117–21 of the series *Biblioteca de Autores Españoles* (hereafter referred to as *BAE*). Carrillo, *Historia General y Natural de las Indias*, pp. 321–44.

[2] Myers, *Fernández de Oviedo's Chronicle*, pp. 1–2.

[3] Oviedo's service in America took him first to Panama, Nicaragua, and finally Santo Domingo, where he held office as *alcaide* of the fort until his death in 1557. He did, however, return to Spain and on numerous occasions. Myers, ibid., pp. 12–23, has an ample and very informative introduction on the author's life, and furnishes a 'Chronology of His Life and Work', pp. 139–41, which allows the reader to get a clear understanding of Oviedo's movements between America and Europe. He returned to Spain sometime in 1534, remaining through 1535 and returning to Santo Domingo in 1536. Antonello Gerbi's *Nature in the New World*, part II, pp. 129 and appendices, is another valuable source of information.

Chronicler of the Indies, entrusted with the charge to write the history of the Spanish in the New World. The salary was minimal, but the post was a distinct honour and, more importantly, it gave him access to all official documents and papers relating to the affairs of the Indies as well as the credentials to interview the majority of the persons involved in the enterprise.[1]

His magnum opus, the *General and Natural History of the Indies*, from the germ of its inception in 1514 was his constant concern until 1548 when, on his last voyage to Spain, he left behind the huge manuscript for publication in its entirety. Prior to this, however, the first part of the same was published in 1535, then reprinted and augmented in 1547. Like his *Summario*, this first part was widely diffused throughout Europe and translated into various languages, gaining the author fame abroad, particularly in Italy. Finally, in 1557 (the year of his death), the twentieth book of Part Two was printed in Valladolid. No complete edition of the lengthy work, consisting of three parts, with fifty books, hundreds of chapters and thousands of pages, was published in Oviedo's lifetime. Some have posited that the publication of the *General and Natural History* was blocked by Oviedo's critics, particularly by the very influential Fray Bartolomé de las Casas, Oviedo's life-long adversary. Certainly Oviedo's demise removed the prime promoter and probably the financier of its publication.

Oviedo's *General and Natural History* was never completely available in print during his lifetime. However, the autograph manuscripts of the entire three parts that Oviedo deposited in a convent before his final visit to Spain were known, consulted, and copied by interested parties from the author's lifetime onwards. Later, over the centuries, the manuscripts were dispersed or lost. Starting in the seventeenth century, there were several failed attempts to publish the entire work. It was not until 300 years later (between 1851 and 1855) that the eminent scholar, José Amador de los Ríos, edited and issued the work in four volumes under the auspices of the Royal Academy of History with the title *The General and Natural History of the Indies, Islands and Mainland of the Ocean Sea by Captain Gonzalo Fernández de Oviedo, the First Chronicler of the New World*. Amador de los Ríos's work was reprinted and revised first in 1944–45 by J. N. González and, in the most recent and most accessible edition, by J. Pérez de Tudela Bueso in vols. 117–21 of the collection *Biblioteca de Autores Españoles*, 1959.[2]

Oviedo compiled his history over a period of some four decades. As source materials came to him and as he was able to interview participants in the various expeditions in Spain or in the Indies, Oviedo had to incorporate new information and correct his previously written sections. Because of his constant revision of his text, there is a good deal of repetition of anecdotal passages throughout the entire work. Additionally, the original manuscripts are often difficult to interpret to the point that at least one Oviedo scholar, Daymond Turner, has suggested that the Ríos-Tudela Bueso edition leaves something to be desired. Nevertheless, the *BAE* edition is the only one currently available.

---

[1] See, *BAE*, vol. 117, pp. cxvi–cxix, for an excerpt of the imperial appointment.

[2] Daymond Turner's several articles and bibliographical monograph listed in the Bibliography were perhaps the first to clear up the muddle of the various copies and manuscripts of Oviedo's works. See 'Aborted First Printing', pp. 105–25; 'Forgotten Treasure from the Indies', pp. 1–46; *Oviedo y Valdés: An Annotated Bibliography*. Jesús Carrillo also has a lengthy account of 'what's what and what's where' in his '*Historia General y Natural de las Indias*', with additional information in his 'Oviedo on Columbus'. Myers, *Oviedo's Chronicle*, includes a very helpful chart locating the various manuscripts, pp. 180–87.

The likelihood of a new critical Spanish edition of the Oviedo history as well as a complete English translation is slim given the sheer size of the work.

From the first, Oviedo was cast as the apologist for the atrocities of the early Spanish colonial era, particularly by las Casas.[1] It is certainly true that in the early days of his writing career, Oviedo (like most other Spaniards) was suffused with nationalistic pride in the discovery, exploration, and colonization of the immense territory of the New World. Indeed, the Pope himself confirmed that it was Spain's destiny and obligation to take on the task. Thus it was considered a sacred God-given task to evangelize and civilize these new souls of the New World in exchange for the right to possess the lands. The Catholic, chivalric spirit of the centuries of the Spanish Reconquest (long celebrated in verse and prose), was imagined by many to be continued in the New World against the 'idolatrous' Native Americans.[2]

But, of course, this dream was not to be fulfilled in a territory so immense, so potentially rich, and so distant from the control of the Spanish Crown. It soon became clear to Oviedo that the opportunity to operate unchecked was enticing to many Spaniards. We see in Oviedo's early impressions of the New World (in 1514 in Darién) a marked sense of triumphalism at Spain's possession of such a vast world. But his initial optimism was soon tempered by his candid observations of the worst motives of the Spanish explorers.

Even in the early days of his residence, Oviedo began to protest at the cruelties inflicted on the indigenous peoples and to call attention to the lawless officials and clergy who preyed on natives and Spaniards alike. During the almost four decades that Oviedo wrote his history, he never hesitated to expose misdeeds wherever he observed them, which injected an increasing tone of disillusionment into the text. The enthusiastic imperial chronicler of the early days of Imperial Spain was not the same as the tired and discouraged Oviedo of 1548 when he stopped writing its history. Kathleen Myers examines in greater detail Oviedo's growing dismay at the situation in the Indies, noting that:

> By the 1540s the conquistadors' greed had completely soured any of the original visions of establishing new societies in America. By then, whole populations in the Antilles and Central America had disappeared, and Spaniards had murdered each other at alarming rates in rebellions and civil wars extending from Tierra Firme to Peru.[3]

After investing some forty years in his *General and Natural History*, and in spite of his failing health, Oviedo turned his attention to other less depressing subjects, including two other characteristically mammoth projects – the oddly named *Batallas y quincuagenas* (*c.*1544),[4] and another *Quincuagenas* (*c.*1556).[5] Although older biographies

---

[1] Myers, ibid., pp. 130–31.

[2] Attesting to the popularity of the genre of the novel or romance of chivalry at the time is the fact that Oviedo's *Claribalte*, published in 1519, constitutes the first novel of the New World. Oviedo was no doubt aware of Emperor Charles V's predilection for this genre. Years later Oviedo disavowed these tales as frivolous.

[3] Myers, *Oviedo's Chronicle*, pp. 130–31.

[4] *Quincuagena* means a grouping of 50 which seemed to appeal to Oviedo, his *Historia General y Natural* also being comprised of 50 books.

[5] The *Batallas y Quincuagenas* was also transcribed by Amador de los Ríos and Tudela y Bueso and published in four volumes. Only one volume of the *Quincuagenas* was published. See, Dille, *Writing from the Edge of the World*, p. 25.

state that the historian died in Valladolid, Spain, official documents show that Gonzalo Fernández de Oviedo y Valdes (long accustomed to the tropical warmth of Santo Domingo), died there at his post on 26 June 1557.

6.   Book XX of the *Second Part of the General History of the Indies: written by Captain Gonzalo Fernández de Oviedo y Valdés, Warden of the Fortress and Port of Santo Domingo of the Island of Hispaniola, His Majesty's Chronicler. The Subject of which is the Strait of Magallanes.* In Valladolid by Francisco Fernández de Córdoba. Printer to His Majesty, 1557.

Oviedo's *Historia General y Natural* follows the path of the Spanish in the New World from their first sight of the islands and the mainland on the Ocean Sea.[1] The nineteen books of Part One of the *Historia General y Natural* begin with Columbus's arrival and subsequent explorations first of the Caribbean islands. Three more voyages to the adjacent areas of mainland Central America and the north coast of South America (or *Tierra Firme* as it came to be known) follow. This general history of the Spanish discovery, exploration, and colonization is intertwined with Oviedo's observations of the exotic fauna, flora and ethnography, the first glimpse of the New World to reach the general public in Spain and Europe through further translations. The encyclopaedic nature of the work has garnered Oviedo many New World 'firsts' as 'the first ethnographer, geographer, sociologist, botanist, zoologist, mineralogist, comprehensive historian and autobiographer ... first novelist and poet and first to propagate visual representations of the Indies'.[2]

In the first book of Part Two, Book XX of his *Historia General y Natural*, Oviedo turns his attention from the discovery of the New World to the search for the westward route to access the riches of the Orient – the goal Columbus had first proposed to the Catholic Monarchs. This book was extracted and published in Valladolid in 1557 under the title *Book XX of the Second Part of the General History of the Indies,* etc. It is not clear how *Book XX* came to be published as late as 1557, given the fact that Oviedo returned to Santo Domingo from his last visit to Spain in 1549. Twice in the introductory material to *Book XX*, Oviedo indicates that he completed it 'in this present year, 1546.' At the end of the text we have the printer's note: 'No more of this work was printed because the author died.' This statement would seem to indicate that Oviedo himself paid for its publication, as he had for his *Sumario* and for the 1535 edition of the first part of the *Historia*.[3]

Whatever the circumstances of its publication, *Book XX*, the first of the nineteen Books that comprise Part Two, concerns the first three Spanish voyages to the East Indies that took place during the period of Oviedo's composition of his history. These voyages were: Magellan's discovery of the Strait that led to the first circumnavigation of the globe (1519–21); the little-known, follow-up armada to that expedition five years

---

[1] The name at the time for the Atlantic as opposed to the Southern Sea, the Pacific.

[2] Dille, *Writing from the Edge of the World*, p. 25.

[3] Myers is of the opinion that he did finance the work, *Oviedo's Chronicle*, pp, 20–22. Pérez de Tudela suggests that the 1547 edition of the first part of the history was made without the author's permission, *BAE*, vol. 117, p. cxxxix, n. 457.

later (1525–35), initially led by García Jofre de Loaysa;[1] and the expedition that Hernan Cortés sent from Mexico in 1527 in search of the Loaysa armada. The information on this third fleet is interpolated in the chapters concerning the Loaysa voyage. It might perhaps be expected that the narrative of Magellan's voyage would predominate in *Book XX*, and Oviedo did recognize the great navigator's accomplishment in charting a western route to the Indies. However, it is instructive that, of the thirty-six chapters that comprise *Book XX*, Oviedo devoted only the first four to this monumental voyage while the remaining thirty-one are devoted to the subsequent Loaysa expedition to the Moluccas.

Oviedo's privileging of the Loaysa expedition seems to reflect the general discrediting of Magellan's reputation by its deserters and the survivors who needed to downplay their mutinous conduct on that voyage. Pigafetta's first account was available to Oviedo who acknowledged him as 'an intelligent man and eyewitness ... worthy of credit.'[2] But, perhaps mindful of Magellan's poor reputation in Spain, Oviedo's overall assessment of the Italian's work is equivocal at best. In one passage, Oviedo subtly questions the writer's authority: 'The Vicentine Antonio Pigafetta, A Knight of the Order of Rhodes, who *says* he was on the voyage.'[3] In Chapter III of *Book XX*, Oviedo reviews the Italian's narrative section by section in an ambiguous fashion – seemingly favourable, but including statements like the following: 'Truly, concerning some things this knight recounts I am either neutral or perplexed, not doubting that what he writes is true even though one could contradict some of the things concerning Trapobana.'[4]

7.   Oviedo's Source: Andrés de Urdaneta

Andrés de Urdaneta y Ceráin was born 1508 in Ordizia, Guipúzcoa (a region of Spain long known for its seafaring tradition), and died in 1568 in Mexico City. His father, Juan Ochoa de Urdaneta, was the alcalde of Villafranca. At the age of seventeen under the patronage of his famous fellow Basque, Juan Sebastián de Elcano, Urdaneta joined the Loaysa expedition being formed in La Coruña. He clearly had impressed Elcano with his intelligence and obvious self-possession. His remarkable memory, literacy, command of Spanish and Basque and general facility in languages, as well as his understanding of mathematics indicate that he had received an excellent education and that his enrolment in the venture was as a supernumary, possibly as an accountant. Even before the armada came to the Strait, he was assuming responsible duties far beyond what one would think fitting or possible.[5] Because of his facility in learning Malay and

---

[1] García Jofre de Loaysa; variant, Loaisa.

[2] Pigafetta's initial account was presented to the King (formerly Charles I, elected as Holy Roman Emperor in 1519 with the title of Charles V) in September of 1521, shortly after his return to Spain. Oviedo obviously had access to it for his history, but Pigafetta's original manuscript has not been found. Skelton examines in detail Pigafetta's subsequent manuscripts, written in French and Italian, in his introduction to the facsimile edition of the Beinecke-Yale manuscript and its translation; *Magellan's Voyage*, pp. 13–26.

[3] Editor's italics.

[4] *BAE*, vol. 118, pp. 223, 231–7.

[5] For biographies of Urdaneta, see Arteche, *Urdaneta*; Cuevas, *Monje y marino*; Miguel Bosch, *Urdaneta en su tiempo*.

native languages and his general fearlessness during his nine years in the Moluccas, Urdaneta was invaluable to the Spanish commanders and to their native allies. Since the Portuguese confiscated all the Spanish expedition records, Spanish officials had to rely on reports made by the survivors upon returning to Spain. Five of these official reports were translated and published by Sir Clements Markham in his 1911 Hakluyt Society volume, *Early Spanish Voyages to the Strait of Magellan.*[1] Two of them are republished here as appendices. Markham's translation of Andrés de Urdaneta's formal official report, personally delivered to the Emperor and Consejo de Indias in Valladolid on 26 February 1537, was the most extensive of those received. Urdaneta's testimony only reinforces Oviedo's opinion of his leadership skills, particularly his ability to assess and intervene effectively in crises, and to observe, process and present strategic and economic data. It provided the Spanish authorities with a detailed, factual narrative of events and the experiences and actions taken by the marooned Spaniards. Urdaneta had played a pivotal role in encounters with the indigenous leadership in the Moluccas. He had a major part in battles with the Portuguese and in the negotiations for the return of the Spanish survivors to Spain. Even though the documents he carried back to Europe had been confiscated in Lisbon, his remarkable memory allowed him to recall the significant detail within them.

After his return to Spain he met Pedro de Alvarado, one of the conquistadores in Mexico. Because of his experiences in the Far East, Urdaneta was invited to join a proposed expedition into the Pacific from Mexico. Oviedo records that he met Urdaneta in Santo Domingo, most likely when the latter arrived in Santo Domingo in March 1539 in the company of Pedro de Alvarado. Oviedo judged Urdaneta to be 'a good and intelligent man who well remembered what he had seen and noted' in his journey to the Moluccas.[2] The personal interviews allowed Oviedo to question and expand what he had gained from the official reports and enrich his own evolving narrative of the expedition. Since Oviedo's narrative relies heavily on Urdaneta's accounts, it is not surprising that his exploits occupy a good part of the history of that period of the confrontation.

In Chapters XXVIII to XXXI Oviedo relates the history of the expedition under Alvaro de Saavedra,[3] sent out from the west coast of Mexico by Hernan Cortes with orders to sail to the Moluccas to discover what had happened to Loaysa's venture. Of the three ships which left at the beginning of November 1527, only Saavedra's *Capitana* reached the Spice islands, and two attempts to return back across the Pacific failed. Saavedra died in the last attempt, and the *Capitana* was found unfit for any further service, leaving her stranded company to make terms with the Portuguese in Ternate. Urdaneta was familiar with these events and was apparently Oviedo's source for them. Vícente de Nápoles, a member of the *Capitana*'s complement, travelled back to Spain via Lisbon with two other companions, All three were clearly in a very ragged condition, prompting the Consejo de Indias to issue each of them with 12 ducats to allow them to buy new clothing and to travel to

---

[1] Hakluyt Society, 2nd ser., vol. 28, London, 1911, pp. 41–89. Archival access to legible images of the original preserved in the Archivo General de Indias, Sevilla, can be found online through the PARES system.

[2] See below, p. 74.

[3] Saavedra: variant Sayavedra.

Madrid.[1] A contemporaneous copy of the transcript of Vícente de Nápoles's actual formal hearing before the Consejo de Indias, comprising his report and answers to questions, is preserved in the Archivo de Indias. This latter document is, as a curator has annotated in the margin, a defective copy. It states that Saavedra's expedition left New Spain in 1526 and so throws out all other dates given in the report by one year.[2]

The lengthy narrative provided by 'Vincencio of Naples, who left New Spain in the said fleet, went through all that has been described, reached Lisbon, and from thence came to. Spain. He was at the Court of His Majesty, and gave an account of the whole voyage', translated by Sir Clements Markham, is republished here as Appendix 2. The narrative appears to have been written after his formal report to the Consejo de Indias but there is no indication about for whom it was intended. It contains more information on his adventures than his testimony to the Consejo de Indias.[3]

8. The Loaysa Expedition to the Spicelands: the Events of the Voyage

a. The Organization of the Fleet

Given the astounding value of the *Victoria*'s cargo, Spanish merchants and the Fuggers, agents for European moneyed interests acting principally as Charles V's bankers and creditors, were eager to continue to develop a spice trade rivalling that of Portugal's. In 1522, the year that the *Victoria* returned, Emperor Charles V authorized the establishment of an agency to occupy and colonize the Moluccas. This new bureaucracy, distinct from the older House of Trade (Casa de la Contratación) in Seville that administered American affairs, was named the House of Spiceland Trade, (Casa de Especierías). It was headquartered in Galicia in the port of La Coruña under the complete control of the factor Cristóbal de Haro. This important figure had previously dealt in spices in Lisbon on behalf of the Fuggers, but in 1516 transferred his dealings to Seville where he cultivated a relationship with Bishop Fonseca, then the all-powerful head of affairs of the Indies.[4] Haro was granted a monopoly of spice sales in all Spain, and thus controlled their legal prices along with other exemptions and tax privileges. This monopoly also extended to the spice trade. As a result, a second expedition was formed to follow Magellan's route to the Moluccas which the Spanish continued to maintain lay in their dominion under the Treaty of Tordesillas.

---

[1] AGI, Indiferente General 422, L. 16, f. 125r–v, Carta acordada a Diego de la Haya, cambio de la Corte, el pago de 12 ducados en total a Vícente de Nápoles, Juan de Mazuecos y Arias de Leon, que han venido de Maluco, para que puedan seguir al rey hasta Madrid, Sept 1534; Indiferente General 422, L. 16, ff. 123v–124r, Recibo de Vícente de Nápoles por la cantidad de 3.791 maravedíes, que pago Diego de Pérez, por orden de los del Consejo, cantidad gastada en ropas.

[2] A contemporaneous copy of the transcription of Vícente de Nápoles's testimony can be found in Navarrete, *Colección de los Viajes*, vol. 5, pp, 476–86. Navarrete noted that numerous inaccuracies had been made by the copyist.

[3] AGI, Patronato 43, N 2, R 11, 'Relación de Vícente de Nápoles: navegación armada del Maluco'. See below, Appendix 2.

[4] Parr, *So Noble a Captain*, pp. 154–71, details Jakob Fugger's important role financing European international ventures, and offers biographies of Cristobal de Haro, pp. 172–82, and of Juan Rodríguez de Fonseca, pp. 183–99.

When the Portuguese learned of a planned second incursion into their domination of the Moluccas trade, they made their opposition firmly known. As a result, the two governments agreed to meet in conference to resolve these disputes. Their delegates met at Elvas-Badajoz in 1524, but in the absence of accurate geographical data, the deliberations could not reach consensus, and Charles V continued plans for the second Spanish armada to the Moluccas.[1] The high hopes of a financial windfall from this second venture were reflected in the increased size of the second fleet, which comprised seven ships with a complement of 450 men. Because of the usual delays in the complicated process of outfitting and manning such an armada, it did not set sail from La Coruña until 24 July 1525. The armada was made up of: the flagship *Santa María de la Victoria* (not the same ship as took part in the Magellan expedition), the *Sancti Spíritus*, the *Anunciada*, the *San Gabriel*, the *Santa María del Parral*, the *San Lesmes*, and the *Santiago*.[2]

One might think that, given the mortality and the horrendous hardships suffered by the survivors of the Magellan expedition,[3] one such voyage would have been enough. However, a few of those men did sign on for the second voyage, chief of whom was Juan Sebastián Elcano. His circumnavigational fame notwithstanding, command of the fleet was given to Frey Don Francisco José García Jofre de Loaysa, Knight Commander of the Sovereign Military and Hospitaller Order of St John of Jerusalem, of Rhodes and of Malta.[4] Don García was selected because of his previous service in the Mediterranean and also because, at that time, his kinsman Fray Juan García de Loaysa y Mendoza[5] was the first President of the newly formed Consejo de Indias. Oviedo later included a dedicatory epistle to this prelate prefacing the first part of *Historia General y Natural*, even though by then the archbishop was long dead. It was common practice to give command of armadas to the highest-ranking member of the expedition who would then generally leave the actual sailing to more experienced underlings. In this case Elcano was the pilot-major, who no doubt chafed at a secondary position, given his fame at bringing home the *Victoria* in 1522. Nonetheless, Elcano did finally assume official command, albeit only briefly.

b. The Difficult Passage through the Strait
Spate correctly characterizes the total voyage as 'a succession of disasters'.[6] In spite of Elcano's previous experience, the second passage through the Strait was much more

---

[1] Among the Spanish delegation were Elcano, Sebastian Cabot, Diego Ribero, Giovanni Vespucci, and Ferdinand Columbus. Herrera y Tordesillas, *Historia General,* Década III, libro VI, chs 1–7, has a lengthy summation of the arguments of both sides in this debate.

[2] Documents pertaining to the Loaysa expedition and the Saavedra relief expedition are included in Navarrete, *Colección de los Viajes*, vol. 5, pp, 196–279. Herrera y Tordesillas, Década III, libro VII, chs 5–6, also provides details on the ships, personnel, and the sailing instructions. Of particular interest are the signals that were used to communicate from ship to ship. Parr, *So Noble a Captain*, pp. 381–3, describes the complement and offensive armament of a royal Spanish ship in 1520.

[3] Only 14 of the original 270 members survived.

[4] This military order dates from the time of the crusades and still exists in Malta, and was the order Charles V gave after the knights were forced from Rhodes by Saracen armies. *Fraile* (meaning friar, monk, or brother) has two apocopes: *fray* and *frey*. The former was the title generally used for members of religious orders, while *frey* was used for members of military orders. Accordingly, official documents relating to the expedition, Navarrete, and *BAE* all use *frey*. However, Oviedo generally uses *fray* in the 1557, which has been retained.

[5] Appointed Master General of the Friars Preachers in 1519, Bishop of Osma 1524, confessor to Charles V.

[6] Spate, *Spanish Lake*, vol. I, pp. 90–91.

difficult than the first, primarily due to the almost constant storms the fleet encountered. Off the Santa Cruz River the flagship, *Santa María de la Victoria*, and the *San Gabriel* were separated from the rest of the fleet. Sailing on south, the other five ships came to the mouth of the Gallegos River which Elcano mistook for the Strait. Later, when they reached Cabo Vírgenes at the entrance of the actual Strait, another storm wrecked the *Sancti Spiritus* and blew the *Anunciada* out to sea. Once again the fleet had to regroup, but in the process the commander of the *San Gabriel* abandoned the mission and sailed for home, only to run into difficulties on the Brazilian coast.[1] A subsequent storm blew the *Parral*, the *San Lesmes*, and the *Anunciada* out of the Strait and into open Atlantic waters, and this time the *Anunciada* was never heard from again. Because of damage to the *Victoria*, that ship as well as the *San Lesmes*, the *Parral*, and the patache *Santiago* returned to the Santa Cruz River, for repairs and resupply, prior to reattempting passage of the Strait. Because the Strait was narrow, deep, and stormy, the Santa Cruz River offered a more protected and safer anchorage, better foraging possibilities, and a place to careen the ships needing repair.

The passage through the Strait took about seven weeks to sail a distance of approximately 100 leagues. Oviedo's sailing directions for the passage of the Strait are probably those reported by crew member Martín de Uriarte and augmented by information from Andrés de Urdaneta, another crew member. The roles these two crew members played in the expedition became more and more significant as the voyage progressed.[2]

c. Losses in the Pacific

The remaining four ships of the armada debouched from the Strait's western entrance, Cabo Deseado (now Cabo Pilar), to enter the Pacific Ocean on 26 May 1526. Soon after the passage they were once more separated by a storm, never to regroup. The *Santa María de la Victoria*, overcrowded with the survivors from the wreck of *Sancti Spiritus*, sailed on in search of the Moluccas. The *San Lesmes* and the *Parral* simply vanished.[3] After the dispersal of the fleet, facing a shortage of provisions because the majority had been stored aboard the larger *Victoria*, the patache *Santiago*, captained by Elcano's brother-in-law Santiago de Guevara, continued up the South American coast in search of the closest Spanish colonies which were in Darién or New Spain. After some fifty days at sea, the desperate crew reached Tehuantepec where they were saved. Oviedo includes a detailed report of this harrowing voyage provided by Father Juan de Areizaga, who experienced the ordeal.

---

[1] The travails of the *San Gabriel*, reported by some of its crew in 1528, can be found in Navarrete, *Colección de los Viajes*, vol. 5, pp. 171–7. See below, pp. 53, n. 2, 139, n. 1.

[2] Since Oviedo's time, topographical names have naturally changed, making the historian's text difficult to follow. The present translation relies heavily on the identifications in vol. 5 of Navarrete's *Colección de los Viajes*, and on Samuel Eliot Morison's and Joyner's maps for explanatory information. Morison himself sailed the Strait to recreate the voyages and identified the various 16th-century topographical sites with present-day terminology.

[3] It seems that the *Parral* made it to the Celebes, where it wrecked on Sanguín Island and the survivors were either killed or enslaved by the natives. It is possible that the *Lesmes* wrecked on the desert island called Tepujoé, first explored in 1772, where an old cross was discovered; Navarrete, *Colección de los Viajes*, vol. 5, pp. 89–94, 163–7.

Out in the vast Pacific, conditions on the lone *Santa María de la Victoria* were very bad for the 120 persons on board. Scurvy took a terrible toll on the passengers and crew. The ship's pilot, Rodrigo Bermejo, died, and was replaced by Martín Pérez de Elcano, Juan Sebastián's brother. The Comptroller General Alonso de Tejada died and was replaced by Alvaro de Loaysa, the Captain General's nephew, who also soon passed away. Captain General Loaysa died on 30 June 1526 and Elcano took charge, only to die on 6 August. The crew elected Toribio Alonso de Salazar to replace him and to head the expedition, but he also died the following month. Subsequently, the command went to Martín Iñiguez de Carquizano, who then led the Spanish until July of 1527 when he was poisoned by the Portuguese in the Spice Islands. Carquizano was replaced by Fernando de la Torre, who commanded the dwindling Spanish forces until 1535 when the remaining Spaniards were forced to surrender to Portuguese forces and were returned to Spain.

Elcano's plan had been to head first for Cipango (Japan), the mysterious and wealthy land reported by Marco Polo (but not visited by him), and whose exact whereabouts were as yet unknown to the Europeans. However, after Elcano's death, because of the desperate conditions on board the ship, the course was altered to make for the Ladrones (Marianas) Islands that had been previously visited by the Magellan expedition. After reaching Guam and the Philippine archipelago, the *Victoria* (the sole remaining ship of the seven) arrived at the Moluccas, landing first at Gilolo and then moving to Tidore on 19 December 1526. Only 105 men survived the ninety-day crossing of the Pacific.

9.   The Years Spent by the Spanish Survivors in the Moluccas

By the time Carquizano and the remnant of the Loaysa expedition arrived in November 1526, the Portuguese had been settled on Ternate for four years, with a stone fortress for their defence and maintained by an annual supply fleet from Melaka. Given the importance of trade with Melaka the sultan had little option but to accept their overarching control or so-called 'protection'. For the Queen Mother Regent of Tidore and the sultan of Gilolo, the presence of the Portuguese on Ternate constituted a threat to the established balance of power between the four sultanates. Informed of a recent Portuguese attack on Tidore, Carquizano took the opportunity to offer Spanish military assistance, and was permitted to install his men on that island, bringing the *Victoria* to anchor there on 1 January 1527. Shortly thereafter an envoy arrived from Ternate, sent by Garcia Henriques, the current Portuguese commander, with directions to assert that the ownership of the Spice Islands fell to the Portuguese crown and that the Spanish intruders should immediately bring themselves under his fort on Ternate. Carquizano's response stated Charles V's claim to the contrary, and that his company would be happy to receive a 'visit' from the Portuguese. Clearly expecting that such a 'visit' would not be a friendly one, Carquizano set his men to building defence works on the shore and was ready for the assault force of 100 Portuguese and native allies which arrived on 18 January. With the support of Tidorean allies and use of the guns aboard the *Victoria*, they were able to repulse the attackers. The *Victoria* could, however, no longer support the reverberations from her artillery, which split her seams. Unable to remove the ship to a safe place to carry out repairs, they had no option but to strip, scuttle and burn her, leaving

19

themselves with no means to send for supplies or instructions from Spain. They were henceforth to be reliant on regional vessels – *fustas*, canoes, *paraos*, junks – and whatever they could build or capture from the Portuguese. The years 1527–32 witnessed ever-shifting conflict between the Spanish and the Portuguese, as each sought to assert the rights of their respective monarchs to the Spice Islands. Although the parties were able to count on the assistance of native allies, the constant hostilities seriously disrupted and damaged the balance of the Moluccan world order, and ultimately provoked indigenous opposition.[1]

After withdrawing his attacking force from Tidore, Garcia Henriques sent to Melaka for reinforcements. In the interim, however, his request was derailed by the unexpected arrival in Ternate of a force of 100 men, led by Jorge de Meneses, who had been appointed to replace him as Captain General. The abrupt change in command provoked factional conflict in the Portuguese garrison as the former commander refused to relinquish his authority. The upheavals largely distracted Portuguese attention for the remainder of 1527, giving the Spaniards an opportunity to establish themselves on Tidore, with an outpost on Gilolo, and fend off minor Portuguese assaults. The sudden death of Martín Iñiguez de Carquizano in July was believed to have been due to poison, plotted by Captain General Meneses, as Urdaneta reported. Fernando de la Torre was elected as the new Spanish commander.

The prospects for Torre and his men appeared to have miraculously improved at the end of March 1528 when Alvaro de Saavedra Céron arrived from Mexico in the *Florida*. The reports that some of Loaysa's fleet had made it through the Strait of Magellan into the Pacific had been carried to Mexico by Captain Santiago de Guevara and Father Juan de Areyzaga. Their report prompted Hernan Cortes to despatch three ships, the *Florida*, the *Santiago*, and the *Espiritu Santo*, to make the voyage across the Pacific to the Moluccas to reinforce and supply them. Departing at the beginning of November 1527, only Saavedra's *Florida* completed the crossing, the other two vessels having disappeared in a violent gale near the Marshall Islands. He arrived at Tidore on 30 March 1528. The arrival of news and supplies from Mexico gave Torre and his men the confidence that they could complete their mission. On 3 June Saavedra set out, planning to recross the Pacific to Mexico carrying a cargo of spices. Unable to make any headway against the contrary north-east trade winds near the Marianas, he returned to Tidore in October. He set out again in May 1529, but died at the beginning of the voyage. His company, having failed in a second attempt to make headway across the Pacific, returned to Tidore in December 1529, only to find that the situation of the Spaniards had changed dramatically.

On 28 October 1529, Fernando de la Torre had only forty Spaniards currently with him on Tidore, having sent, as Urdaneta reported, thirty of his men to join 'a fleet of the Moors of Gilolo and Tidore ... to destroy some towns of the enemy some 50 leagues from Maluco' to the eastward of Gilolo.[2] Urdaneta alleged that Fernando de Bustamente, Torre's official contador or accountant, had treacherously alerted Jorge de Meneses to the reduction of the Spanish force, prompting him to bring a 'great fleet' against Tidore,

---

[1] Andaya, 'Los primeros contactos', pp. 69–74.
[2] Oviedo uses the alternative name, Batochino de Moro.

sacking its city, killing 'many natives' and wounding 'more Spaniards'. The latter group retreated to a defensive earthwork. According to Urdaneta, it was Bustamente who 'went about, stirring up a mutiny, saying that they were now at the end of the year 1529, and had been five years away from Spain, and that no fleet of His Majesty had come, or was likely to come, so that it would be better to go over to the Portuguese'. Undermined by his subordinates, Torre negotiated what he considered to be a binding agreement. He and the men who stood by him were to be permitted to take ship for the settlement of Camafo on Gilolo, taking only one piece of artillery, their arms, and property. All else was surrendered to the Portuguese. The Portuguese took all the spices which had been collected for transports and burned both the royal and Spanish settlements. Urdaneta and some eighteen others, who had been absent with the fleet, on learning of these events made for Gilolo, and assisted in the transfer of some of the Tidorean nobility thither. Torre could not be persuaded to abandon his agreement with the Portuguese, until he learned that the company of *Florida* had again failed to find a route At this point the argument that it was important to assemble a stronger Spanish contingent on Gilolo so that it would be able to assist any Spanish vessel which might subsequently arrive, overcame his earlier scruples.

Despite efforts by Jorge de Meneses to break the relationship between the Spaniards and their Gilolo hosts, ultimately it was the information that indigenous leaders were planning to combine to rid themselves of the Portuguese that in turn forced the two European parties to cooperate for their own survival. Plans to massacre the Portuguese on Ternate were provoked by an insult, a ritual profanation of a Muslim *cadi* and kinsman of the sultan. When rumours of this reached the Spaniards on Gilolo, Urdaneta was sent to inform Jorge de Meneses. The latter immediately inflamed the situation by imprisoning the boy ruler of Ternate and extracting confessions by torture from, and ultimately beheading, four or five leading notables. The Queen Mother declared total war, bringing all the island rulers to join her, except those of Gilolo. The arrival of a ship carrying a replacement Captain General brought about the arrest and departure of Meneses, but, for the Spanish, also carried the devastating news that Charles V had made a monetary settlement which effectively pawned his claim to the Moluccas to the Portuguese.[1] The small force with Torre on Gilolo recognized that, should the indigenous forces overcome the Portuguese on Ternate, they would likely turn against them next. Reduced in number by death and desertion to about twenty, living on Gilolo with their native concubines and children, they were destitute, shoeless, and in rags, subsisting on the wild boar they hunted and upon handouts from the local sultan who had grown weary of subsidizing them. In January 1532, an envoy was sent to Goa[2] to negotiate terms for their repatriation to Spain. Receiving consent from the Viceroy in 1534, and a provision of 2,000 ducats for their support, the survivors and their families left for Malacca and thence to Cochín. Urdaneta remained behind with the pilot Macías

---

[1] The Treaty of Zaragoza, 22 April 1529. Juan III of Portugal – taking advantage of Charles V's perennial need for cash – proposed pawning Spain's claim on the Moluccas for 350,000 ducats with the right of redemption. Herrera reproduces the provisions of the contract in *Historia General*, Década 14, libro V. Herrera excuses Charles's inattention to the plight of the Loaysa survivors, holding that the Portuguese kept the details of their tribulations secret.

[2] Goa, on the west coast of India, was taken by the Portuguese in 1510, and remained the headquarters of Portuguese holdings in Asia for 450 years; Disney, *Portugal and the Portuguese Empire*, vol. 2, pp. 129–34.

del Poyo vainly hoping to collect clove owed to the Spanish crown, but they too were forced to leave in February of 1535. They travelled via Banda, Java, and Malacca to Cochin. Two years later, only seven men returned to Spain, an even worse record than that of the previous Magellan expedition and without a valuable cargo of spices to cover expenses for the fiasco. All the Spanish expedition records, logs, charts, correspondence, pertaining to the expedition were confiscated by the Portuguese authorities so as to keep secret the particulars of the spice trade and the route to the Moluccas.[1] Pérez-Mallaína, calculates that, of the 450 men who sailed with Loaysa and excluding the 85 who returned via Mexico, and those who lived out their life in India, 'only a few more than half a dozen crewmen returned to the metropolis after having spent between eleven and twelve years in faraway lands'.[2]

The returning survivors, and the heirs of those who had died, presented petitions for the wages owed to the Casa del la Contratación in Seville. Pérez-Mallaína notes that, while 'the king's justice' could generally be relied to uphold salary contracts made between private parties, they were much more parsimonious when it came to settling claims made by those who had served on voyages of discovery or expeditions that the Spanish Crown had 'patronized'.[3] The Loaysa claimants received an ungenerous response of two years' salary.[4]

10. Urdaneta and the *Tornaviaje*, 1565

During and after Magellan's voyage to the Moluccas there were five other attempts to find a sea route back across the Pacific to Mexico (referred to in Spanish as the *tornaviaje*) and all had failed disastrously. Finally, the *tornaviaje* was thought to be impossible to accomplish, and even no less an authority than St Francis Javier warned against attempting it. Given the Portuguese pre-eminence in the Indian Ocean and the Indonesian archipelago, the only alternative for Spanish ships to return from the Moluccas was by the Carreira da India around Africa. This route was too long, too risky, and also a violation of the Treaties of Tordesillas and Zaragoza. The improbability of a viable eastward return voyage from the Spice Islands to Mexico made its commercial value doubtful, and was in part a reason that Charles V gave up his claim to the Spice Islands in the Treaty of Zaragoza.

However, some twenty-five years later, in 1559, King Philip II revived interest in the possibility of establishing bases in the Philippine Islands (later named for him) to initiate trade with China and the Far East. In spite of the fact that those islands lay (as did the Moluccas) in the Portuguese demarcation, it appeared that Portugal was not very interested in the Philippines and made no serious objection to Spanish explorations there. Philip ordered two ships to sail from the west coast of Mexico to explore the islands and establish a foothold there, and, above all, to find a reliable return route to

---

[1] Nowell, 'Loaisa Expedition and the Ownership', pp. 325–36. Various official reports and documents relating to the Loaysa and Saavedra expeditions (in Spanish) are found in Navarrete, *Colección de los Viajes*, vol. 5, pp. 193–486.

[2] Pérez-Mallaína, trans. Rahn Phillips, *Spain's Men of the Sea*, pp. 197–8.

[3] Ibid.

[4] Nowell, 'The Loaisa Expedition and the Ownership', p. 335.

Mexico. By then Urdaneta had retired and joined the Augustinian Order in Mexico, but he was a logical choice to participate in the undertaking. The king ordered Urdaneta (now Father Urdaneta) to accompany an expedition under the command of fellow Basque Miguel López de Legazpi. Initially, Urdaneta refused to take part in this venture, objecting that that he was too old to go, and that the territories were in the Portuguese sector. He was finally lured to participate in the voyage by a false promise that the armada was headed to New Guinea. Only after the fleet of four ships sailed in November 1564 and was far out to sea was he informed of its true destination. One vessel, the *Navidad* commanded by Alonso de Arellano and piloted by Lope Martín, parted early on from the fleet and made its own separate voyage arriving first in the Philippines and making no attempt to rejoin Legazpi's fleet. The latter arrived in the Philippines in January 1565.

In June 1565, Urdaneta was despatched in the *San Pedro* to identify the return route to Mexico. This time, by sailing north to latitude 39°N and then east in an uninterrupted voyage of 7,644 miles, he found the prevailing winds and currents that brought the ship to northern California and then down the coast to Acapulco in November and so dispelled the belief that a return route was impossible. The following year, Urdaneta sailed to Spain to make his report and then again returned to Mexico, where he died in 1568. Urdaneta's discovery of the path back across the Pacific was one of the greatest contributions to maritime navigation.[1] He made possible the famous fleets known as the Manila galleons that brought Mexican and Andean silver to the entrepôt of Manila to purchase spices, fine textiles, porcelains and other prized goods from all over South East Asia and China. The galleons returned to Acapulco where the goods were transported throughout the Spanish Empire and beyond to Europe. These treasure fleets made their annual voyages starting in 1565 and continued as late as 1815.[2]

11. The Significance of the Loaysa Expedition.

As there are many existing works on the subject of Magellan, the present translation of Oviedo's *Book XX* does not include the chapters on Magellan that are disjointed, perfunctory, and disappointing. Their interest today is not in the chronicle per se, but rather how Oviedo grudgingly deals with the material of his best-known informant, the Italian Pigafetta. The comparison of Oviedo's Magellan material with the lengthy and detailed account of the second expedition under the Spaniard Loaysa reveals a tendency to xenophobia in Oviedo, as well as his desire to always be in control of the chronicle of the Indies. Ironically, western history has been more focused on Magellan and Pigafetta.

---

[1] A claim to have made the return to Acapulco 2 months earlier was lodged by Arellano and Martín. After inquiry no action was taken against him but neither was their claim countenanced. See Spate, *Spanish Lake*, pp. 104–5; Nowell 'Arellano versus Urdaneta', pp. 111–20. Nowell argues that they were denied their due in finding the return route because 'in their day both these men had the reputation of being decidedly shady characters'. Because Arellano had separated his ship from the armada without permission, apparently with the intention to explore alone, he was also charged with mutiny by Legazpi.

[2] The classic work on this topic is Schurz, *Manila Galleon*, first published in 1939. Schurz notes (p. 15) that 'No other regular navigation has been so trying and dangerous as this, for in its 250 years the sea claimed dozens of ships and thousands of men and many millions in treasure.'

They have received the full attention they merit, whereas the longer and ultimately more influential Loaysa expedition (1525–35) is little known outside of Spanish language historiography.

Oviedo's narrative of the second expedition to the Spice Lands is a lengthy and fascinating adventure tale of men who undertook enormously long and hazardous voyages to the other side of the world to challenge the Portuguese South East Asian monopoly of the spice trade. After a long and hazardous crossing of two oceans, only one ship of the fleet of seven reached the Moluccas. Without contact and supplies from their government and stranded by the loss of their ships, these few Spaniards tenaciously held out for years against superior Portuguese forces and native islanders who were alternately their friends and then their enemies. Their dwindling numbers were constantly engaged in battles on land and sea in service to an emperor who, unbeknownst to them, had already relinquished his claim to the islands when it was to his advantage.

Whether in terms of men and ships lost or as a commercial and territorial failure, the Loaysa expedition was a disaster. Although no valuable quantity of clove was brought back, something equally or more precious was – knowledge. The few survivors returned with a wealth of information about the area that greatly expanded what was discovered on the relatively short Magellan-Elcano visit there. The Loaysa returnees had acquired knowledge of the Portuguese operations and trade routes that had previously been kept as a closely guarded secret by the Portuguese Crown. The confiscation of the Spaniards' papers on their return to Lisbon, and the Spanish ambassador's fear that Urdaneta would be murdered before he could exit Portugal for Spain, underscores Portuguese concern to suppress any outside knowledge of their trade secrets.

Additionally, Urdaneta and his surviving companions brought back a wealth of experience of the region's society, politics, resources, navigation, customs, and language. This was information that would prove vital to future Spanish involvement in the area. Perhaps the most valuable lesson learned was that the establishment of a viable Spanish presence in the Spicelands, and surrounding areas, hinged on discovering a reliable return route across the Pacific to Mexico – the *tornaviaje*. Although the resolution of that problem by Andrés de Urdaneta was some decades off, it was finally accomplished as a direct result of the Loaysa armada.

12. This Translation

The source text for this translation is the 1557 edition of *Book XX* whose folio numbers (recto and verso) are indicated in [ ] throughout to facilitate cross reference. The original Spanish text has been compared to the text of modern Spanish text edition edited by Juan Perez de Tudela Bueso, published in five volumes for the *Biblioteca de Autores Españoles* in 1959.[1] This latter edition contains references to the preceding 1851–5 edition of José Amador de los Ríos. With a few exceptions noted, the 1557 text and the Ríos-Tudela edition are substantially the same. Where differences occur, most seem to be due to orthographic printing errors common to sixteenth-century texts. The numbers in < > throughout the text of the translation signal page numbers of the *BAE* text for

---

[1] Henceforth *BAE*, vols 117–21.

comparison. In footnotes the reference to the chapter and page numbers in the original 1557 printing is followed by the relevant volume and page numbers in the 1959 *BAE* edition.

One error in the 1557 text is in the sequence of chapter numbers where two chapters are given the number III. This English translation reflects the correct order in line with the 1557 *BAE* edition. There are three types of footnotes. Oviedo's marginal references in the 1557 printing are presented as footnotes and identified by that date. Those of Los Ríos and Tudela Bueso, are identified by their author's name. The remaining notes reflect the work of the present editor.[1]

Proper names are as given in the 1557 printing. The Portuguese are identified with Spanish spelling (e.g. Serrano for Serrão). The Spanish spelling, Magallanes, is used for the explorer's surname and the Strait throughout the Ovideo text. The names of the other various participants are as Oviedo recorded them. These names are obviously phonetic equivalents of what the Spaniards thought they heard and, consequently, their spellings vary (often greatly), according to what text or source one reads. The regal titles are also as Oviedo recorded them – king, prince, sultan, emirs, raja. Toponyms are given as written by Oviedo, Urdaneta, and Vícente de Nápoles in the texts, with variant spellings and the modern identifications listed in a reference at the first occurrence. The maps also note the present-day denominations when identifiable.

As opposed to my two previous Oviedo translations, here the historian's prose is markedly easier to follow and translate, principally because Oviedo is reproducing the oral and written reports supplied by participants in the expeditions. By the nature of their informants – soldiers, sailors, other adventurers – these accounts tend to be quite straightforward and generally free from the rhetorical flourishes that often characterize Oviedo's works. The difference will be obvious when the reader compares his highly stylized introductions (especially the dedication to the Emperor) with the simpler prose of the text. True to form, however, Oviedo is ever in control of the narrative, interjecting himself into the history with comments on the proceedings, his informants, and on his own personal experiences in the New World Indies. The historian's 'I' is never far from the surface and in this way Oviedo always tacitly claims possession of the chronicle of the Indies, as befits its imperially designated Official Chronicler. All translations are my own except where indicated by credit to another translator.

Oviedo's chapter titles are often lengthy summaries of a variety of events, commonly concluding with 'etc.' for things he did not refer to. His titles are presented in full in the body of his text. They have been shortened in the Table of Contents to include what Oviedo clearly considered to be the most significant events. Only elisions in the middle of a chapter heading in the Table Contents are marked with an ellipsis.

The footnotes to Oviedo's text are from three sources. First, there are those that appear in much abbreviated form in the margins of the 1557 edition, and are often quite vague as to the exact work cited in them. Presumably, those references were supplied by Oviedo. Most of those annotations were included as footnotes in Amador de los Ríos's edition and retained in Juan Pérez de Tudela Bueso's *BAE* reprinting. The substance of those notes is identified by (1557). They are here translated and adjusted to conform to English usage with additional information for more clarity when possible. Notes supplied by

---

[1] With some subsequent additions and amendments by the Series Editor.

Amador de los Ríos are identified by the notation (Ríos). The main body of the notes not attributed to either Oviedo or Amador de los Ríos were supplied by the late Professor Dille, with some additions provided by the Hakluyt Society Series Editor with additional information for more clarity when possible.

Appendices 1 and 2 were originally translated by Sir Clements Markham and included in his edition of *Early Spanish Voyages to the Strait of Magellan*, Hakluyt Society, series 2, vol. 28, 1911. His translations are republished here with some minor amendments to the text as a result of comparison with the originals held in the Archivo de Indias, and to the footnotes in respect of the content of references provided earlier in this volume.

Book XX of the Second Part of the General History of the Indies.

Written by Captain Gonzalo Fernández de Oviedo y Valdés,
warden of the fortress and port of Santo Domingo of the Island of Hispaniola,
and his majesty's chronicler.
The subject of which is the Strait of Magallanes.

In Valladolid by Francisco Fernández de Córdoba.
Printer to His Majesty.
In the year MDLVII

Prologue

Holy Caesarean Catholic Royal Majesty:
I now return to the work of this *General and Natural History* of your Indies and western empire which includes so many new, great and marvellous things detailed in this Second Part I present to your Caesarean Majesty that will move the reader and all Christians to give thanks to Nature's Master, and in which many admirable things in the Universe will be presented to faithful Catholic intellects, so as to cause them infinite delight to see amplified the Christian Republic in such great and countless kingdoms of yours, where for so many years and centuries Satan and Hell augmented their condemned company with a multitude of lost souls. All of which Divine Mercy is now remedying and your Monarchy overflows with glory, praise and eternal fame at your triumphs; and with inestimable favour and renown, a great part of this good is attributable to the bellicose and noble Spanish nation, and all together to the good fortune and personal excellence of its Prince.

And although for many long centuries, truthful and eminent authorities have written of the vigour, soldiery, high-mindedness and excellencies of this our nation, in the present day what your Spanish vassals have wrought in these Indies should merit greater credit, fame, and title, as much in the exercise of arms on land as on the vast waters of the Ocean Sea as brave veterans dauntless in the face of fatigue, constant peril, innumerable hardships, famine and disease and with all this, the majority of them unsalaried and unrewarded. The result of their efforts has acquired for your Majesty another hemisphere and half a world, no less land than all that which the ancients called Asia, Africa and Europe.

Neither Alexander the Great nor his soldiers ever lost sight of the Arctic pole, even when they found themselves most distant from their native land, Macedonia. Now opposite that pole in the other Antarctic region your Castilian banner possesses more kingdoms and [f. 2r] states and unites under one sceptre more diverse languages and peoples than all those many princes together since God created the world. What Assyrian monarchy, what power of the Sicyonians[1] or of great Alexander and his Macedonians, what power of Darius and Cyrus and the Persians, what power of the Mycenaeans or Corinthians, what power of the Athenians or Thebans, what of the Parthians or Egyptians, what potency of the Carthaginians or of the Romans whose famous and much praised dominions are solemnized in many volumes of grave and worthy authors can compare? All these realms as well as others I omit are encompassed in the Arctic hemisphere, but yours comprehend the one and the other pole.

---

[1] Sicyonians or Sikyonians (*Sicionios*): inhabitants of Sicyon, Sikyon or Sekyon, an ancient Greek city in the northern Peloponnese about 11 miles north-west of Corinth.

The fabulous tales of Jason and Medea and the Golden Fleece cannot compare with the things your Spaniards have experienced in these new lands.[1] Let those who praise Theseus and the labyrinth with its Minotaur be silent since, truth be told, <p. 213> those metaphors faced with real history are childish fairy tales compared with what has been seen and continues to be seen every day in our time in these our Indies.[2] So that in this and future ages envious enemies of such a valorous and experienced nation, so praiseworthy for its virtues, will not be able to gainsay what my own eyes and those of many others have seen.

Writers have much praised the Romans and rightly tell of their glorious deeds in conquest of a great portion of the world. Trogus Pompeius and Justinus proudly trace the Romans' origins to the famous Trojans, and principally to Aeneas who settled in Italy where he took a second wife, Lavinia, daughter of King Latinus.[3] (As you will recall from Livy, his first wife was Creusa, daughter of King Priam.[4]) However, that famous man from whom the Romans claim descent I find not so highly celebrated in Trojan histories as the Romans would have him, but rather with Antenor vituperated as unfaithful to their king and country.[5] Another origin more honest, greater, and better, another more noble and ancient, another more famous and esteemed can be attributed; because it is widely believed that the Spanish *Brigos* were the ancestors of the Phrygians who are the very same Trojans, as I said in Chapter III, Book II, Part I of this *General History of the Indies*, and so says Pliny.[6] Thus many centuries before Aeneas, the Trojans would be descended from our Spaniards because the *Brigos* are themselves Spanish and derive their name from Brigo, the fourth king of Spain. It is from this origin and beginning, better than Aeneas's, which one ought to revere and acclaim the Romans. But, be it this or another founding, however they may like, our Spanish origin had its beginning in Tubal who came to populate Spain soon after the universal flood.[7]

But let us leave these very ancient beginnings and return to the Romans. Some partisan modern Italian historians, thinking to honour Spain, say that our Spanish ancestors [f. 2v]

[1] Publius Ovidius Naso (Ovid), 43 BCE–17/18 CE, *Metamorphoses*, bk VII, 1557.

[2] Titus Livius Patavinus (Livy), 59 BCE–17 CE, *History*, Decade I, bk I, 1557.

[3] Justinus (Marcus Junianus Justinus), fl. 3rd cent. CE, *Epitome*, Bk XLIII, 1557. Pompeyo Trogus's *Historiae Philippicae* exists in a paraphrase written two centuries later by Justinus. An English translation is available through www.attalus.org.

[4] Livy, *History*, Decade I, ch. IV, 1557.

[5] Antenor: counsellor to King Priam, said to have treacherously opened the gates of Troy to the Greeks.

[6] Pliny (Gaius Plinius Segundus), 23–79 CE, *Naturalis Historia*, Bk V, ch. XXXIII, 1557. Phrygia, a kingdom in west central Anatolia. According to Herodotus, the Phrygians initially lived in the southern Balkans and were called Bryges, Briges, or Brygians (hence Spanish *Brigos*) and allies of the Trojans. Oviedo (Bk II, ch. III; *BAE*, vol. 117, pp. 17–20) labours mightily to justify Spain's claim to the New World, writing that in ancient times the lands were the Hesperides so named for the twelfth king of Spain Hespero and thus already Spanish property. If that were so, then Columbus's claim of discovery would be questionable and could undercut the long-standing lawsuit his heirs brought against the Crown for abrogating the admiral's rightful revenues from the Indies. Naturally, Ferdinand Columbus's biography of his father is sharply critical of Oviedo's knowledge of ancient history, writing that his claims are irrational and baseless; *Life of the Admiral*, ch. 10, pp. 28–34. However, in other sections of his history, Oviedo highly praises the Admiral. See below, p. 35, n. 2.

[7] Tubal: Tubal-Cain the son of Lamech and Zillah (Genesis, 4:22), 'an instructor of every artificer in brass and iron'. In a marginal note Oviedo indicated the source as Berossus. Berossus wrote a history of Babylonia, *c*.290 BCE which has only survived through citation by others; for example, Eusebius of Caesarea, whom Oviedo often cites. In 1492, Annius of Viterbo published what he claimed were the lost books of Berossus, which was probably known to Oviedo.

inherited from Rome the art and science of war, political institutions, and other honourable customs, thus refining and correcting Spanish rusticity or ignorance. This I deny as completely false and said by men of little credit and no authority. The truth is quite the opposite. Even though some of the Roman captains, leaders, and consuls came to Spain and, accompanied by no more courage but with more fortune, subjugated the greater part of it, the Romans did not contribute as much of the virtues that they say. 'Virtues' such as martyring Christians and teaching men to suffer their tyranny and to be idolaters like the Romans, who abominated many Spanish saints and virgin martyrs, friends of God, who, by their merits, populated part of the celestial seats that Lucifer and his minions lost. The sacred histories of the Catholic Church are filled with examples. Leaving aside innumerable other saints, my point is supported by martyrs such as the Saint Acislus, Saint Victoria, Saint Faustus, Saint Januario, Saint Martial, Saint Zoilus, Saint Eulegius, Saint Pelagius, Saint Lucretia, Saint Nunilus, Saint Alodia, Saint Justa, Saint Rufina, Saint Emeterius, Saint Celedonius, Saint Facundus, Saint Primitivus, Saint Claudius and Lupercius and Victor (noble knights of the noble city of León), Saint Fructuosus, bishop, Saint Augurius, Saint Eulogius, Saint Sabina, Saint Fides, Saint Olalla [Eulalia] of Mérida, Saint Leocadia, Saint Felix, Saint Olalla of Barcelona, Saint Eufemia, Saint Centolla, Saint Narciso [Narcissus], Saint Juste [Justus], Saint Pastor, Saint Engracia, and the many virgins and others who were martyred with her in Zaragoza in Aragón.[1] These friends of God and many other martyrs and saints resplendent in their constancy in the Christian faith through which our countrymen and women, suffered countless torments for not <p. 214> accepting the rites and idolatries of the Romans.

Later, the Goths expelled the Romans from Spain, the first of them being Athanarico [Athanaric]. His lineage endures today in your Majesty and your children by direct descent through your predecessors. This exalted lineage that will continue for centuries in your successors and descendants had its origin in Scythia (which is east of your German empire) in the year of our Lord 343. Some hold that Alaric the son and successor of Athanaric, was the one who came to Spain, as I detailed in my *Royal Catalogue of Spain* that your Caesarean Majesty ordered placed in your private chambers.[2]

Of Roman origin was the traitor Count Julian who, in 720 in the time of the unfortunate King Rodrigo, let the Moors into Spain to destroy it.[3] After its destruction, he who began and was the first king of the restoration was the sainted Goth, Pelayo. By

---

[1] Although the roll call of martyred saints is meant to support Oviedo's argument against the glorification of Spain's Roman inheritance, some of the martyrs in his list (Eulegius, Pelagius, Lucretia, Nunilus, and Alodia, for example) were early victims of the Moorish occupation. The spelling of the names in this translation follows modern Catholic norms where identifiable.

[2] *Cathálogo Real de Castilla, y de todos los Reyes de las Españas e de Nápoles y Secilia, e de los Reyes y señores de las Casas de Françia, Austria, Holanda y Borgoña; de donde proceden los quatro abolorios de la Cesárea Majestad del Emperador don Carlos, nuestro Rey e señor de las Españas, con relación de todos los Emperadores y Summos Pontífices que han sucedido desde Jullio César, que fue el primero emperador, y desde el apóstol Sanct Pedro, que fue el primero Papa, hasta este año de Cristo de MDXXXII años.* Like several others of Oviedo's lengthy works, this genealogy was never published, however, the manuscript of this extravagantly titled tome has been transcribed and edited by E. A. Romano de Thuesen in an unpublished PhD dissertation, University of California, Santa Barbara, 1992.

[3] Oviedo's marginal note cites Eusebius (Bishop of Caesarea, Palestine, 263–339 CE), *De los tiempos*. Oviedo cites him frequently also using the work's Latin title *De temporibus*. This may refer to Eusebius's *Ecclesiastical History* or perhaps his *Chronicle*. The date of the Moorish invasion of Spain was 711 CE.

his very sword and those of his successors, all native Spaniards, was Spain recovered and returned to its own seignory and Christian republic once the evil, tyrannical sect of perfidious Mohammed was dissipated and expelled. The restoration lasted [f. 3r] until 1492, the year in which the Catholic Monarchs, your grandparents of immortal memory, Don Fernando and Doña Isabel took Granada (which I witnessed).[1] In truth, one can say the Re-conquest lasted until your Caesarean Majesty extirpated and expelled from Spain the remaining subjugated Moors practising their damnable sect. Then was their name totally extinguished and expelled from all your kingdoms, expunging all trace of their Ishmaelite rituals and ceremonies.

Thus, Spain should glory much more in its Goths and in its own native Spaniards than in the benefits, contributions and customs of the Roman people. Because of the many hardships and evils that happened to Spain under the Romans, we should glorify more the Goths whose feats of arms the Romans experienced to their harm and shame several times, especially when King Alaric sacked Rome. Paulus Orosius's history relates how in the same way that God saved the innocent Lot from Sodom, he also saved Pope Innocent I when Alaric came to besiege Rome.[2] St Jerome says that, during that siege, the starving Romans ate each other, the mother not pardoning the infant at her breast but from hunger returned it to her belly where it had recently been.[3] And as cruel as some historians make him out, King Alaric proclaimed that those taking refuge in the churches would be unharmed in the sacking, especially those inside the Church of Saint Peter and Saint Paul. Nevertheless, thousands of Romans were put to the sword or imprisoned. Likewise, it is written that the Gothic King Teodoric took Rome and also the Goth King Totila destroyed Rome so that this royal lineage was very hateful to the Romans.

Let us leave this topic to return to our history and principal intent. Goths and Spanish are those who find themselves in these our Indies, vassals of your Majesty and of the Royal Crown of Castile, all guided by the industry of that memorable first admiral, Don Christopher Columbus of eternal fame. Even though all that is now and will be written may perish on earth, such a famous history will be perpetuated in heaven where God wills that everything good be rewarded for the eternal praise and glory of such a famous man.

It seems to me just and right that your Majesty and all the kings of Castile remember to continually honour, reward, and protect the succession and house of Columbus and to sustain, augment, and esteem it <p. 215>, a jewel and ornament of your realms as the cause of so many good things, particularly that Christ and the Catholic faith be served, increased, and preached in these Indies where, since time immemorial, it was unknown in so many foreign kingdoms. From these strange lands Columbus caused innumerable treasures to be delivered to your Royal Majesty's treasury in Spain to be well employed by your Majesty in God's service against infidels, and in many holy ventures and pious works that your Caesarean Majesty undertakes. I leave it to the erudite historians [f. 3v]

---

[1] In his youth, Oviedo was a page in the household of the duke of Villahermosa, King Ferdinand's nephew, and was present in 1492 at the siege and capitulation of Granada, the last Moorish kingdom in Spain. There he also witnessed Columbus receiving his commission to sail west.

[2] Oviedo's marginal note cites Paulus Orosius (c.375–c.418 CE), *Ormesta mundi*, Bk VII. Perhaps from *Historiarum Adversum Paganos*, seven books of history against the pagans, one of the most widely copied books from the medieval period. Alaric besieged the city of Rome in 410 CE.

[3] Oviedo's marginal note cites Saint Jerome (c.340–420 CE), Epistles, *Ad principium*.

who attend upon your Majesty to more specifically detail your works, as I can only speak authoritatively about things in these Indies.

One of the things that I have especially desired to make known by my pen is the correct account of the positioning and geography of Tierra Firme. To that end I divided this *General History* into three parts – the first in nineteen books, the second in nineteen, and the third in twelve, for a total of fifty books. Of these, this is the second part commencing with the twentieth book which deals with the discovery of that famous and long strait by Captain Ferdinand Magallanes, and also related is his death at the hands of the Indians. After that the book continues with the events of the second fleet, your Majesty sent to the Spice Islands under Commander Fray García Jofre de Loaysa and also relating some particulars of the Moluccas and of that voyage and the people of those parts.

Ending Book XX, I will progress to Book XXI. I will describe the coast, commencing from the eastern mouth of the Strait at 52½ degrees south of the Equator in the other hemisphere of the Antarctic pole. From there I will proceed to the Paraná River (improperly known as the Plate) moving up in the direction of the Artic pole to Cabo San Agustín.[1] From that cape, I will describe the coast of Tierra Firme towards the west, crossing the Equator (or the Torrid Zone) and then to New Spain.[2] I will continue along that coast northward until turning east rounding the mainland in the land of Labrador and the Bacallaos towards the north, arriving at 60 or more degrees north of the Equator.[3] After this book, I will proceed in the following books to detail the journeys, voyages, and histories of the diverse governmental territories included in this vast Tierra Firme. This will conclude Book XXXVIII, the last of this second part of the *History*. All this will be to confound the opinions of the ancient cosmographers and writers who held that the land underneath the poles is uninhabitable.

After concluding Part II, I will proceed to the third in another volume of this *General and Natural History* of your Indies. This part will concern areas other than Tierra Firme and the southern lands and seas, and the rest of the information gathered by my laborious studies of the Indies, or at least what in my time I have been able to see or been informed of these materials, as your Majesty orders me and in which I am constantly occupied.

The last part will comprise twelve books to bring the total to fifty and will conclude these histories (as far as what is known to the present). However, my work will not stop, but rather continue to expand in some of the [f. 4r] books with what may be learned during my lifetime as doubtless in time there will be more information. Nevertheless, the number of books will remain the same –fifty– in three volumes by the end of this present year 1546.[4] I say this with the confidence that the Holy Spirit will inspire me so that in everything God and your clement Caesarean Majesty will be pleased with me. <p. 216> I will count my time very well spent if I have succeeded in contenting your sacred person.

[1] Cabo San Agustín is close to the Brazilian city of Recife at 8° 20′ S.

[2] New Spain: now central Mexico. *Tierra Firme*: the name originally given to the northern coast of South America and which became known in English as the Spanish Main.

[3] Bacallaos: supposedly discovered by the Portuguese João Vaz Corte-Real, who named the island Terra Nova de Bacalhau (the new land of codfish), or Terranova, which in English became 'new found land' and finally Newfoundland. The present-day Canadian province of Newfoundland comprises Newfoundland Island and the coastal area named Labrador.

[4] Here *BAE*, vol. 117, gives '1544', but it is corrected in the *Prologue* to 1546.

May Jesus Christ ever be my guide and ever praised, and I beg Him to make up for my defects. To Him I commend myself and all that I write I put under the correction and protection of the Holy Apostolic Mother Church of Rome so that my treatises, accepted by Her together with your Caesarean Majesty's favour, may be inspired and inspiring as they are offered for the reader's good and praiseworthy edification. Nevertheless, I confess the weak preparation of my rude intellect for such an arduous undertaking, as well as my stylistic poverty to know how to explicate so many strange histories and novel events with the appropriate pleasure that these histories require. That aside, I will not desist telling what I have learned in compliance with your Caesarean Majesty's mandate and that of your Royal Council of the Indies. And since one naturally fears the dog-like tongues of one's critics, I intend to shelter myself against them in the prudent council of Seneca who says: *Stultum est timere, quod vitare non posis* – it is foolish to fear what cannot be avoided.[1]

---

[1] Lucius Annaeus Seneca, 4 BCE–65 CE: *De Remediis fortuitorum*, 1557.

PROLOGUE[1]

The preceding General Prologue is dedicated to the Emperor, our Lord King. This following Prologue is the introduction to Book XX of the *General and Natural History of the Indies*, the first book of the second part of histories of them.

Introduction to Book Twenty

My conscience charges me to begin this second volume of these histories pertaining to Tierra Firme with the first admiral, Don Christopher Columbus, discoverer, author, and foundation of all the discoveries of the Indies, islands, and Tierra Firme of the Ocean Sea as to him alone and to no other is due such glory. However, historical order requires me to begin this book not with the admiral but with Captain Ferdinand Magallanes who discovered the great and famous southern strait of Tierra [f. 4v] Firme itself. This is necessary so that I relate in an orderly fashion the disposition, limits, and degrees of latitude of that area to be better understood by the learned as well as unlearned reader. Those famous beginnings in the New World related in the first part of these histories justly belong to the Admiral.[2] As I have related, it is well known that he first discovered and navigated the lands and seas of these Indies, as I have related in the year 1492 of the nativity of Our Redeemer. But let no one complain of me when I write of other captains and individuals who, after the great and principal discoverer, continued to voyage and to build upon that first beginning other discoveries that will be related with the dates, places, and provinces of each. In this manner the pre-eminence of the memory of the Admiral as first discoverer will be safeguarded, and the deeds of others given their due. So, God willing, I hope to relate all that to His praise and glory and to the consolation and recreation of faithful Christians and to manifest the truthfulness of the *General and Natural History* of these Indies if the reader be pleased to wholeheartedly accept the work as faithful to the author's intent. That being the case, all persons who may see these treatises will not fail to give thanks to Our Redeemer for all that they are notified herein and which comes to their attention for the first time.

This first book (the twentieth of this second volume or part) treats the famous Strait of Magallanes and what is known of it to this present year of 1546. In it will be related the voyage of the fleet of Magallanes; the islands of the Moluccas, the Spice Islands, where <p. 217> and how this captain and others were killed; how one of the ships returned laden with spices; how the ship sailed west and returned from the Levant to

---

[1] Before this, the *BAE*, 117 text inserts: 'Here begins the twentieth book of the *General and Natural History of the Indies, islands and Tierra Firme of the Ocean Sea* which concerns the *Strait of Magallanes*' – not in the 1557 edition. The two sentences following Prologue are omitted in *BAE*.

[2] Oviedo covers Columbus in Part I, Bk II and chs I–IX of Bk III; *BAE*, vol., 117, pp. 13–74.

circumnavigate the globe following the path of the sun. This vessel was the *Victoria*. Also to be related is the voyage through the Strait of another fleet commanded by Fray García Jofre de Loaysa, his death, and the events of this voyage as well as many details of those islands and peoples, according to the testimony of eye-witnesses from both expeditions, well-known persons worthy of credit.

CHAPTER V

Which treats of the second and infelicitous voyage to the Spicelands, with the second armada that the Emperor, our lord, sent there in the second discovery commanded by Captain General Fray García Jofre de Loaysa, Knight of the Order of Rhodes, citizen of Ciudad Real

Our lord, the Emperor-King, briefed by Captain Joan Sebastián del Cano, captain and pilot of the famous nao *Victoria*, and by Fernando de Bustamente and other hidalgos who went with Magallanes and returned to Spain in the said ship with Joan Sebastián, ordered his factor, Cristóbal de Haro, to outfit a second armada in Galicia in the port of La Coruña. Six ships and a galeón were made ready, very well provisioned with all that was necessary. His Majesty appointed as his captain general Commander Fray [f. 20v] García Jofre de Loaysa of the Military Order of Rhodes. A native of Ciudad Real, this man was a good knight, experienced in land and sea warfare. The chief pilot and guide was Joan Sebastián del Cano who, as I have related, had been pilot of one of Magallanes's ships and returned in the famous ship *Victoria*. This ship, in my opinion, <p. 240> is one of the five most renowned vessels of the world which are:[1]

The first and principal was the ark that God ordered Noe to build in which he and his wife; his sons Sem, Cam and Jafet;[2] and his daughters-in-law escaped the great flood so that human lineage would be restored. This ship is praised for its size, form, voyage, and divine artifice, for being constructed by God's mandate, for His mercy and for so high a mystery and such good.

The second famous ship was Jasón's, called the *Argos* for the name of the master who built it and in which Jason went to the island of Colcos[3] in search of the Golden Fleece. This venture was successful due to his love affair with Medea. This ship is celebrated for its voyage and for the noble princes who sailed in it.

The third was the ship that Sosi, king of Egipto, had built.[4] That huge vessel was two hundred and eighty cubits long. It was of cedar wood, entirely gilded on the exterior and silver plated on the interior. The ship was dedicated to the god of Thebes. This ship is notable for its great magnificence and richness but not for its voyages of which nothing is recorded.

---

[1] As Amador de los Ríos notes, the listing here of the five famous ships is a virtual repeat of what Oviedo included in Pt I, Bk VII, ch. XL; *BAE*, vol. 117, p. 199.

[2] Noah, Shem, Ham, and Japheth.

[3] Colchis.

[4] The source for the Egyptian ship is given as from Diodorus Siculus (*c.*60–30 BCE), *Bibliotheca historica*, bk II. Diodorus calls the king Sesoösis, perhaps now known as Sesostris or Senusret.

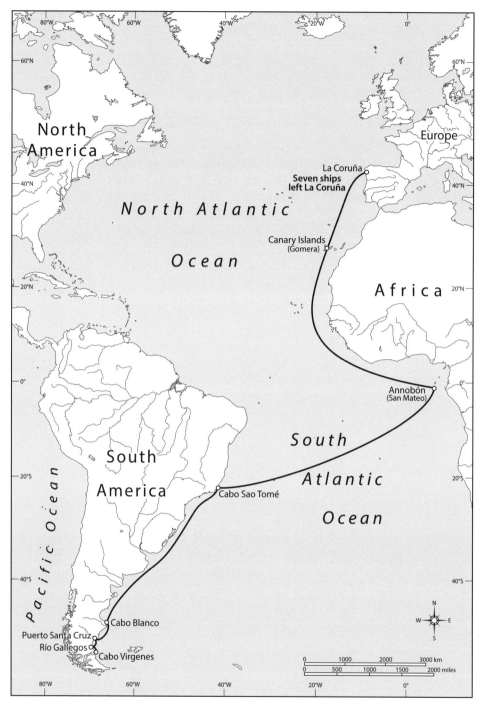

Map 1. The track of Loaysa's fleet to the Strait of Magellan.

The fourth famous ship in which the first admiral of these our Indies, Don Cristóbal Colom, discovered these parts and islands of Tierra Firme, called the *Gallega* first mentioned in the first part of this *General History of the Indies*.[1]

The fifth famous ship I say is the *Victoria* that in which captain and pilot Joan Sebastián del Cano returned from the Spicelands, for that ship circumnavigated the entire world in the longest journey made by any ship to date since the beginning of the world.

Let us return to our subject. In July of the year 1525, Commander Loaysa, Caesar's[2] captain general, set out for the Spicelands from the Guadalquivir River and the port of Sanct Lúcar de Barrameda.[3] The flagship in which the general sailed, was called, the *Sancta María de la Victoria* of 300 tons burthen. The nao *Sancti Spíritus*, of 200 tons commanded by Juan Sebastián del Cano as captain and chief pilot who is mentioned in the *History* in various parts as the one who returned to Castile in the nao *Victoria* laden with spices. Another nao of 170 tons, the *Anunciada*,[4] was captained by a gentleman named Pedro de Vera. The fourth nao, was named the *Sanct Gabriel* in which Don Rodrigo de Acuña went as Captain and she was of 130 tons.[5]

The fifth nao, named *Sancta María del Parral*, of 80 tons, captained by a gentleman [21r] named Don Jorge Manrique. The sixth nao, the *Sancto Lesmes* also of 80 tons, and Francisco de Hoces went as captain. The seventh ship, of fifty tons was called the *Sanctiago*, a *galeón*[6] or patache of 50 tons and her captain was Sanctiago de Guevara.

These seven ships carried four hundred and fifty men. On 2 August of that year they came to the island of Gomera which is one of those of the Canaries where they stayed twelve days taking on water, food, and other provisions for their long journey. The Eve of Our Lady, 14 August, they set sail along the southern route, and on 20 October they came to the island of Sanct Mateo where they remained until the end of that month.[7]

That island, according to the charts of the cosmographer Alonso de Chaves, is two degrees south of the equator but, according to Diego de Ribero and others, it is one and a half degrees south. The man who set down and verified the report of this journey was a cleric named Don Joan de Areyzaga, a Basque whom I met and talked with in Madrid in 1535[8] <p. 241> at the time he gave his report to Caesar and the gentlemen of his Royal Council of the Indies. Don Joan said that the island of Sanct Mateo was at two and a quarter degrees south of the line and was more or less four leagues in circumference. He

---

[1] The *Gallega*; so named because she was probably built in the shipyards of Galicia. Later renamed the *Marigalante*, and then renamed again the *Santa María* as Columbus's flagship when she was chartered from her owner, Juan de la Cosa.

[2] This is a short form of the full title, 'Caesarean Majesty, Emperor-King' by which Oviedo refers to the Holy Roman Emperor Charles V who was also King Charles I of Spain.

[3] The fleet sailed 24 July 1525, not from San Lúcar but rather from La Coruña where, as Oviedo correctly noted, it was outfitted, and where la Casa de la Contratación de la Especería (the House of Trade for the Spicelands) was established after the Magellan expedition had reached those parts. Navarrete, *Colección de los Viajes*, vol. 5, p. 5.

[4] Variant: *Anuciada*.

[5] Elsewhere in both the original 1557 and *BAE* editions the name of the captain of the *Sanct Gabriel* is given as Jorge de Acuña; see below, p. 41, n. 1.

[6] See above, p. xvii.

[7] Morison, *Southern Voyages*, p. 479, identifies this island as what is now Annobón in Equatorial Guinea at 1°30′S, 5°40′E. See below, p. 141, n. 3, for Markham's commentary on earlier attempts to identify the same.

[8] See below, pp. 58–9. Oviedo spells the given name of the priest as either Joan or Juan. The information gathered from Father Areyzaga is found in Chapters V–XIII.

said that the island consists of high and mountainous ground covered with trees, among which are many palms and orange trees. Around the island are five small islands projecting into the sea – three on the southern side and two on the north where there is a very good anchorage and a large and fine river. On the island are many birds, especially frigate birds and boobies[1] that are easily captured. They clubbed to death many of the latter in their nests that contained only one egg, a number they verified after examining various nests. There were also swifts breeding in those small islands. In the forests, they found many hens and roosters like those in Spain as well as many wild swine like ours. They found many human bones and skulls, and a Portuguese crew member said that the island had been populated by Portuguese who were all murdered by their black slaves. They found ruined houses, a large wooden cross set up like those generally found along roads, and a tree with an inscription reading 'Pe[d]ro Fernández passed through here in the year 1515'. In the waters of the harbour there were many fish, particularly all the sea bream or red mullet they could wish for. One day a fish resembling a sea bass was caught. It was as large as a twenty-pound salmon. All those at the captain general's mess who ate it became so sick, they thought they would die. It is believed that they would have had they not been treated with theriac and other remedies; as it was, they were sick for many days.[2] The reverend father cleric Juan de Areyzaga said [f. 21v] that he saw the fish and it had teeth like those of a large dog. He reported that he himself killed another similar fish weighing more than fifty pounds, but because of what had happened with the others he did not dare eat it, and threw it overboard.

The fleet left Sancto Mateo Island on 13 November 1525, but this father called it Sancto Tomé. On 4 December they sighted the Brazilian coast of Tierra Firme. The next day at twenty-one and one half degrees, they were three leagues offshore at high and forested land.[3] This priest said, that comparing their charts, they discovered from those of the cosmographer Diego Ribero that the Brazilian coast from the cape of Sanct Agustín to Cabo Frío was sixty leagues more to the west than what it was supposed to be; and on the charts of cosmographer Nuño García, Cabo San Agustín was sixty-eight leagues west of what was indicated.

This priest, writing about catching flying fish, said that the tunas flushed them out of the water and that some tunas jumped after them to a height of one or more *estados*. The albacore tunas are so large that one would weigh two hundred or more pounds.[4] They killed some of the largest of these with heavy baited hooks let out from the stern of fast moving vessels.

Thursday, 28 December, the Day of the Innocents: because of a sudden squall, the ships were separated but after the storm they regrouped in convoy with the exception of the flagship. That night in search of the missing ship, all set out their lanterns and sailed

[1] There are currently 5 existing species of the genus *fregata* found in the tropical oceans and capable of soaring for great distances above them. The brown booby (*Sula leucogaster*) is found on the coast and islands of Equatorial Guinea.

[2] Theriac (*triaca*), 'treacle': an antidote to poison, especially snake venom, dating from ancient Greek physicians, compounded from various drugs mixed with honey.

[3] Morison, *Southern Voyages*, p. 479, identifies the Brazilian landfall as the Banco S. Tomé off the cape of the same name at 22°S.

[4] Tunny (*Thunius alalunga*), can weigh as much as 30–40 kilograms. There are numerous species of flying fish (Exocoetidae). Pepperell, *Fishes*, pp. 78–80, 227–9.

with only the foresails. During this time, the *Sanct Gabriel*, captained by Rodrigo de Acuña became separated from the others.[1] Two days after losing contact with the flagship, the five ships continued on their route, believing that it had travelled on ahead of them.

On 5 January 1526 they sighted Cabo Blanco.[2] This reverend father said that it is at forty-six degrees, but our cosmographers put it at only forty-five degrees south of the equator. From this cape this cleric <p. 242> determined the distance to the Strait at one hundred and six leagues, whereas our cosmographers say one hundred and twenty-five, more or less. But one should not confuse this with the Cabo Blanco at the mouth of the Paranaguazú (or Plata) River that is three hundred and seventy leagues away from the Strait.[3] (With regard to cosmography and latitudes, I will disregard what this father says as I do not believe he was as expert with the astrolabe as he was in the rest of what he reports. Nevertheless, from time to time I will report his observations since he said that with the quadrant and observation of the sun and North Star he took the latitudes he affirmed.)

On 9 January, seeing that there was no sign of the flagship or the *Sanct Gabriel*, the remaining captains agreed that Santiago de Guevara should go in his galeón or patache to the harbour of Santa Cruz that the priest reported as at fifty degrees south (others call it the River of the Cruz and put it at fifty-one [f. 22r] degrees).[4] There he was to place messages as specified by instructions they had from the captain general. The captains agreed that the fleet should go on to the Strait to make repairs and await the flagship[5]

Sunday, 14 January: They sighted a great, wide river that, by all signs, seemed to them to be the Strait. They drew so near that they were in four fathoms of water and the nao *Sancti Spíritus* touched the shoals several times. (Those shoals extend three and four leagues out to sea and at low tide are exposed to reveal great gullies and high ground two and three fathoms high.)[6] Likewise, on the same shoals the *Anuciada* touched bottom. Because the tide was coming in, Captain Juan Sebastián del Cano ordered the ships to anchor. Once anchored, he had the skiff[7] brought out and sent it to land to see if it were the Strait. On board the skiff were Pilot Martín Pérez del Cano, Treasurer Bustamante, the priest Don Juan, and five other men with orders that if it were the passage they would light three fires and, if not, not light any. The treasurer and gunner Roldán went to reconnoitre as previously they had been there and in the Maluco on the voyage of Magallanes. Entering the river, the treasurer said that without doubt that area was the

---

[1] Here both the original 1557 and *BAE* editions give the captain's name as Jorge de Acuña, but the roll of ships and their captains and subsequent references indicate it should be Rodrigo de Acuña.

[2] Both the 1557 text and *BAE* give the date as 1522, an obvious error that is corrected at the start of Chapter VI.

[3] Cabo Blanco, Argentina, lies at 47°12′18″S.

[4] Río Santa Cruz, here refers to what is now Puerto Santa Cruz, Argentina, 50°7′44″S, 45 leagues N of the Strait. where the Ríos Santa Cruz and Chico enter the South Atlantic. The coastal approach and entrance to the river is shoaled with many sandbanks.

[5] For details of the route and sailing directions, see Navarrete, *Coleccion de los Viajes*, vol. V, p. 14 and docs 9 and 26. The other ships sailed on to the Strait because they wanted to transit the passage before it became too dangerous.

[6] According to Navarrete, ibid., p. 14 and docs 9, 10, 26, this river was 5–6 leagues north of the Strait. It may refer to Río Gallegos, 51°35′51″S, 20 leagues N of the Strait.

[7] *Esquife*, a small rowing boat.

Strait, and that they should light the signal fires for the ships to enter. The gunner said the same. But the chaplain and the pilot refused until they were certain it was, in fact, the Strait. So they proceeded and landed, and said it was not and began to argue like confused guides because the one side said yes and the other no. Finally, they agreed to continue ahead to a point farther on to better decide.

The ships, seeing these men continue on without building a signal fire, hoisted sail and went on in search of the Strait, leaving the pilot, treasurer, cleric, and gunner on land and the others in the river.[1] The land party moved on to the point but the gunner said it was necessary to continue farther on. After another three leagues, they realized that this was not the Strait. When they returned to the skiff, they found it grounded very far from the river channel so they had to wait for the water to rise so they could follow the ships. However, that night the weather was so bad the skiff sank. When the weather cleared the next day it was low tide and the boat was stuck on the river bank. They disembarked and lit a fire, and the next four days they ate roots and some shell fish. On the fifth day, recovering the skiff, they went to an island in the middle of the river to catch the birds they saw feeding there. Once on the island, they killed many white birds resembling doves with red beaks and feet. On the same island, they found an infinite number of flightless marine geese, covering completely a space one half league long and one half or one quarter [f. 22v] wide.[2] They killed so many of these birds that they filled the skiff completely. Each of these birds <p. 243> plucked, skinned, and gutted weighed seven or eight pounds. With these provisions, they left in search of the Strait and the other ships. That day they made it to the river's mouth where they had to stop and beach the skiff because of adverse weather.

The next morning, while they were preparing to continue their journey, there arrived a certain Bartolomé Domínguez, a citizen of La Coruña, with four other men. They were sent by Joan Sebastián del Cano to search for them and inform them that the ships were now in the Strait. Domínguez brought a letter from the captain informing them that the ship *Sancti Spíritus* unfortunately had been lost, and that on receipt of his letter, they should set out right away to come to him. So, they abandoned the skiff and the birds and walked twenty leagues through very rough terrain that, although not mountainous, was very thickly forested.[3]

The ship[4] was lost near the Cabo de las Once Mill Vírgines at the entrance to the Strait. By the time these companions arrived there, Captain Juan Sebastián del Cano had gone on to find safe harbour for the other ships. At midnight on the fourteenth (which was the same day that they discovered the aforementioned river, Río Gallegos), after they anchored, a terrible storm blew up that swept away all the ships' boats and the ships began to drag their anchors. Finally, the *Sancti Spíritus* sank on the coast with the loss of nine men. The survivors barely managed to save themselves. They built huts on land and recovered the greater part of theirs and the king's cargo and belongings. The next day they were more fortunate than the first. Captain Juan Sebastián on the *Anunciada* with

---

[1] While the landing party searched upstream, the incoming tide freed the other ships which went out to sea and moved on to Cabo Vírgenes, 14 January 1526; Navarrete, ibid., pp. 13–14.

[2] Penguins; possibly Southern rockhoppers (*Eudyptes chrysocome*) or Magellanic (*Spheniscus magellanicus*).

[3] It is not clear why the party went overland. There is no explanation as to why they could not return with Bartolomé Domínguez. Perhaps their skiff was too damaged to be used or the weather was too bad.

[4] *Sancti Spíritus*.

its boat and cables lost returned after being blown out to sea. The other ships set about to make repairs, unloading all the artillery they had. The *Anunciada* re-entered the bay of the Once Mill Vírgines on the eighteenth of the month. Now with good weather, the three ships, *Anunciada*, *Santa María del Parral*, and the *San Lesmes*, entered the Strait to anchor.

CHAPTER VI

How Captain General Fray García Jofre de Loaysa rejoined the other ships of the armada, and of other events that happened to them, and of the giants and people of the Strait of Magallanes to whom Magallanes gave the name Patagones

On 22 January 1526 the flagship *Santa María de la Victoria*, the *Sanct Gabriel*, and the patache arrived on the route to the Strait.[1] After rounding Cabo Vírgenes, the patache's skiff landed and picked up Treasurer Bustamente and the cleric Don Joan. They then went to the flagship to report how the nao *Sancti Spíritus* was lost and say that the captain general should not even think of landing there but rather, since the weather was good, should enter the mouth of the Strait. And so he did. After giving this warning, the priest departed in the patache for the bay where the three other ships were.[2] Once entered into the mouth of the Strait, they anchored because of the currents that are very strong there. Captain Joan Sebastián arrived with the skiff and boarded the patache to pick up the priest. They went to the flagship and agreed with the general that the two caravels, the *Parral* and the *San Lesmes*, and the patache should go back for the people and salvage the things that had escaped the sinking of the nao *Sancti Spíritus* at the Cabo de las Once mill Vírgenes with the said Captain Joan Sebastián del Cano. This plan was put into effect, and the people and salvage were collected, even though with a great deal of effort because of wind and sea conditions. The weather was so bad that they had to abandon the operations and put out to sea.[3]

The flagship *Victoria* and the others in Victoria Bay were so afflicted by this storm that the flagship foundered on <p. 244> the coast, and for three days the stern-post beat against the shore, breaking off all the ship's upper-works and the rudder. They jettisoned the gun carriages, hogsheads and other things at hand. The captain general and crew escaped to land, only the master, the boatswain, and four or five sailors remained on board in great danger awaiting whatever God would do with them.

Three days later the weather cleared with a fair wind and they brought out the flagship and with the other two, the *Parral* and the *San Lesmes,* set out to sea to return to the Santa Cruz River. All five vessels went to Santa Cruz, except for the patache that stayed in the aforementioned bay where Captain Sanctiago de Guevara and father Don Juan were.[4]

---

[1] Navarrete, *Colección de los Viajes*, vol. 5, p. 25 gives the date as 24 January.

[2] The anchorage was in Victoria Bay, now Bahía Santiago, on the north side of the Strait after the First Narrows. The other ships present were the *Anunciada*, *Sancta María del Parral*, and *San Lesmes*.

[3] According to Navarrete, ibid., p. 15, the smaller *Sanctiago*, and the *San Gabriel's* boat, took shelter in a narrow defile that would not accommodate larger vessels; the *Parral* re-entered the Strait, and the *San Lesmes* was blown out to sea to 55°S.

[4] Navarrete, ibid., pp. 15–16, clarifies the confusion of this part of the Oviedo text as follows. The *Victoria* was taken back to the Santa Cruz River, where there was a wide beach to careen the ship and make repairs. On

Not knowing of the storm related above, they thought that all the ships were in the Strait in Victoria Bay which was a good twenty leagues inside the Cape.[1] Captain Sanctiago and the priest agreed that the cleric and three companions should go by land in search of the captain general and the ships, taking provisions to last four days and a forty-league march. And so the plan was put into effect because the cleric, according to what I judged from his manner, was accustomed to hardship. When I met him in the year 1535 he was probably thirty-five or so years old. I heard him say that when he and his companions travelled along the coast on route to the Strait, they saw many herds of large wild tapirs that fled from the Christians whinnying like colts and jumping like deer.[2] Also, they saw many tailless rats that this priest believed, or was informed by his companions, were called *hutias*. However, I believe that these animals were no other than *corís* because they seem rat-like [f. 23v] and are tailless, while the *hutia* has a tail like a rat (as I reported in Book XII of the first part of this *General History*).[3]

The path this cleric and his companions followed was difficult, crossing through many lagoons and swamps, but of good water. Along it they found many wild sloe bushes that were edible if you did not have anything else. After four days they came to Victoria Bay where they expected to find the captain general. But, of course, he was more than fifty leagues away in Sancta Cruz, as reported above. So, they went on a league farther past Victoria Bay, and there they found many huts of the *patagones*[4] who are men thirteen palms tall and their women the same. As soon as the women saw them they came out, yelling and signalling for the Christians to go away because their men were out hunting. But the Christians, as they were accustomed to make peace with them, began to shout 'oh, oh, oh,' raising their arms and throwing their weapons on the ground. The women likewise put down their bows and made the same signs, and then both parties ran to embrace each other.

---

13 February the *Victoria, Parral* and *San Lesmes* arrived at Santa Cruz. Those on the pinnace *Sanctiago* and the *San Gabriel*'s boat sheltered in the defile. Not knowing of the move to Santa Cruz and supposing them all in Victoria Bay, they sent the cleric, Santiago de Guevara and the others overland to Victoria Bay where they found nothing except evidence of the damage done to the *Victoria*. Returning to the arroyo, they saw the *San Gabriel* which had come to inform them of the fleet's whereabouts and recover its ship's boat and then sailed off presumably to return the Santa Cruz River. The priest and party on the pinnace went to Victoria Bay to salvage items jettisoned from the wreck of the *Victoria*, and then returned to Puerto Santa Cruz. During the time it took to make repairs to the ships, there was no sign of either the *Anunciada* or the *San Gabriel*. See below, pp. 53, n. 2, 139, n. 1.

[1] Markham, *Early Spanish Voyages*, p. 91, n. 1, identifies this as Bay of Virgins or of Santiago on the north coast between the First and Second Narrow.

[2] Guanacos; *Yanaques* (*Lama guanicoe*).

[3] Possibly rabbit rats (*Reithroden physodes* (*auritus*)). For Oviedo's discussion of *hutias* and the *corís*, see Bk XII, chs I and IV; *BAE*, vol. 118, p. 29. *Corí*, is Oviedo's name for guinea pigs which he had first encountered in Santo Domingo. They were native to the Andes. *Hutias* or *jutias* (*Capromyidae*), cavy-like rodents but larger than guinea pigs, were also found on the Caribbean islands.

[4] The Giants said to live in Patagonia were reported by Antonio Francesco de Pigafetta to have been encountered and named by Magellan when he came across them at Saint Julian in 1520. The name may have related to their allegedly large feet (*patones*), Alternatively the name may have been drawn from the giant Pathoagón who appeared in the popular novel of chivalry *Libro segundo de Palmerín* (the *Primaleón*), published in 1512 by Francisco Vázquez and which Magellan is said to have read. See Duviols, 'The Patagonian "Giants"', in McEwan et al., *Patagonia*, pp. 127–38. Spanish Jesuit missionaries in the mid-18th century named the peoples of this region Southern Tehuelche. Anthropologists now generally use the name Aónikenk, meaning 'people of the south'.

This father, Don Joan, said that when they embraced, neither his head nor those of any of the other Christians came up to within a hand-breadth of the women's privates, and this padre was not a small man, rather one of good stature.[1] Then the Christians gave the women hawks bells, needles and other trinkets. They strung the bells on threads and put them on their legs. When they heard the sound of them as they moved about, they jumped and capered with much laughter, enjoying the bells marvellously. (I wanted to find out how those Christians and the cleric knew that the above was the custom of making peace with those giant people, and he told me that he had seen it before from these men as will be reported in the following chapter.)

The natives' bows were short, sturdy and wide, made of a very strong wood. Their arrows are like those of the Turks, each with three feathers and the tips were of flint like well-made harpoons. The Patagones are great marksmen, shooting as accurately as or better than our crossbowmen. <p. 245> Around their heads, they tie some cords above their ears in which they stick arrows like a garland with the feathers up, and from the cords they draw the arrows to shoot. In this fashion those women came out to face us. They are well-proportioned people of the height mentioned. They go about nearly naked, only covering their genitals with some pieces of tapir hide.[2]

The Christians gave the name tapir to those hides not because they know they are from tapirs (which, in truth, they are not) but rather from some animals like tapirs that have thick or even thicker skins. Ahead, when the things of Castilla del Oro are discussed, more will be said [f. 24r] about what kind of animals are these because, according to what I understood from this padre cleric, they are the same animals that are called *beorí* in the province of Cueva in Tierra Firme where I have seen and eaten them.[3]

---

[1] The good father certainly must be exaggerating for, with the palm at 8.2 inches (Phillips, *Six Galleons*, p. 72), these giants would be just shy of 9 feet tall. Even at that height, one supposes the Christians would come up to higher than 'their privates'. This exaggerated representation of the height, numbers, and prodigious strength of the Tehuelche encountered continues throughout the following chapters.

[2] Subsequent travellers through the Strait marvelled at the capacity of the indigenous peoples to withstand the rigorous climate. Those encountered here would have been a family band of Aónikenk, terrestrial hunters who inhabited eastern Patagonia south of Río Santa Cruz. In addition to loincloths, they also wore loose cloaks, caps, and foot coverings, made from guanaco skins by their women. See, Campbell, Bradley, and Lorimer, *Narbrough*, pp. 43–4.

[3] Oviedo describes this animal called *danta* or *beorí* in Bk XII, ch. XI; *BAE*, vol. 118, pp. 42–3. Manning and Owen, *Knowledge in Transition*, notes that 'danta', the Spanish name for elk, was transferred to the New World tapir. *Beorí* was the indigenous name for the same.

CHAPTER VII

What happened to the cleric Don Joan de Areyzaga among the giant Patagones, and of the continuation of their journey in search of the ships of the armada

As has been related, after the giant-women made peace with those Christians, they took them to their camp and lodged them distributed one by one among the dwellings.[1] They gave them certain roots which at first are bitter tasting but then become less so. Also they gave them some large and tasty mullets, the flesh of each weighing more than a pound. Not more than after a half hour in those dwellings, the men of those women came back from the hunt bringing a tapir they had killed. The animal weighed twenty or thirty *arreldes*[2] which one of them carried on his back as effortlessly as if it were ten pounds. The women went out to meet their husbands and tell them of the presence of those Christians. Then the men embraced the Christians in the manner reported above and shared their kill with them. After skinning the animal they commenced to eat the raw flesh. They gave the cleric a piece weighing almost two pounds which he put in the fire to roast but right away one of the giants snatched it back, thinking that the padre did not want it. The giant ate it up in one bite to the dismay of the cleric who was very hungry and needed that food.

After eating, they and the Christians went to drink at a pool some distance away from the camp. One by one, the giants drank from a skin bag that held more than a *cántara*[3] of water and perhaps even two *arrobas*[4] or more. There were some among those Patagones who emptied the skin three times uninterruptedly but until one was satisfied the others waited. The Christians also drank from the same skin. One full skin was enough for them all with some left over, leaving the giants to marvel at the little the Christians drank. Then all returned to the huts and when night fell the Christians were lodged apart as previously reported.

The dwellings were made from tapir skins like well-tanned and polished cowhide, but smaller. They suspend the skin from two poles positioned against the wind. Everything else is open to the sun and rain so that the 'house' is nothing more than what is described.[5]

---

[1] The word Oviedo uses is *rancho* which usually means a camp or hut, but from the woodcut illustration he supplied the 'dwelling' appears to be a simple lean-to or windbreak shelter of branches covered by guanaco skins.

[2] A weight of 4 lbs usually used in reference to meat.

[3] Here meaning that the skin was about the size of a large churn or vessel.

[4] *Arroba* is used here as a liquid measure, between 12 and 16 litres.

[5] The Aónikenk encountered by the Spaniards were mobile terrestrial hunter gatherers, organized in small family bands, who inhabited Eastern Patagonia south of Puerto Santa Cruz. Their shelters consisted of brushwood windbreaks or rough tents consisting of a framework of sticks, over which they cast a cover of guanaco skins sewn together with gut. They managed to endure the frigid temperatures of the region, going largely naked except for hats, foot coverings, and large blanket-like cloaks, all fashioned from guanaco skins by the women. Borrero, 'Origins of Ethnographic Subsistence Patterns', pp. 60–81.

Thus, all [f. 24v] night long they are whimpering and shivering from the excessive cold. That land is marvellously frigid of necessity, lying as it is at $52^1/_2$ degrees on the other side of the Equator, towards the antarctic pole. The Patagones live in a constant state of war, and so do not light fires at night for fear of being seen by their enemies. For the slightest reason they fold up their dwellings and, carrying them on their shoulders, move wherever they like.

This community was composed of sixty or more households, each one <p. 246> of more than ten persons.

Those few Spaniards passed the entire night in a state of fear and anxiety, awaiting daybreak to depart in peace if they could to go where they had left the ship. The ship was more than forty leagues away, and they had no food or money to buy it and, even if they had, those people had no idea what money was. Come morning, they took leave of the giants with poorly understood sign language. The Spaniards made their way to the coast searching diligently for any sign or remnant of the flagship and the two other ships anchored there.

According to this cleric, those companions firmly believed that those giants would have done what they later did if not for a dog the Christians had with them. Those people greatly feared the animal because it behaved so fierce and brave against the Indians the Christians could barely restrain it.[1]

When they returned to the coast of Victoria Bay, they came upon pieces of wood, gun carriages, and water casks that the *Santa María* had jettisoned during the storm I described earlier.[2] With this they suspected what had happened and resumed their journey. At night they went to the coast and found some shellfish and barnacles that they ate raw. They dug holes in the sand to sleep in, covering themselves except for their heads and passed that night very cold, hungry and exhausted.

The next day, they crossed valleys and hills thinking to shorten their journey. On the way they found only some small berries that grow in those regions, an unknown fruit but not bad tasting. Also, they found some wild and not very tasty sloes, and some rats with which they sustained themselves and staved off death by starvation. They resumed their march, but had to leave the dog behind as it was exhausted and overcome by hunger, thirst, and lameness. Some thought it would be a good idea to eat it, but the cleric and others dissented. They passed that day in hunger and hardship, but at least they found much good water. They spent that night in a valley where they had no other refreshment than some hay with which they covered themselves and which was a great relief against the intense cold they suffered.

The following day, continuing their journey, they lost a companion, Juan Pérez de Higuerola, leaving only the cleric and two other men. At dawn they sighted more than two thousand Patagones or giants. (This name *patagón* was erroneously [f. 25r] given to

---

[1] Large dogs trained for war were unknown in the Americas and were used by the Spaniards to devastating effect against indigenous opponents. Oviedo frequently mentions the importance of dogs in battles with much larger numbers of indigenous warriors. Oviedo recalled seeing Vasco Núñez de Balboa's dog Leoncico, which he noted 'gained Vasco Núñez a thousand gold peso ... because like any other participant he was given an equal share of the booty in gold and slaves'. He recorded that, after taking part in many raids (*entradas*) and siring many other fearsome dogs, it was mysteriously poisoned; *Historia General y Natural*, Bk XXIX, ch. III; *BAE*, 119, p. 211

[2] See above, p. 44, n. 2.

these people by the Christians because of their large feet which, although much larger than ours, are not disproportionate considering their body height.)[1] The Indians advanced towards the Christians, raising their hands and yelling, but without arms and naked. The Christians did the same, throwing down their weapons and moving toward them because, as reported previously, this is the manner of peaceful greeting that those people use when they come upon others and they embrace in a sign of confidence or love.

After this ceremony, the Patagones picked up the three Christians, raised them one by one over their heads and carried them a quarter of a long league to a valley where there were a large number of lean-tos set up like a large city. The Patagones brought out their bows and arrows and put on feather ornaments for their heads and feet. After that, they again picked up the Christians and moved on a long league from the encampment where they could not be seen and set them down and stripped them. They felt the Christians all over, examining them in wonderment at their small size and whiteness. They grasped their genitals and examined and considered each Spaniard's body part by part. In this way, they passed them among themselves with great excitement, so much so that those poor Spaniards suspected that, wishing to eat them, the Indians were trying to ascertain the taste of that meat, seeing what they were like inside and out. And so, greatly afraid <p. 247>, the cleric Don Juan de Areyzaga and his companions commended themselves to God's mercy.

Many times the Indians put arrows to their bows, making signs that they were going to shoot them, but Our Lord was pleased to come to their aid in such distress and free them from the savage giant race. After three or more hours of this play, there came a young man of boyish appearance with another twenty giants, each with bows and arrows and their stomachs covered with soft, woolly hides like those of very fine sheep and wearing very beautiful white and red ostrich-feather headdresses. Then all the giants sat on the ground, lowered their heads and talked a while among themselves as though praying in a low voice. None raised his eyes from the ground, even though there were more than two thousand of them who had stripped the three poor Christians, who at each moment expected that their days were over. The Christians thought that the giant young man was probably their king come to put an end to them. As much as they could understand, it seemed that the boy-giant was reprehending the others. He then took father Don Joan by the hand and lifted him to his feet. Although the Indian seemed to be eighteen to twenty years old and Don Joan was twenty-eight or more and not short but of average height, the priest did not come up to this boy's privates. [f. 25v] The boy-giant called the other two Spaniards and signalled with his hand that they all should depart. One of the twenty who came with that captain or boy-king placed a large feather plume on the cleric's head. And so, those three companions went off naked, not daring to ask for their clothing. Seeing the liberality of that principal Indian, they imagined that he intended them to leave in that manner and if they were to try by signs to recover their clothing, that although he would order them given their clothing, he would become angry

---

[1] See above, p. 47, n. 4. Oviedo's comments reflect the currency of the description of giant Patagonians first circulated in Antonio Francesco Pigafetta's account of Magellan's expedition. More recently, research published by Hernandez, García-Moreno, and Lalueza-Fox, 'Brief Communication', pp. 545–51, states that measurement of Aónikenk postcranial remains indicates a stature of between 6 feet 8 inches and 6 feet 10 inches (174–8 cm), which would have put them some 4 inches (10 cm) taller than 16th-century Spaniards.

and punish the first group of giants who took them. So, thinking it best not to anger the boy, they left without their clothing but with their lives.

The Spaniards continued their journey along the coast, suffering horribly from hunger, thirst and the cold. Reaching the sea, they came upon a dead fish washed ashore that looked like a conger eel. They ate it raw and it did not taste bad to them.

Those giants paint their faces white, red, yellow and other colours. They are enormously strong. The cleric Don Joan said that with one hand each one could lift over his head three iron cannon carriages, each weighing two quintals or more. They wear very beautiful feather ornaments on their heads and feet. Their diet consists of raw meat, some roots grilled or raw, but no bread that these Christians could see. They eat raw or very hot grilled fish, a good deal of shellfish consisting of barnacles, mussels, and very big oysters that the Christians imagined produced large pearls. Likewise on that coast they eat many dead whales washed ashore by the great waves.

The cleric said that, before all the above happened, six of these giants were visiting a ship of the fleet and the cleric and two other companions came ashore with them to observe something of their customs. In a valley, they came upon some of these giants who sat down and signalled the Spaniards to join them which they did. Then they brought out a huge fetid piece of whale meat weighing more than two quintals. They put portions of it before the cleric and his companions but it was so awful they had to refuse it. However, the Indians commenced to cut it up with some flint knives that each had, and with each mouthful ate three or four pounds or more. The Spaniards then returned to the ship with the Indians and gave them hawk's bells, pieces of broken mirrors and other trinkets which they happily took away, thinking themselves very rich. They were astonished by the artillery fire and at all the other things the Christians had.

Returning to the account of the journey of the cleric and his two companions: he said that <p. 248> arriving naked at the beach, they saw the ship *Sanct Gabriel* that was searching for its boat and that was with the patache. And on informing Captain Santiago de Guevara that the ships were in the Sancta Cruz River and that [f. 26r], if there were time, they should go to the bay where the ships had jettisoned the bronze anchor stocks and gun-carriages of the artillery and recover them and then proceed to Sancta Cruz, and so they did. And this was 2 March 1526. The cleric Don Joan and his two companions returned to the patache, giving infinite thanks to Jesus Christ for freeing them from those giants in the way that was reported above.

CHAPTER VIII

Of some particulars of the people called the giants, and of the birds, fish and other things that those of this armada observed

According to the cleric, Don Juan Areyzaga, these giants are so fleet that there is no wild or Spanish horse however fast that can match them. When they dance, they hold some small bags of tough tapir hide filled with pebbles in each hand. Three or four of the giants line up facing another group of three or four dancers, and then they jump toward each other with their arms wide, shaking the bags to produce sound. This movement they keep up as long as they please without any singing. It seems to them an extremely beautiful musical melody in which they take great contentment, not desiring Orpheus's lyre or his song that the poets imagine lulled Pluton and mitigated the torments of Tantalo, Sísifo, and other suffering ones in the abyss.[1]

Returning to the topic: These giants are great throwers. With tremendous force they hurl a two or more pound stone a long distance and with great accuracy. In general they are a happy and festive people.

Don Juan de Areyzaga, wishing to avenge the humiliation of being stripped naked, as related in the previous chapter, tried to take away their bows and mistreat some of the giants who came out to the patache. One day one of the giants came to the shore and called for them to take him on board and the priest and others went to get him. But, being a priest, his anger abated and he did not want to mistreat the Indian and, even though the other Christians wanted to kill him, he did not permit it. They took him to the ship and fed him very well with meat and fish. He refused the bread as these giants do not eat it and likewise the wine. That night they bedded him down below deck. When he lay down they closed the hatch and placed on it two or three large gun carriages for lombards[2] and a large crate full of goods. Anxious at being down there in the closed sleeping space, the giant decided to come out. He put his shoulder to the hatch with everything on it, lifted [f. 26v] it and came out. Witnessing this, the Christians put him in another place where all night long he did not stop singing and yelling. At midnight when he thought the Christians were all asleep he tried to leave but the cleric had stowed his bow and arrows in a chest and so in exchange the Indian stole a nice hat from him. But the Christians were on to him and detained him until morning when they gave him his bow and arrows. He put the cleric's hat between a piece of hide he wore and his stomach and left.

---

[1] Oviedo's comment refers ironically to the pleasure that they took in their music, comparing it to the power of Orpheus's lyre which mitigated some of the suffering of figures of Greek mythology such as Tantalus and Sysphus, who were both subjected to unbearable endless torments in the Underworld.

[2] Bombards or lombards: a large calibre, wrought-iron, hooped barrel, breech-loading cannon, used in Western Europe in the later Middle Ages, possibly first in Spain.

51

They are so primitive they think that everything is held in common, and that the Christians do not get angry about what they take. So, later this same giant returned, and happily by signs gave us to understand how he had stolen the hat.[1]

Along that coast there are abundant stocks of good fish of many kinds. There are diverse large and small birds in great flocks. The diet of these giants is what was reported – tapir, whales and other fish. Also, there are roots resembling parsnips that are very nourishing and make a nice staple food <p. 249> that can be eaten sun-dried, raw, grilled or boiled.

There are some large birds like geese that cannot fly because instead of wings they have appendages like the dolphins and similar fish. They have beautiful plumage.[2] The Spaniards captured, skinned, and ate many of these birds. The cleric reports that they were a good source of food, but were not very tasty.

---

[1] Martinic Berros, 'Meeting of Two Cultures', p. 111, notes that the first encounter between Aónikenk and Magellan's crew in April 1520 was marked by initial apprehension followed by wary trusting curiosity. This would seem to characterize the encounters described here, although accounts of violent skirmishes and clashes are found in later 16th-century accounts.

[2] Probably rheas (*Pterocnemia pennata*).

CHAPTER IX

Continuing the journey of the armada that went with Commander Fray García de Loaysa, and of some particulars of the river and harbour of Santa Cruz and of that land

On 8 March 1526, the patache left the Cabo de las Once mill Vírgenes and anchored half a league south of land but, because of the strong winds, the ship was dragging its anchor and almost struck the coast until God allowed them to move off. With great effort and jettisoning cargo, they moved from bank to bank all night long in extreme danger. Not ceasing to vow pilgrimages, they thought themselves lost. But once they escaped this peril, they sighted the land of Sancta Cruz where the other ships were. On 11th of that month of March, the patache entered the harbour to find the flagship,[1] the nao *Sancta María del Parral*, and the nao *Sancto Lesmes*. Neither the captain general nor the others on that river knew anything of the nao *Anunciada* or of the nao *Sanct Gabriel*. For that reason the general sent the flagship's boat to the patache even though they were anchored a half league apart to bring Master Sanctiago de Guevara and the cleric Don Joan [f. 27r] to the flagship. On arrival, they told the general that Captain Sanctiago de Guevara had sent to request that the Captain of the nao *Sanct Gabriel* send five to six quintals of sea biscuit to him because they needed it, but the request was ignored. Not only did he not send the biscuit, but he took the boat and its fourteen-man crew and sailed off for that very harbour of Sancta Cruz where the captain general was. Since he had not arrived, there they believed that he had returned to Spain.[2]

That river was given the name Sancta Cruz. It lies at twenty leagues north of Cabo de las Once mill Vírgenes.[3] It is one and a half leagues wide and the tide there rises six fathoms, the current is so strong that no boat can make it to land against it until the high tide is reached. At low tide, the river's depth is five fathoms and at high tide twelve. When the tide is out, the river water is fresh, and so they replenished their water supply by drilling through the ships' hulls and running a leather hose to the taps of the hogsheads they needed to fill, in this way taking in all the water they wished.

---

[1] The *Victoria*.

[2] Navarrete, *Colección de los Viajes*, pp. 166–76, provides information on the *San Gabriel* and the *Anunciada* after their separation from the armada. The former sailed back up the coast to Brazil with the intention of returning to Spain with a cargo of Brazil wood. After experiencing numerous hardships (see Markham's note below, p. 139, n. 1), the ship limped back to Bayonne, Galicia, on 28 May 1527 with only 27 Castilians and 22 Indians as survivors. The *Anunciada*, after meeting up with the *San Gabriel*, sailed off without a pilot, anchors, or the ship's boat, intending to reach the Moluccas via the Cape of Good Hope. It was never seen again. Markham, see below, p. 139, n. 1, states that its captain had tried to rejoin the fleet.

[3] See above, p. 41, n. 3.

A league upstream from this river's mouth there is a small, low, flat island.[1] At low tide when it is dry, some large and shapeless sea lions weighing more than two quintals congregate there. They managed to kill six of them and they tasted like beef. Their hide is so thick and tough that no man can penetrate it with a thrown lance, even though some strong men tried.

In the harbour there they caught many sardines like those of Castile and many large, nice skates. With these they completely filled more than fifty hogsheads. At low tide one finds huge quantities of anchovies in some pools one handbreadth deep. Innumerable seagulls eat these fish. There are so many flying about that their numbers completely block the view of the sky.

A companion brought on board an animal he found ashore. It was the size of a suckling pig with a pig's muzzle, cloven hooves and a body covered with a shell like the armour for a horse. When it wished, it covered itself completely under <p. 250> that shell and grunted like a pig. They named it 'armoured horse'. (Before these Spaniards saw this animal I had eaten a number of them in the Tierra Firme in provinces of Cueva and Nicaragua that are the first lands discovered. The Spanish call these animals *encubertados*.[2] In 1532, I brought the coverings or shells of these animals to Spain from Nicaragua where there are many of them.)

So, returning to the narrative and to the Sancta Cruz River: In that area are many *adives*.[3] These are animals like wolves, and howl like them, but have a distinctive noxious characteristic that nature has given them for their defence which I will now relate. [f. 27v] When some crossbowman or any other person menaces them, they raise a leg and shoot out a strong stream of urine at their pursuer. The stench is so horrendous and intolerable, no man can continue on from nausea and abhorrence.

On the bank of this river are found many jaspers, some like those that staunch bleeding and some of a different sort.[4]

There they careened the flagship and made repairs to the other ships. Before the armada entered the river from the sea, they had seen many fire-lights at night on a mountain. So some of the Spaniards went inland to see if there were any settlements, but in four days they came across no signs of people or towns save some remains of campfires.

On 29 March the armada departed from the river and harbour of Sancta Cruz to continue the journey.

---

[1] In earlier times the sand and mud flats of the estuary attracted sea lions (*Otaria flavescens*). Isla de los Leones, 47°45′14″S, was formerly the site of a sea lion colony.

[2] *Encubertados*: armadillos; more fully described by Oviedo in Bk XII, ch. XXIII; *BAE*, vol. 118, pp. 47–8, and illustrated in plate V, *BAE*, vol. 121.

[3] *Adives*: skunks. Oviedo provides a lengthy description of this animal and its defence system which he compares to a small fox (*zorrilla*); in Bk VI, ch. XXXIV; *BAE*, vol. 117, p. 193–4. Humboldt's hog-nosed skunk (*Conepatus humboldtii*), also known as the Patagonian hog-nosed skunk, is found in open grasslands.

[4] Oviedo provides no reference for the belief that jaspers have the ability to stop bleeding. Isidore of Seville's *Etymologies*, Bk XVI, p. 323 (on carbuncles), notes that 'Some people think the gemstone jasper provides good fortune and protection to pregnant women'. However, he warned that, although 'Certain believe that the jasper gives both attractiveness and safety to its wearers, ... to believe this is a sign not of faith but of superstition.'

CHAPTER X

Of the continuation of Commander Loaysa's journey to the Spicelands, and of some particulars of the river of San Alfonso where he had been before, as reported in Chapter IV, and how the armada returned to the Strait of Fernando Magallanes

On the 29th of March, after hearing mass, the armada left the Santa Cruz River to continue its journey. On the 2nd of April, during the first night watch, and because of bad weather, the patache alone separated from the flagship to enter the Sanct Alifonso River.[1] The following day, Monday, on a small island there, those on the patache killed so many birds that they filled eight hogsheads of them skinned and pickled in brine. They clubbed these flightless birds (described in Chapter VI)[2] and selected the ones that seemed the youngest as being the most tender and best for eating. Not one of these birds skinned and gutted weighed less than eight pounds. Their livers are as large and tasty as those of sheep.

In this river there are white tunas, whales come in there, and much good fishing. But this time no ship entered there other than the patache which left the following Wednesday, 4 April, and on the following Friday, the sixth of this month turned into the Cabo de las Once mill Virgenes[3] which is the mouth of the Strait. That night they anchored next to a large cape. The following Saturday they set sail in fair weather but could not enter the first neck of the Strait for lack of wind. They anchored on the south edge of the Strait a league away from the said gorge. Some Spaniards went ashore in the ship's boat. They found no people although they came upon large footprints of the giants or Patagones described above and they saw many tapirs. So it is that both coasts of the Strait are populated by these giants.

Sunday, 8 April, with a fresh breeze, the patache passed through [f. 28r] the said [*first*] neck and, the weather being fresh, were about to enter the second neck or better called second narrows when they saw behind them the flagship and the other ships entering from the first. So, the patache anchored to await them and on Monday <p. 251> Captain Sanctiago and father Don Juan went to the flagship to excuse themselves for having gone ahead because of weather conditions and to receive the general's orders.

From that place they discovered some anchorages in the Strait, and all the ships went to shelter in a very good one. There they found a canoe made of tree bark over a

---

[1] San Alfonso: called the San Ildefonso by Navarrete, *Colección de los Viajes*, vol. V , p. 25, which on the modern map could be either the Río Coig or Río Gallegos which is immediately north of Cabo Vírgenes.

[2] *BAE*, vol. 118, refers to Ch. VI, although the actual description is found above in Ch. VIII, p. 52, n. 2.

[3] Cabo Vírgenes. Named the Cape of the 11,000 Virgins after the legend of the 11,000 virgins said to have accompanied St Ursula from Britain to Rome and been martyred at Cologne as they returned.

Map 2.   The approach to and through the Strait of Magellan.

framework of whale ribs, five *nahes* or oars like spades for paddling,[1] and they found the point of a deer's horn indicating that these animals inhabit that land.[2] There they gathered a quantity of good dry firewood and saw many camp fires inland on both sides of the Strait.

The following Wednesday they anchored in a good harbour that they named Sanct Gorge.[3] (I do not find this place on the navigation charts, but that is what the cleric Don Juan called it.) He said that there they resupplied with water, firewood, and much green cinnamon that abounded there and was edible though somewhat tough.[4] There the armada's ailing factor named Cuevas Rubias, died on the twentieth of the month and was buried in a coffin at the foot of a large tree near a river.[5]

This cleric said that while in this harbour on three or four nights, two animals were sighted on land that were said to be carbuncles whose gem stones were alight like resplendent candles. They kept watch for them and diligently tried to capture them but they never again appeared.[6] This was on the northern coast in the interior of the Strait which, as I have said, is 52½ degrees south of the equator.

(I have not found anything written about such an animal. I have seen that Isidoro writes: '*Omnium ardentium gemmarum principatum carbunculus habet.*' He also says that there are certain dragons that have in their head a precious stone that cannot be taken while the creature is awake. So, to obtain it, magicians trick the dragons into eating certain bait that they are fond of and which puts them to sleep. Once asleep, the stone can be taken easily.[7] Plinio speaks at length about carbuncles, a term he uses for all precious stones that are fiery, like rubies and spinels but does not say they are found in animals.)[8]

Let us return to the narrative. From that place, the captain general reconnoitered the southern bank for harbours and found many good ones in which ships could shelter almost without having to moor the vessels. This was the 23rd of April, and that night two canoes of Patagones or giants approached. The Patagones spoke in a menacing tone to which the cleric responded in Basque. (You can imagine how well they understood each other!) But they did not come very close. It was useless to try to go to them in the ship's [f. 28v] boat because their canoes are generally much faster than boats, and especially so if they are rowed by men of such great strength. So, it was impossible to catch up to them. As they left, they displayed some burning torches. The Christians rightly thought that

[1] The text gives no indication of their precise anchorages. The 'canoe peoples', Kawéskar, who inhabited the western reaches of the Strait were maritime hunters who used bark canoes. They relied for their construction on the southern beech forests and therefore inhabited the western part of the Strait as far east as Isla Isabela. Borrero 'Origins of Ethnographic Subsistence', pp. 64–77.

[2] Pampas deer (*Ozotoceros bezoarticus*).

[3] San Jorge.

[4] Green cinnamon (*Canela verde*): identified by Morison, *Southern Voyages*, p. 396, as wild celery (*Apium australe*), and noted as an anti-scorbutic for the scurvy that afflicted sailors on long voyages.

[5] Diego de Covarrubias. Navarrete, *Colección de los Viajes*, vol. 5, pp. 36, 224, 265, indicates that he died on 23 April.

[6] Presumably their eyes were, or shone, like fiery carbuncles.

[7] [*1557 marginal note*: *Ethimol.*, lib. XVI, cap. XIII]. Quoted in Isidore of Seville, *Etymologies*, ed. Barney et al., 2006, p. 326, as 'Of all the fiery gems, the carbuncle holds the principal rank.'

[8] [*1557 marginal note*: Plinio, lib. XXXVII, cap. LVI] Oviedo's 1557 note refers to Bk XXXVII, ch. VII, of Pliny the Elder's *Natural History*. Spinels are described in *NOED* as a hard glassy mineral occurring as octahedral crystals of variable colour.

those giants planned to set fire to the ship but they did not dare come close enough to do so.

On Wednesday, the 25th of the month, they left the harbour they called San Jorge to continue their voyage. San Jorge is likewise not noted or recognized by our cartographers. This cleric named another harbour Puerto Bueno, another on the northern side Sanct Joan de Porta Latina. On the 24th of May they went to another harbour they called Puerto Frío because the padre said it was so very cold there that many people died. On Friday, the 25th of May, they sailed out of the Strait to continue their voyage to the spicelands.[1]

The majority of the above harbours are not listed on our charts and so, when I have finished writing this report which the cleric Don Juan de Areyzaga gave of this voyage (as far as he was with it), <p. 252> I will list the harbours named by our cosmographers. I am sure that the one or the other is correct, because this priest made his deposition as one who was present. Those who make the charts say nothing except what is reported to them or from what they found out from the first voyage of Magellanes, who discovered the said Strait in the year of Our Lord 1520.

The names given by the discoverers to the rivers, harbours, promontories, and other features ought to be retained and continued. However, the discoverers who come after them, maliciously wishing to appropriate to themselves more than what they do, change the names to obscure the fame and praise of their predecessors. I myself am eyewitness to some of these evils, having seen them practised by some governors and captains in Tierra Firme.[2] Nevertheless, if I live long enough to finish these histories or at least in what I will be able to write, each rightful name will be preserved.

---

[1] On 26 May 1526, according to Navarrete, *Colección de los viajes*, p. 45.

[2] Oviedo criticized Governor Pedrarias Avila for having done this in Panama to claim Balboa's discoveries for himself.

CHAPTER XI

Of some particulars of the famous Strait of Ferdinand Magallanes

At the present time it is impossible to know all the secrets of the Strait of Magallanes, but in time these things will be better known the more they are seen and reported.[1] Nevertheless, I will relate the particulars brought to the attention of His Caesarean Majesty and to his Royal Council of the Indies by the cleric Don Juan Areyzaga who participated in the voyage to the Spicelands of Commander Fray García de Loaysa. What was reported of this account previously and what I will now relate was signed and sworn to as a priest by Don Juan de Areyzaga.

The padre said that the length of the Strait [f. 29r] is one hundred and ten leagues, more or less, from Cabo de las Once mill Vírgenes, which is its eastern entrance to its western end at Cabo Deseado.[2] In it are three roadsteads about seven leagues wide from bank to bank.[3] Of the three narrows, each half a league wide, one is a league in length, another two leagues. The third passes through very high mountains that seem to reach the sky.[4] Those mountains run along both sides of the Strait up to its exit. In that place there is no sunshine almost all year long, the nights lasting more than twenty hours. The cold is extreme with constant snow, which is as blue as fine turquoise or blue cloth. The vegetation consists of groves of oak and many other species of trees as well as abundant wild cinnamon, as reported previously.[5] The trees are very fresh and green but burn easily on contact with fire. The waters are very warm and teem with fish stocks – whales, *serenas*, swordfish, tuna, white sharks, *votes*, sharks, hake, very large carp, abundant sardines, anchovies, large mullet, oysters, and many other diverse fish.[6]

In the Strait there are many good anchorages fourteen to fifteen fathoms deep, while the main channel is more than five hundred fathoms. There are no shoals. The width of the Strait is generally two leagues, although one league or less in some parts. The tides from both seas enter and rise for fifty or more leagues to meet in the middle of the Strait producing a great and marvellous roaring sound. From high tide to low there is an hour's

---

[1] For a detailed mid-17th-century description of the topography of the Strait and navigation through it, see Campbell, Bradley, Lorimer, *Voyage of Captain John Narbrough*, pp. 62–72, 257–72. Morison traced the passage of the Strait by air and includes detailed maps and bibliography of its exploration in *Southern Voyages*, pp. 380–401, 474–98.

[2] The Strait is approximately 310 nautical miles long.

[3] There are numerous anchorages throughout the Strait and it is not possible to identify those intended here.

[4] The First Narrow, Primera Angostura, is 10 miles long and 2 miles wide. The Second Narrow, Segunda Angostura, is 12 miles long and 4 miles wide. The Third Narrow is the passage from Passo Inglés east of Isla Carlos III and through *Passo Tortuoso*, about 18 miles long and 1.1 miles wide at its narrowest point.

[5] *Drimys winteri*. Navarrete, *Colección de los Viajes*, vol. V, p. 44, speaks of the presence of a tree with laurel-like leaves and bark tasting like cinnamon.

[6] *Serenas* are likely to refer to a type of seal. It has not been possible to identify what he refers to as *votes*.

difference, so that in one part they run and in another they do not. This Strait has many gorges that were not named or explored fully because of the time involved and the lack of sufficient provisions to do so.

In addition, there are many fine rivers and creeks, especially in the harbours that they named. All this <p. 253> Strait is populated by the aforesaid giant Patagones bowmen who go about naked. In the western mouth there are many islands and islets on both the northern and southern sides. The land that runs along on the north cuts off sharply to the north-east and nothing more is said of this undiscovered coast. In truth, I believe that of necessity it runs up to and forms part of the coast of Panama that Adelantado Vasco Núñez de Balboa discovered, being the first Christian to reveal to us the Southern Sea. This coast, before coming to where Vasco Núñez encountered it, has to join that one discovered by the Adelantados Don Diego de Almagro and Don Francisco Pizarro and later that of Peru and other provinces, reaching the Gulf [f. 29v] of San Miguel, where Balboa first sighted the South Sea. From there the coast runs eastward along land discovered by Gil González de Avila, then along the provinces of Nicaragua, Chorotega, Malalaca, Nequepio, Goatimala, and the Gulf of Guazotán and then the southern coast of New Spain discovered by Don Fernando Cortés, now the marquis del Valle, as will be recounted in the appropriate place in the third part of the *General History of these Indies*.[1]

---

[1] A fascinating passage in which Oviedo demonstrates to his readers how the various areas of Spanish settlement in Central America (New Spain, Yucatan, Guatemala, Honduras, Nicaragua [Choluteca Malaka])were linked in a continuous Pacific coastline running northwards from the western end of the Strait of Magellan. The conquests by Hernan Cortés are found in in Bk XXXIII; *BAE*, vol. 120, pp. 7–267.

CHAPTER XII

Of what happened to Captain Sanctiago de Guevara and to Chaplain Don Juan de Areyzaga and the other Spaniards aboard the pinnace *Santiago* in their journey beyond the Strait and how they lost sight of the other ships of the armada that they never again saw or had knowledge of

After exiting the Strait of Magallanes into the Southern Sea and being at 47½ degrees south of the equator, the armada changed course to a northerly direction searching for the route to the Spicelands. On Friday, 1 June 1526, they lost sight of the flagship and the *Santa María del Parral*. Aboard the patache they could see the *Sancto Lesmes* and believed the other ships were on ahead.[1] For the men on the pinnace the worry was that they had only four quintals of hardtack, eight hogsheads of water and nothing else to eat for fifty persons and they estimated that they were two thousand leagues from the first land where they could find food. As this ship had only a small storeroom, their main food supply was on the flagship.

Because of the extreme cold they made all possible haste toward the equator. They were not able to fish in that great gulf of water, but they did see many different types of birds. Don Juan said they had one rooster left and one hen that laid one egg per day save in the Strait where because of the cold she did not produce. However, turning toward the equator, she resumed laying. He said that Captain Francisco de Hoces of the *Sancto Lesmes* tried to buy the chickens when they were in the Santa Cruz River for fifty Flemish ducats. At that rate, by the time they arrived at the Spicelands they would have been worth more than a thousand ducats to their owner, Captain Santiago de Guevara. But he refused because those eggs were a great remedy for the sick and there were no other chickens left in the entire armada.

The patache continued its journey to the equator. After crossing it, many days later they came to 12 degrees [f. 30r] north and, in their estimation, three hundred and forty leagues from the first land discovered by Christians that this reverend father thought would probably be the Isla de las Perlas. (To my mind, this was impossible because that Island is east <p. 254> of Panamá at 7 degrees north, fourteen or fifteen leagues off the coast of Castilla del Oro.[2])

Furthermore, this father says that on 11 July they saw two land masses, the one an island and the other either an island or mainland. But the day before they saw the sea

---

[1] Four of the seven vessels that constituted the armada made it through the Strait – the flagship *Santa María de la Victoria*, the *Santa María del Parral*, the *Sancto Lesmes*, and the pinnace *Sanctiago*. The patache became separated from the rest 157 leagues out from Cabo Deseado.

[2] Oviedo refers here to the Island of Cubagua, Venezuela, 10°8′79″N, 64°10′34″W. Castilla del Oro was the name given to the Isthmus of Panamá, reflecting the value of the merchandise carried from it to Spain.

filled with large and small snakes at 13 degrees north and there they killed three tunas and other fish.

(What he says of the snakes I can well believe because going from Panamá west to the province of Nicaragua on that coast is a gulf called Culebras so called for the innumerable snakes there and through which I have sailed. It could be that, although I saw them closer to land than what the padre reports, these snakes extend farther out to sea. But the truth is that this ship passed the coast at a distance and made port in New Spain as will be related on ahead. When I write concerning the Gulf of Culebras I will testify to what I have seen there.[1])

So, returning to the topic of this cleric and the voyage, he relates that on 12 July they came to land and saw smoke and many people coming along the coast toward where the patache anchored, a quarter league offshore. The Christians fired some blank shots with their harquebuses and the Indians threw themselves on the ground but afterward resumed coming toward the ship. The next day they sailed close to the land to find an anchorage and saw many people along the coast and many white towers but had no skiff or boat to go ashore.

On 21 July, while the ship was running close to shore, the Indians signalled and called to them showing a white flag. They came to a small island with many birds which they named Magdalena because it was the eve of her feast day. The next day, Sunday, they set sail again. And to conclude this account, its author, Don Juan de Areyzaga, said that on 25 July they anchored off a wide cape in fifteen fathoms to a clean sand bottom. There it was necessary either to run the ship aground or send a man ashore. To do this they agreed to remove the top of a chest and put into it the sounding lines and other thin cables with one end tied to the ship. The man who would set out in the chest would play out the rope little by little as the tide and wind carried him to shore. In case the chest capsized, he would hang on to the rope and those on the ship would pull him back. They agreed that this person would carry mirrors, scissors, combs and other trade [f. 30v] items to give to the Indians so that they would not kill or eat him. With this plan decided, the chaplain begged Captain Sanctiago de Guevara, who was his cousin, and the other people to be so kind as to let him set out in the chest. They tried to dissuade him but, at his insistence and seeing his firm resolve, they agreed and he got in the chest wearing breeches and a doublet and with a sword (instead of his breviary).

Halfway to land the chest capsized, leaving the cleric swimming vigorously a quarter league from shore. Thinking the shore closer than it really was, he determined to go there, considering it shameful to turn back. He soon became exhausted, disoriented, and half-drowned but God deigned to help and put in the Indians' hearts a desire to go to his aid. So, five strong young men jumped in the water which was quite rough and pulled him out. They laid him half-dead on the beach and moved away from him. An hour or more later, he came to, stood up, and signalled them to come to him. Still they did not wish to and threw themselves on the ground, embracing it. The cleric did the same, thinking that was a sign of peace and friendship. Then some Indians swam out and brought back the chest and a hemp basket tied to it containing the gifts <p. 255> and trade items and set

---

[1] Oviedo mentions the Gulf of Culebras in Costa Rica in several places throughout the *General and Natural History*, but the most complete description is found in Bk XXXIX, ch. II; *BAE*, vol.120, p. 344. The sea snake (*Pelamis platurus*) is found in the Pacific waters off Central and South America.

it near the cleric. Don Juan untied the bag and tried to give them what it contained but they refused and made signs that he was to go with them. As he was now dried off, he put on the sword and set out with them. One of the Indians preceded him carrying the bundle on his head. In that manner they marched along the coast to a valley where they lost sight of the ship. On ahead they climbed a small hill from which could be seen a league away a large city or settlement with many towers surrounded by pleasant forests. As he descended the hill, the padre saw coming from all sides many people who covered the field and made a great deal of noise. They brought water in pitchers sprinkling it before them as they approached him. After he advanced half a league, the padre was surrounded by more than twenty thousand men, some with bows and arrows, some with sharp-tipped spears, and others with shields and swords. More than two thousand men preceded the cleric to clear the ground before him.[1]

(It is true what he said concerning the Indians having swords. But, the swords of those people in that land are not of steel or other metal but of wood with the cutting edges set teeth-like with flints sharp enough to cut the throat of a bull in one stroke as easily as would a sword of fine steel.)

Returning to the history: The cleric Don Juan, accompanied as described, proceeded to that large settlement. The king or cacique, the lord of that land, attended by two thousand warriors came out to meet him at the foot of a cliff under a large shady tree by the path the cleric [f. 31r] was travelling. The Indians who had pulled him out of the sea by signs indicated to him that this man was their king and lord and the cleric understood them. When he came near to the king he doffed his bonnet and bowed low and immediately the king responded with the same courtesy then embraced him and took him by the hand. In that manner, they proceeded to the city with more than two thousand men sweeping the path before them, the cleric and the cacique speaking to each other in their own languages without understanding each other.

Close to the city there was next to the road a wooden cross sunken in the ground. Later he found out that Christians had erected it there nine years before. Drawing near the king said 'Santa María', pointing out the said cross. As soon as the cleric saw it he burst into tears of joy, uncovered and knelt at the foot while the king and the others watched. After he finished his adoration and prayers, he stood up and bowed deeply to the cross. Then the king took his hand and they continued to the city. They led him to some large palaces where they gave him a very nice chamber. They sat down on many small, finely worked palm mats placed on the floor and food was brought. There were quantities of cooked and roasted venison, some large shrimp and langoustines; quantities of corn tortillas; cherries, plums and *guayabas*;[2] and to drink – good water; a beverage made from toasted corn flour; and another, highly prized among them, called *cacaguat* made from a certain fruit that resembles almonds and which also circulates in that land as money.

(In addition they ate other things that the cleric Don Juan could not name. Neither did he understand what this *cacaguat* was. When I asked him what was this fruit or money, he told me that each year the Indians planted and harvested it. That is false because the fruit that passes for money in New Spain, Nicaragua, and other places grows

---

[1] The account in Navarrete's is even more exaggerated, reporting 12,000 men clearing the path; *Colección de los Viajes*, vol. V, p. 180. Other numbers in his narrative are also unbelievably high.

[2] Guavas.

on trees. I have seen many of them as will be related in the appropriate place.[1])<p. 256>
Returning to the history: After they had eaten, the chaplain presented to the king or
cacique all the trade items he brought from the ship and the king received them with
great pleasure. Then the cleric by signs communicated that he wished to return to the
ship with some food for those who stayed on board. Immediately that lord had brought
three very large deer and many other things and everyone including the king started out
for the coast. Arriving at the sea, they climbed a small hill because it was high tide. From
there Don Juan called out to those on the ship, telling them this was good land and to
take heart and give thanks to God because He had brought them to where there was
much bread, meat and other things even though he had not understood where they were.
When those on-board the ship understood him they fired [f. 31v] all the artillery in
celebration. At the first shot, the king and the others immediately threw themselves on
the ground, but the cleric raised up the king with his hand, laughing and telling him not
to be frightened. The others followed suit, although not without fear of the shots. At
nightfall the cleric, the king, and the more than ten thousand bowmen returned to the
city because they could not enter the sea at that time.

The cleric dined very well on the abovementioned items, and afterward three or four
large fires were lit in the patio of the palace. The king went to repose in his house and the
cleric remained in his chamber. The presence of more than five hundred men to
accompany and guard him made him very fearful and he passed that night with little
sleep.

At dawn the next day, the king returned with many people and they went to the coast.
Three men swam out to bring back the end of the sounding line tied to other cables from
the shore to the ship, a distance of seven hundred and fifty fathoms. With the king and
cleric tied to one end, the ship's captain reeled them onto the deck. More than five
hundred swam around them, carrying along much food in barrels taken from the ship
for that purpose as well as balancing food on their heads as they are expert swimmers. (I
greatly marvel that where there were so many Indians, *canoas* were lacking to transport
the king and the padre to the ship.) With all on-board, they raised sail, rounded the wide
cape or promontory and anchored before that city.

The next day the Christians disembarked via a nice raft made by the Indians.[2] They
gave garments and other trade goods to the king. Captain Santiago de Guevara and those
on-board went ashore to construct huts and lean-tos on the beach and they were
handsomely fed. After this, only the chaplain, the captain and six other Spaniards went
with the king to the city; the others remained on the beach. In the city the Christians
were lodged in the same palaces where the cleric Don Juan had spent the night.

So many people came out to see these Christians that it seemed to them a multitude
not only for a city but enough to populate an entire kingdom. Lodged in this fashion the
Indians kept them good company and generously fed them quantities of food. They were

---

[1] *Cacaguat*: cacao. Oviedo speaks of it at length in Bk VIII, ch. XXX; *BAE*, vol. 117, pp. 267–73. J. Amador
de Ríos, *BAE*, vol. 118, p. 256, notes 'When the author abstracted the report of the cleric, Don Juan Ariezaga,
he had not yet come to the final line of his manuscripts, for which reason he does not cite this passage that he
already explained thus the use of *cacao* or *cacaguat* in the description of chocolate as beverage as well as its
application as money: Oviedo wrote this second part of his *General History* in 1544 and revised the first in
1548.'

[2] Clearly this was the form of sea transport commonly used.

there five days pleasantly entertained by *areitos* or dances of those Indians.[1] They wrote letters to Hernando Cortés or to his governor or captain, because they came to understand that land could be none other than New Spain. Three Indians took the letters to a city twenty-four leagues away to a Christian that the Indians indicated by signs they would find there. Four days later the messengers returned, signing that the next day the Christian would come there.

And so it was that the next day as the captain and cleric were strolling along the coast near the ship they sighted many [f. 32r] people almost <p. 257> a league away. They suspected that it would be the Christian because the same Indians who carried the letters signalled them to come. So, with certain companions, they approached those people and saw a Christian reclining in a litter made of a hammock borne by twelve Indians. He was the governor of that entire province. As soon as he saw the captain, the cleric, and the other Spaniards the governor got down from the hammock and went to embrace them and they him. He asked them who they were, who sent them to that land, if they were Christians and of what nation they were. They responded:

'We are Christians, Spaniards, and vassals of the Emperor Don Carlos. Because of contrary weather we were separated from an armada that His Majesty is sending to the Spicelands and the Molucca Islands. We have come ashore here in great need, desiring to know what land is this since God is pleased that we come upon someone to tell us.'

To this the Christian responded:

'Gentlemen, we are all vassals of Caesar and you are in his lands. Give thanks to Our Lord for He has brought you here where, as His Majesty's vassals, you will receive all courtesy and pleasure. This land is part of New Spain where Their Majesties' captain general and governor is Hernando Cortés. It is one of the best lands and lordships in the world, with many great settlements and cities and great lords of the indigenous Indians.'

Then, with much pleasant conversation they all went to the city and, although the Christians of the ship had been well served before, from then on, because of the governor's presence, they were even better treated.

After they had related their journey and past events, that Spaniard told them that Captain Sanctiago de Guevara was to go to Mexico City where Hernando Cortés was – a distance of three hundred and seventy-five leagues.[2] He said that the captain would be very well treated by him and generously provided with all he might need. Likewise, in his absence his ship and people would be cared for. The governor said that he would give the captain a litter and people to transport him to Mexico City in comfort as well as all else he would need. However, the captain responded that he was in very ill health, as in truth he was, and thought he would not arrive there alive. Nevertheless, he would speak with padre Don Juan, his cousin, and beg him to undertake this arduous task, like many others

---

[1] *Areitos*: traditional songs accompanied by dances. Oviedo describes the *areitos* he witnessed in Panama in his *Summario*, 1526. Myers, *Oviedo's Chronicle*, p. 296, n. 29, notes that Oviedo tended to homogenize aspects of indigenous culture, here applying the term generally although it originally applied to the customs of indigenous groups in the Caribbean Islands.

[2] The distance of 375 leagues would be well over 1,000 miles. Navarrete, *Colección de los Viajes*, vol. V, p. 181 reports a more plausible distance of less than 150 leagues.

he had undertaken to serve Their Majesties, and go to Mexico to pay respects in his name to Hernando Cortés. And so it was done and the padre left the following day.

(That city where these people came to land in the patache is called Macatbán and the governor resided in another city or large town called Tegoantepeque.[1] According to the cleric, in the first city, Macatbán, there were above one hundred thousand residents. That is not so marvellous, because those towns or settlements are like neighbourhoods as are the settlements in the valleys of some Spanish provinces in Vizcaya and Guipúzcoa and in Las Montañas.[2] Everything would seem to this cleric [f. 32v] and to the others as if it were one town, notwithstanding that, there are great adjoining populations. The town Tegoantepeque is on the coast of the Southern Sea, in New Spain, 12 degrees north of the equator.)

---

[1] Spelled Macatán, Tecoantepeque in Navarrete, ibid. Oviedo locates the towns at 12°N, which would place them somewhere on the Pacific coasts of El Salvador, Honduras, and Nicaragua, a very long distance away from Cortés in Mexico City. Navarrete writes that the pinnace was at 13°N on 10 July, but travelled on until 25 July. It is more likely that they landed at closer to 16°N, especially if Navarrete's estimate of the distance to Mexico City were correct. Tecoantepeque is probably present-day Tehuantepec.

[2] Las Montañas: referring to the Spanish province of Santander.

CHAPTER XIII

In which is the conclusion of the account of the cleric Don Juan de Areyzaga

Padre Don Juan de Areyzaga departed Tegoantepeque 31 July 1526 for Mexico City where he found Hernando Cortés. The governor received him very well and this padre highly praised him for his courtesy and good treatment. There the padre made an account for His Majesty sent by the first ships, about this caravel which made port at New Spain,[1] and of the armada under fray García de Loaysa. At that time it was thought that the rest of the armada had arrived at the Spicelands, but what happened to those ships will be reported farther on. There Commander Fray García de Loaysa died and <p. 258> the Captain Juan Sebastián del Cano, and the Treasurer Bustamente, as well as other gentlemen and *hidalgos* were lost in the manner that will be related during the course of these histories in the appropriate place of the discourse of these matters.

Later, Gonzalo Gómez de Espinoso (of whom I spoke in Chapter II of this book) returned from the Spicelands and gave the report included in that chapter.[2] Afterward padre Don Juan de Areyzaga came to Spain to make his report. Here I will not bother to relate many other things that the padre saw in New Spain as I am more fully informed about this area from many residents and people who have been here longer than the padre. With regard to what the padre told of New Spain, he could not see or understand it because of the short time he was there. But because I heard him testify to the manner in which he saw a large lizard or crocodile killed (of which I have seen more than the padre) and it seems to me that the art of capturing the animal is notable, I will include it here, reserving for their appropriate places other things that I have seen of these fierce animals in the Tierra [Firme].

The padre said he saw that the Indians drove a heavy stake in the ground near water and tied to it a three-fathom-long rope. Then they took a dog and introduced into its body through the mouth a wooden stake as thick as your wrist, very strong and as long as the dog's body. The ends of the stake were sharpened in the fire. Making a hole in the dog's side through the ribs, they tied the stake inside the dog to the other stake sunk in the ground. When the lizard left the sea and swallowed the dog whole, immediately the sharpened ends of the stake inside [f. 33r] pierced its throat so that it could neither sever the rope with its teeth nor spit out the dog. Then many Indians surrounded the trap and with their slings (although not instructed by the Mallorcans, they are very skilled in their

---

[1] The *Santiago*, usually referred to as a *patax* or *pataje*, is here identified as a caravel.

[2] The information on Gonzalo Gómez de Espinoso is found in ch. IV; *BAE*, vol. 118, pp. 238–9. Gonzalo Gómez de Espinoso sailed with the Magellan expedition, but remained in the Moluccas when the *Victoria* departed for Spain. He was captured by the Portuguese and was four years a prisoner in India before returning to Spain to report to the emperor and his Royal Council in 1528. Oviedo interviewed him in Seville.

use) they killed the beast. The padre was present for this and measured the creature at eighteen feet in length.

Above I said that the Indians of New Spain are skilled in the use of slings without having been taught their use by those of the Islands of Mallorca because the invention of use of slings is attributed to those inhabitants of the islands of Mallorca. So says Vegecius in his treatise *The Art of War*, where the women there do not allow their small sons to enjoy a delicacy which they have not first hit with a stone from their sling.[1] This, even though Pliny credits the Phoenicians with the invention of the sling.[2] But Isidoro in his *Ethimologias* credits the invention to the Mallorcans.[3] Vocieno Montano, the orator from Narbonne, being exiled by Tiberio César to the Island of Baleare (that is Mallorca) in the sea of Spain, was the first to use the sling to hurl stones.[4] My opinion on this is that neither those of Fenicia[5] nor the Mallorcans taught the Indians of New Spain, or those of Peru, or those of other parts of Tierra Firme where they use slings and are very skilful in their use; rather, those Indians came across them by their needs and defence as manual arms, and that rustics by nature use slings and master their use better than other arms.[6]

Let us now pass on to relate the continuation of what I promised in the prologue or introduction of this book.

[1] [*1557 marginal note*: *De re militari*, lib. I, cap. XVI] Oviedo's note refers to the work of Publius Flavius Vegecius Renatus (fl. 4th cent. CE).

[2] [*1557 marginal note*: Plin., lib.VII, cap. LVI] In his *Natural History*, Pliny the Elder notes that the sling was invented by 'the Syrophoenicians'. A note to the text reads 'Strabo ascribes the invention of the sling to the Aetolians; he informs us, that the inhabitants of the Balearic Isles, so famous for their dexterity in the use of this instrument, originally obtained it from the Phrygians.'

[3] [*1557 marginal note*: Isidoro, lib. XVIII, cap. X]. Oviedo refers to Isidore of Seville's *Etymologiess*, Bk XVIII, ch. X, where is no mention of the sling as an invention of Mallorcans, but rather the statement that 'The sling (*fundum*) is so called because from it stones "are poured" (*fundere*), that is, cast.'; see p. 354 in the 2006 translation of *Etymologies*, ed. Barney et al.

[4] [*1557 marginal note*: *Supplementum cronicar*, lib. VIII.] Oviedo refers to the work of Vocienus Montanus Narbonensis, *Supplementum chronicarum*, Bk VIII.

[5] Phoenicians.

[6] The frequent interjection of a totally unnecessary display of classical erudition, is one of Oviedo's least admirable tendencies. Worse, once composed, he repeats these gratuitous nuggets throughout the *General and Natural History*. See, for example, following Ch. XVI, where he provides a shortened reference to the sling and Mallorcans.

CHAPTER XIV

Of the Strait of Magallanes, its length and width, its notable parts, the giants that inhabit it and other particulars

As already reported in preceding chapters, both coasts of the Strait of Magallanes are inhabited by <p. 259> giants whom our Spaniards called Patagones for their large feet. They are thirteen palms in height, enormously strong and can run as fast as or even faster than good horses. They eat two- or three-pound mouthfuls of raw meat and grilled fish. They go about naked and use bows and arrows among other particulars that the reader will have noted. However, lest you think that these men are the tallest the world has known, let the reader consult Pliny who will inform you that, according to Onesicritus, in India where the sun is directly overhead there are men as tall as [f. 33v] five cubits and two palms. These men do not age. They live one hundred and thirty years and in death they appear as if they were middle aged.[1] Moreover, Plinio [Pliny] in his *Historia Naturalis* tells of a group of Ethiopian shepherds called Syrbotæ living along the northern bank of the Astrago River who grow taller than eight cubits.[2] So, these men are taller than those of the Strait of Magallanes. And, with regard to speed, the same author writes that Crates of Pergamon referring to Etiopía says that there live the Troglodytes who outrun horses.[3]

Returning to our history: This strait, which is the subject here, is one hundred and ten leagues in length and at its widest seven leagues and, according to the eyewitness account of the cleric Don Juan de Areyzaga, it narrows in some places to a league or less.

Now I will report what I find in the recently amended charts and many others I have seen by different authors worthy of credit.

Starting with the western mouth[4] is the archipelago of Cabo Deseado, called an archipelago because of the great number of large and small islands in close proximity there running toward the equator. This cape is at 52 degrees or slightly less south of the equator.[5] From the said cape, twenty leagues east of the coast, is the channel called Todos

---

[1] [*1557 marginal note*: Plinio, Bk VII, ch. II] In his marginal note Oviedo refers to Pliny the Elder's, *Natural History* Bk VII, ch. 2. Assuming the cubit at about 20 inches and the palm at 8.2 inches, their height would be about 10 feet. Onesicritus (*c*.360–290 BCE), was a Greek Cynic philosopher who served on Alexander's campaign to the East and was sent by him to interview Indian philosophers.

[2] Oviedo makes a second marginal note to the same book and chapter of Pliny the Elder's *Natural History*. The estimated height would be about 12 feet.

[3] Oviedo's third marginal note to the same source. Crates of Mallus or Pergamon (2nd cent. BCE), a Greek language grammarian and Stoic philosopher, leader of the literary school and head of the library of Pergamum, described as the Crates from Mallus to distinguish him from other philosophers by the same name.

[4] The Series Editor is particularly grateful for the assistance she received from Captain Richard J. Campbell in identifying landmarks in the Strait.

[5] It stands at 52°45′S.

Sanctos. Opposite this on the other coast is a bay called the Campana de Roldán.[1] Returning back half way from this bay to the western mouth are found the Nevadas Islands, and the point opposite Cabo Deseado which is also called Cabo Deseado.

From the channel of Todos Sanctos up the coast twenty leagues is North Bay from which projects a point a little higher that turns southward. On the opposite coast of this point is another bay, the Bahía Grande. From Bahía Grande following back down the coast to the west, one returns to the Campana de Roldán and in between these two places are the Sierras Nevadas.[2] So that, from these bays North and Grande, we have gone forty leagues up both coasts of the Strait.

From the point at North Bay thirty leagues along the coast to the east is Bahía Victoria, and on the southern side across from it Bahía Grande from which going back thirty leagues is another bay called Bahía Grande (the one mentioned above).[3] The land in between is called De los fuegos.[4] Up to this second Bahía Grande and its facing Bahía de la Victoria we have passed through seventy leagues of both coasts of the Strait toward the east.

[f. 34r] From Bahia Victoria to Cabo de las Vírgenes[5] there are forty leagues. This cape is the principal eastern entrance to this Strait and is at 52 degrees south of the equator.[6] The cape opposite it is called Tierra or Cabo de Fuegos.[7] From there it is forty leagues along this coast west to upper (or more easterly) Bahía Grande.[8] <p. 260> Halfway between these two points is the land called Lago de los Estrechos.

So that from western Cabo Deseado, the western mouth, to the eastern, Cabo de las Once mil Vírgenes, there are one hundred and ten leagues.[9] In the Strait the cartographers

[1] Monte Campana da Roldán is a mountain named by Magellan after his gunner Roldán de Argote (who also sailed with Loaysa); Markham, *Early Spanish Voyages*, pp. 16, 40, 43. It lies on the southern shore of the Strait, 53°57'43"S, 71°46'25"W across from Cabo Froward, the southern tip of the Brunswick Peninsula. The latter cape is also the southernmost point of the continent of South America. There is no channel (here named Todos Sanctos) opposite Campana da Roldán. It is unlikely that this refers to the main channel between Cabo Froward and the Segunda Angostura, that is Passo del Hambre and Passo Ancho. It may be Canal Jerónimo, the only major channel opposite Campana da Roldán.

[2] On f. 34r, Oviedo discusses the Islas Nevadas and refers back to what he names the Sierra Nevadas on f. 33v. The latter designation may be a misprint, since the index to the *Historia General y Natural*, BAE, vol. 121, assumes that both references are to the islands of that name. Given that they are said to lie about halfway between Campana de Roldán and Cabo Deseado they may be the islands in the Third Narrow around Isla Carlos III. If the reference to Sierra Nevadas is as intended, then it may refer to the hills at the western ends of Tierra del Fuego and Isla Dawson.

[3] There are two Bahía Grandes mentioned here. The one said to be opposite Bahía de la Victoria, may be Bahía Lee. The second is said to be opposite North Bay. The description of the latter 'from which projects a point a little higher and turns southward', would appear to be Puerto del Hambre which suggests that the second Bahía Grande may be Bahía Lomos.

[4] Presumably thus named because of the numerous fires of the natives they reported in Ch. X. Later in this chapter it is referred to as Cabo de Fuego or de Humos (that is smoke, fumes).

[5] Uriarte's description of Bahía de la Victoria, in Markham, *Early Spanish Voyages*, pp. 16, 40, 43, notes that 'when you are in it, the bay is so landlocked that you will not see where you entered'. Markham identified it as Bahía Santiago. Since the latter is a wide open bay on the north coast between the First and Second Narrows, it does not fit the case. It may have been the anchorage north of Isla Isabel.

[6] It stands at 52°20'S.

[7] Punta Catalina 52°32'S, 68°46'W, the northern point of the coast on the south side of the entrance to the Strait, from which the coast of the Isla Grande de la Tierra del Fuego leads away south-east; Campbell, Bradley, and Lorimer, *Narbrough*, p. 255, n. 6.

[8] Bahía Grande lies to south-west of Río Santa Cruz on the Atlantic coast, approaching the Strait.

[9] See above, p. 59, n. 2.

place some islands, especially twelve or thirteen, and the charts only call them Las Nevadas, as previously stated. The largest of the twelve is located in the Bahía de la Victoria.[1]

As I have said, at its widest point at the interior mouths, the Strait is seven leagues wide and in other places three, two, one, and in others less than one. But in the eastern entrance, the chart indicates its width at ten leagues from bank to bank and a little more in the western mouth. So, the southernmost Cabo de Fuegos (or Humos) of the eastern mouth is a 53 degrees south in front of Cabo de las Vírgenes.[2]

This is enough regarding the measurements of the sea and land of the great and famous Strait that Captain Ferdinand Magallanes discovered with the armada of our lord Emperor-King in the year one thousand five hundred and twenty of the Nativity of Christ, Our Redeemer, for His glory and praise in augmentation of the sceptre and lordship of the royal crown of Castile.

[1] Oviedo's comment is very vague but this may be a reference to Isla Isabel 52°53′S, 70°44′W.
[2] See above, p. 70, n. 4.

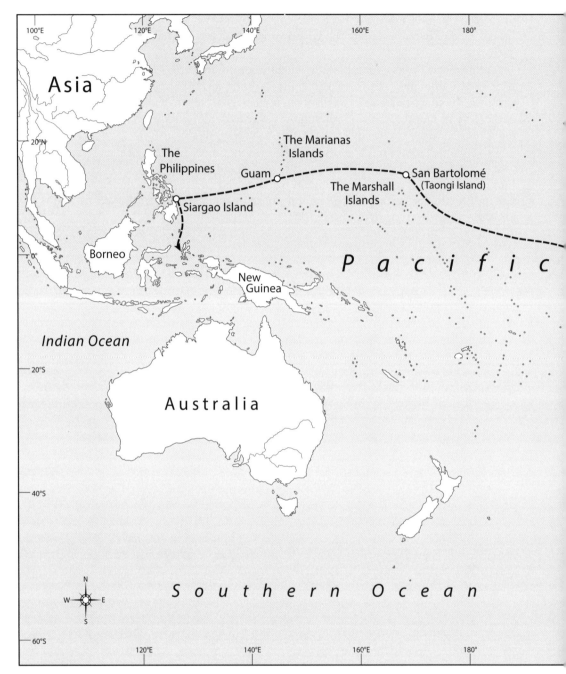

Map 3.   The voyages of the *Santa Maria de la Victoria* and the *Santiago* after entering the Pacific from the Strait of Magellan.

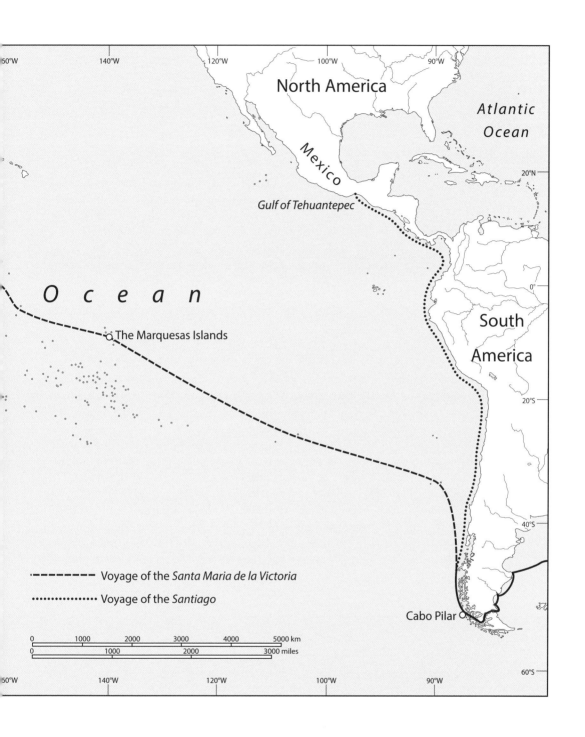

160°W	140°W	120°W	100°W	90°W	

North America

Atlantic
Ocean

Mexico

Gulf of Tehuantepec

20°N

O c e a n

○ The Marquesas Islands

0°

South

America

20°S

40°S

‑‑‑‑‑‑‑‑‑ Voyage of the *Santa Maria de la Victoria*
············· Voyage of the *Santiago*

Cabo Pilar ○

| 0 | 1000 | 2000 | 3000 | 4000 | 5000 km |
| 0 | | 1000 | 2000 | | 3000 miles |

60°S

| 160°W | 140°W | 120°W | 100°W | 90°W |

CHAPTER XV

Of the voyage and armada of Commander Fray García de Loaysa and those who sailed with him; of this voyage several reports were made some years ago by Captain Andrés de Urdaneta, native of Villafranca in the province of Guipúzcoa, by another hidalgo named Martín de Islares, native of the town of Laredo, and by other persons who sailed with the said armada and were witnesses. The said account of the voyage comprises twenty chapters, this being the first. This book ends with the final chapter, XXXVI

In Chapter V of this twentieth book a good deal was said of the calamitous voyage of Commander Fray García de Loaysa to the Spicelands which he undertook in the year 1525 with seven ships and four hundred and fifty men. Chapter XII related how one Friday, 1 June 1526, having exited the Strait of Magallanes into the great Southern Sea and being at $46^1/_2$ degrees south [f. 34v] of the equator on a northerly route, the pinnace *Santiago* lost sight of the flagship and subsequently wound up in New Spain. On board the pinnace was the cleric Don Juan (whose report is included above), and who after the separation knew nothing more of the armada's fate.

Now I will recount what I learned in 1539. The Adelantado Don Pedro de Alvarado passed through this city of Sancto Domingo on the Island of Española[1] on the way to his governorship in Guatimala[2] where he intended to outfit a fleet in the South Sea to sail to China.[3] Travelling with him were two men who had been on that voyage of Commander Loaysa. One was Captain Andrés de Urdaneta, a Vizcaíno (or more properly Guipuzcoano), a good and intelligent man who well remembered what he had seen and noted on that voyage. The other man was an hidalgo, native of the town of Laredo, Martín de Islares, likewise a man of intelligence. In addition to what I had already understood about the route and purpose of that armada, those two men gave me a thorough report and answered some questions I had, being persons who experienced the course of that voyage and were engaged in the travails and wars in those parts with the Portuguese and with the native Indians. I will report their information as briefly as possible because it contains notable things pertinent to the conclusions of the history of that armada.

You should know that five days after Commander Loaysa and his ships left the Strait of Magallanes and entered the Southern Sea, <p. 261> they ran into a violent storm that

---

[1] Hispaniola.

[2] Guatemala: variants, Goatimala, Guatimala,

[3] Pedro de Alvarado (1486–1541) was one of the captains who went with Cortés in the conquest of Mexico. He was infamous for the massacre of the Indian nobles in Tenochtitlan that led to the uprising called *la Noche triste*. Later, he went to Guatemala and became its adelantado and governor in 1530, and after that to Peru with Diego de Almagro in 1534. His plan to take an armada to China came to nothing and in 1541 he died in Jalisco during the Mixtones rebellion.

dispersed the four ships of the convoy never to see each other again. The tempest lasted four or five days, during which time those on the flagship were in great peril because they could not use the sails. Also, because previously nine or ten cubits of the keel near the stern post had been broken, even with the damage repaired the best they could, the ship was taking on so much water that twenty men constantly manning the two pumps could not staunch the flow.[1]

At the end of July 1526, at 4 degrees north of the equator, Commander Fray García de Loaysa, captain general of this armada, died after a grave illness. He died commending himself to Our Lord as a Catholic and fine gentleman in his office. His death brought great sadness and pain to everyone on board the flagship for, besides being a good, wise, and experienced captain, he was of genteel conversation and very well liked.

After his death, accompanied by the Paternosters and Ave Marias of all aboard and his body was committed to the sea, they opened the sealed instructions of his Caesarean Majesty which ordered that [f. 35r], in the event of Commander Loaysa's death, everyone was to obey as general Juan Sebastián del Cano (that captain who in the *Victoria* circumnavigated the world, as related elsewhere). And so it was done as His Majesty provided. But he (del Cano) was also in bad health and, four days after they made him general, God carried him off and they gave him the same burial as they did the Commander and cast him into the sea. A month before they had done the same for Alvaro de Loaysa, the commander's nephew and replacement for the chief comptroller Tejada who died in the same sea.[2]

Upon Juan Sebastián del Cano's death they made captain an hidalgo named Toribio Alonso de Salazar, native of Santander, who was comptroller on one of the galleons.[3] Because Commander Loaysa suspected that Salazar planned to mutiny with the galleon in the Strait and sail back to Spain, the captain general had him transferred to the flagship. In the midst of that great sea, the pilot Rodrigo Bermejo and other good men also died, more than thirty-five in all. This third captain general, Salazar, was himself in poor health and, seeing that the pilot was not very experienced ordered them to change course in search of the Ladrones Islands.[4]

On this course on 13 September they discovered an island they named Sanct Bartolomé.[5] However, as much as they tried they could not come ashore there. The coast they first approached was high and mountainous terrain running north-east–south-west,

---

[1] The ship was overloaded with the survivors of the *Sancti Spíritus*. There were 120 aboard, and the rations were cut to the minimum. Many died, including the comptroller Alonso de Tejada and the pilot Rodrigo Berjemo. Commander Loaysa fell sick, dying on 30 July; Navarrete, *Colección de los Viajes*, vol. V, p. 46; Spate, *Spanish Lake*, pp. 81–109.

[2] Navarrete, ibid., p. 46 reports that Loaysa's nephew died the same day as Elcano,

[3] Toribio Alonso de Salazar had served as contador on the *San Lesmes*. Navarrete, vol. 5, p. 46, notes that after he took the captaincy he appointed Martin Iñiguez de Carquizano as contador general.

[4] Islas Ladrones (The Islands of Thieves); first discovered by Magellan on 6 March 1521. So named by Magellan because of the natives' unsettling disregard for private property. Now Rota and Guam in the Marianas island group. Urdaneta reported that Elcano's intention was to sail to discover Cipango (Japan), but after his death, because of their desperate need of food and water, the crew voted to make for the Ladrones whose position was known.

[5] Navarrete, ibid., p. 47, states that island named Isla San Bartolomé was sighted much earlier on 21 August. The sighting raised hopes that it might be the mythical island where King Solomon was said to have brought treasure to build his temple; Ballantyne, *Science, Empire*, pp. 96–8.

and from the south-west end running north-west. The next day they edged away from the island and sighted a narrow sandy point eight leagues away. They approached it so closely that they could have hit it with a cannon shot, but they could not find bottom even at one hundred fathoms.

At that island were many boobies that would alight on the hands of those on board.[1] Also there were abundant supplies of bonito, albacore and dorado.[2] That island is at 14 degrees north of the equator and three hundred and twenty-eight leagues from the Ladrones Islands.

[1] See above, p. 40, n. 1. The red-footed booby (*Sula sula*) and the masked, or blue-faced, booby (*S. dactylatra*) are found throughout the tropical and sub-tropical Atlantic and Pacific Oceans.

[2] The Atlantic bonito (*Sarda sarda*) was common in Pacific waters. Albacore, longfin tuna (*Thunnus alalunga*). Pacific mahimahi (*Coryphaena hippurus*), commonly referred to as dorados.

CHAPTER XVI

How they discovered the Ladrones Islands and came upon a Christian Spaniard who had sailed in the first armada with Captain Ferdinand Magallanes; the man knew well the language of the Indians where he was and his company was very beneficial; and of other particulars of those islands

When Captain Salazar and the others saw that they could not land on Sanct Bartolomé Island <p. 262> they continued on in [f. 35v] search of the Ladrones. They arrived at the two closest to the equator at 12 degrees north. These Ladrones are a group of thirteen islands, all running north–south. The most northerly of the islands is at 21 degrees. One of the first two islands is called Botahá.[1] There a Christian came out to them in a canoe and greeted them in Spanish: 'Welcome, captain, master and company.' Those onboard returned the greeting with pleasure and asked with whom he had come to those parts to which he responded:

'Gentlemen, I am one of the crew of Captain Magellan's armada. I left the ship of Captain Gonzalo Gómez de Espinosa when he returned to Maluco, not being able to go to New Spain because, at that time, they were dying of a certain sickness on the ship.[2] Two Portuguese companions and I, fearing death, jumped ship on the island closest to the north.[3] There the Indians killed my two companions because of certain outrages they committed. Later I left there with some Indians for this island of Botahá. I am Galician; my name is Gonzalo de Vigo, and I know very well the language of the islands.'

Having said this, he refused to come aboard ship without a promise of amnesty, which they gave him. He sailed with them to the Maluco and was very useful to them as he knew the languages of those lands and something of Malay.[4]

In those islands, before you can anchor, there arrive many canoes carrying coconuts, water in gourds, fish, bananas, yams, rice, salt and many other fruits of that land. The only thing they want in return is iron like nails or whatever pointed thing. They call iron *herero*.[5]

---

[1] Botahá. The island of Guam (Guajan) in the Marianas group. Navarrete, *Colección de los Viajes*, vol. V, p. 48, notes that they arrived there on 5 September.

[2] The ship was the *Trinidad*, Navarrete, ibid., pp. 48–9. The two ships of the Magellan armada that made it to the Moluccas were the *Victoria* and the *Trinidad*. The *Victoria* returned to Spain via the Cape of Good Hope, but the *Trinidad* stayed behind for repairs and missed the favourable winds to follow her. Captain Gonzalo Espinosa tried to sail back across the Pacific to Panama, but was unable to find a route back to New Spain and was forced to return to the Moluccas, where he surrendered to the Portuguese.

[3] On the return of the *Trinidad* to the Ladrones, he and his comrades jumped ship on the island of Rota; Navarrete, ibid., p. 49.

[4] The lingua franca of South East Asia in those days was Malay.

[5] *Herero*: from the Spanish *hierro*. See Quimby, 'The Hierro Commerce', *passim*.

Their canoes are four to five fathoms long, some smaller or longer, and probably two cubits or less wide. Some are made from one tree and others of several but each has a wooden outrigger along one side made in the shape of a dolphin about half the length of the canoe. The outrigger is firmly tied to two poles projecting from the canoe about a fathom away. There is no difference between bow and stern. They have lateen sails made of very well woven mats and when they want to go back they simply turn the sail about and make the stern the bow and vice versa as they wish. These canoes are as deep as a man's knee. The hull planks are fitted together as follows: holes are drilled on the edges of the plank through which it is tied to another with cords made from tree bark. On the interior, they leave some drilled wood pieces on which they tie poles to strengthen the boat. The outside is treated with a pitch made of lime and oil, which closes up all the seams so that water does not [f. 36r] enter.[1]

The Indian men of all these thirteen islands go about stark naked. The women wear a cord about their waist from which they hang green leaves to hide their privates. They are all heathens who worship their ancestors' bones, which they keep in their homes with much veneration and well anointed with coconut oil.

They have one notable custom never before heard of any other people. It is that any young single man who has reached puberty carrying a small wand painted white is at liberty to enter the house of any married man. Upon entering, if the husband is at home, right away the visitor gives him a small basket containing some nuts, a leaf and some lime, all of which is eaten and in Moluccan is called *betre*.[2] Then the host gives the same to the visitor and leaves the house, allowing the young man to be with his wife as long as he pleases and treating her as if he were her husband. (All the male and female Indians carry always with them similar little baskets of *betre*.) <p. 263> The poor cuckold cannot enter his house while the adulterer is with his wife unless they call him. Nor does the husband have the right to go to another house to exchange baskets, or to act similarly, under pain of death.[3]

On those islands there are no domesticated animals or birds except for some small birds like doves. These are highly prized and kept in cages. They encourage them to fight each other, the owners placing small bets on the outcome. (This game I saw practised with quail in Italy during the migration of those birds.) On those islands there are some gulls and pelicans, although few. They have no metals and work wood with stone tools.

They are a handsome people. Both men and women wear their hair very long; some men let their beards grow as we do; and they go about well-anointed with coconut oil. They have no other weapons than slings and lances sharpened in the fire. Some of the spears are tipped with pieces of thin sharp leg bones from enemies killed in battle shaped into points or serrated. (Obviously the Mallorcans could not have instructed these people

---

[1] Pigafetta's account of Magellan's voyage provided a clear and precise description of the single-outrigger canoes with triangular matting sails used by the inhabitants of the Marianas; see Skelton, *Magellan's Voyage*, p. 26.

[2] *Betre*: betel nut: the seed of the Areca palm (*Areca catechu*), chewed with lime throughout the East Indies.

[3] It is interesting that Navarrete, *Colección de los viajes*, vol. V, p. 46, describes the indigenous inhabitants of Guam, the Chamorro people, as 'malos', following up his statement in that sentence that they all go stark naked. The reason for his opinion is perhaps explained by the fact that he also chose not to include Oviedo's description of their sexual practices. On the Chamorro in the first century of contact with Europeans see Lévesque, ed., *History of Micronesia: A Collection of Documents*, vol. I.

in the use of the sling, since there is no way they could have passed to them the invention of such a weapon that Flavius Vegecius and other authors attribute to them.)[1] Returning to the topic: those Indians use no money whatsoever: they highly value tortoise shells to make combs and fish hooks and iron they value above all other things.

The flagship was five days on Botahá Island, taking on water. From there it continued its journey to the Maluco. But before they left they kidnapped eleven Indians on the captain's orders to work the pump. Since they were [f. 36v] sorely plagued by leaks, they had to be constantly vigilant until God would lead them to a place where they could make repairs or be where they could sustain themselves and be secure.

---

[1] [*1557 marginal note*: Veg., lib. I, cap. XVI]. See above, p. 68, n. 1.

CHAPTER XVII

How the third captain general named Salazar died, and Martín Iñiquez de Carquizano was elected to fill the position and continued the voyage to the Maluco; how they came upon a rich island called Vendanao and what happened to them there

After leaving Botahá, on 10 September 1526, Captain Salazar died and was buried at sea with the same honours given to his predecessor captains.[1] There were great differences of opinion among the people concerning the election of another leader. Some wanted Fernando de Bustamante who was one of the hidalgos present with Captain Magallanes at the discovery of the Strait and who returned to Spain with Captain Juan Sebastián del Cano on the *Victoria*. Others wanted Martín Iñiquez de Carquizano, the fleet quartermaster. When everyone agreed to put it to a vote, Martín Iñiguez was the winner.

On 2 October, they discovered the island of Vendanao[2] and anchored near a small island in the harbour of Vizaya.[3] They then broke out the ship's boat and a group chosen by the captain landed to see if they could find an interpreter. They walked almost all that day without coming upon a town or person until in the afternoon they saw some Indians on the beach. They sent the Galician to ask where the town was. He spoke to them in Malay which they did not understand. After a while, the Indians went by canoe up the sound, the ship's boat following. After nightfall they came to a town on the river and the next day they parlayed with the Indians and were understood because there were some among them who spoke the Malay language. They offered quantities of nice Spanish-type chickens and pigs in trade but until then, the Spaniards were given much cooked rice, very good palm wine, <p. 264> fish, and some hens. With this the Spaniards returned well pleased to the ship, which was a good two long leagues from there.

The following day they returned to the town with much trade goods to buy chickens and other food items, but they found very little supply of provisions, and many Indians who were closely reconnoitring the Christians. Finally, they could not buy anything from those people who said that the next day people would come from the mountains bringing rice, pigs and other [f. 37r] food items. But, it was all a ruse and false as they intended to take the Spaniards' boat, and for this were gathering the most people they could.

With this, our men determined to wait until the next day and at dawn, the armed Indians came to the river bank. Via the interpreter, the Indians told the Christians they were suspicious and did not trust them and for that reason they brought nothing. The Christians responded that the Indians should send a principal man as hostage in exchange

---

[1] Navarrete, *Colección de los Viajes,* vol. V, p. 51, notes that Captain Salazar died on 13 September 1526. See above, p. 75.

[2] Vendanao: Mindanao in the Philippines.

[3] Navarrete, ibid., p. 53, notes that the vessel may have been anchored in the Bay of Banculin, 7°25′27″N, 126°21′38″E.

for a Spaniard so that both parties would feel secure and they could trade for what they wanted. The Indians agreed, and later sent to the boat an Indian dressed in a beautiful silk cloth and carrying a dagger with a gold hilt. He left on the ground the cloth, dagger and scimitar and got in the boat.

For their part, the Spaniards sent the Galician they found on the Ladrones Islands. The Galician left the boat and went to meet the king who said that those Christians must be *faranguis* (the name they gave in those parts to the Portuguese) and were bad people because wherever the Portuguese arrived they did evil things.[1] The Galician said that they were not *faranguis* but other people, rivals opposed to the Portuguese and that they would not anger or harm them in their land, wanting only to openly and fairly trade for what they brought. The king then said they were welcome. But, on his return to the river bank, the Galician saw a large contingent of Indians in ambush, ready to attack the boat when it came close to land. At the river bank, the Indians did not allow him to approach the Christians, but rather said they would deal with them from a distance. The Indians brought a small pig and some chickens for this purpose. The price they asked was thirty times what they were worth and, as the Galician saw this, he told our men what was afoot and warned them that he was going to escape to the boat even though he was surrounded by twelve Indians on guard with scimitars and shields. This notwithstanding, as he was a good runner, he took off, cleverly evading his guards and ran to the boat where our men picked him up in spite of the pursuing Indians. Then the Christians jumped ashore, grabbed the pig and chickens on the bank and embarked, taking the Indian hostage with them.

The next day Captain Martín Iñiguez sent them back to land to demand that they sell them some food for their trade items, and then the Spanish would return their Indian. But although they went there, they accomplished nothing with the Indians and returned to the ship. The following day, the captain came ashore with sixty men determined to do battle with the Indians if they did not willingly give food. Again this accomplished nothing except to antagonize the Indians. There was no fight because the weather was bad and the Indians did not appear. So, the captain returned to the ship.

The Indian hostage, observing all that, was very angry with his people. He said that if the captain wished to land with his men, as soon as they fired shots, the Indians would flee [f. 37v] and they could take possession of the place. Further, he said that he knew where the king had a great quantity of gold. The captain then landed with his men in good order and they went to where the Indians were, but they, observing the Spaniards' determination, took fright and dared not await them. The captain, seeing that they fled, ordered a return to where the boat was. They ate on the river bank and then returned to the ship, taking along the well-guarded Indian hostage.

A few days before, there had come alongside a *calabuz*[2] in which was a noble Indian dressed in crimson satin who brought <p. 265> some gold bracelets to sell. He gave many hens that he had with him to the captain, who reciprocated with some cheap Spanish trinkets that greatly delighted the Indian. The Spaniards refused to buy the gold because the captain ordered them not to, and the Indian left. He was from the same island but a

---

[1] According to Navarrete, ibid., p. 53, the natives were informed by a visitor from Malacca that the Europeans were Portuguese and they should not befriend them or trade with them because the strangers would kill them; which, of course, the Spaniards were prepared to do.

[2] *Calabuz*, or *calaluz*: described by Navarrete, ibid., p. 102, as a large canoe.

different province. According to him, those of his land were at war with the people of Vizaya where our men were.

Every night the Indians of Vizaya came to try to cut the ship's anchor cables so that it would wreck on the coast, but they were never successful because the Christians were always vigilant.

That island's circumference is two hundred and eighty to three hundred leagues.[1] When the ship departed they coasted along the southern shore for part of that distance. The island's largest city is Vendanao on the western side. This is one of the islands of the Archipelago of the Célebes.[2] Quantities of gold are gathered on this island, according to what the Indian hostage informed the Christians. They also learned that the Castilians lost in Sanguín were on this island.[3] The island is divided into the following provinces – Vaguindanao, Parazao, Bituán, Burre, Vizaya and Malucobuco – which are constantly at war with each other.

They have many sorts of arms such as bows, scimitars, shields, and daggers. Even the children carry iron-tipped javelins as long as darts but wider. Also, they have harpoons like those to hunt dolphins, though more elegant and well made. These harpoons have an attached cord and if they make a strike, they can reel in the fish. In addition, they have some spears called *calabays* with tips sharpened in the fire and with many spikes. These they can throw very far by setting them in a throwing stick a cubit and a half long. These heathen Indians are bellicose, clever, and false. They go about constantly very well-armed, with their javelins, scimitars, and daggers, even within their own towns.

The eleven Indians on board ship the Christians had taken from the Ladrones islands escaped to that island. However, they were then killed by the Vizayans who did not understand their language and thought them pirates come to raid.

That port is at 8 degrees 4 minutes north of the equator [f. 38r] in the province of Bituán. In Burre province there are quantities of very good cinnamon.

---

[1] Mindanao is the second-largest island in the Philippines at 97,530 square kilometres.

[2] In Oviedo's day, the archipelago was known by the name of the large island of the Celebes to the south of it. The chain became known to the Spaniards as the Philippines when so named by Ruy López de Villalobos in 1543, in honour of King Philip II. The actual colonization began in 1565 under Miguel López de Legazpi.

[3] Sanguín is identified in the following chapter as one of the islands south of Mindanao on the way to the Moluccas. Perhaps these Spaniards were survivors of the massacre at Cebu following Magellan's death at the battle of Mactan, 27 April 1521, described in Bk XX, ch. I; *BAE*, vol. 118, pp. 223–4.

CHAPTER XVIII

Which treats of the province of Cebú and of the trade there with Chinese merchants and in the other islands of the Celebes archipelago, and of the voyage of this flagship, and what islands they saw, and how they came to the islands of the Maluco, and of other things pertinent to this history

On Monday, 15 October 1526, the flagship (the sole remaining vessel of the armada Caesar sent out under Commander Loaysa) departed the above mentioned port of Vendanao with the intention to go to the island of Cebú as these Spaniards understood that it was a very wealthy place. However, lacking a north-easterly wind they changed course for the Maluco. From Vendanao, Cebú Island is seventy-five leagues north-west of the port of Vizaya and ten leagues from the second island Baguindanao.[1] Cebú is a very rich island in which the Indians say much gold is gathered. Captain Magallanes came very close to it at Matán where they killed him.[2] The Cebú Indians are trading people and very bellicose, having the same defensive and offensive weapons of others described in the preceding chapter. Every year very large Chinese junks come to Cebú, Vendanao and other islands. They bring quantities of silks, porcelains, objects of brass, small chests or boxes of aromatic woods, and many other things highly esteemed by the Indians. In exchange <p. 266> for what the Chinese bring them they take away from these islands gold, pearls, mother of pearl, and slaves. These numerous islands form a great archipelago called the Célebes Archipelago. Gold is found on many of the islands and pearls on others.

Leaving Baguindanao Island, the ship headed south in sight of many other islands, among them Sandinguar, Carraguán and Sanguín.[3] On Monday, 22 October, they anchored at an island called Talao[4] which is almost halfway between Ternate (one of the Maluco islands) and Baguindanao. The Spaniards were peacefully received on Talao and were able to trade for many pigs, goats, hens, fish, rice, and other food items. They sent carpenters ashore to cut wood to make carriages for lombards, and other things they had to jettison during the storm in the mouth of the Strait of Magallanes during the time of Commander Loaysa (as reported in the fifth chapter). In Talao, the Spaniards

---

[1] Described in Blair and Robertson, *Philippine Islands*, vol. XXXIV, as a great source of pearls.

[2] More than just coming close, Magellan arrived at Cebu on 7 April 1521 where he found a friendly reception from Sultan Humabon (whose name Oviedo does not mention). To cement their friendship, Magellan agreed to attack the sultan's enemy, Lapu Lapu, on neighbouring Mactan (Mathan, Matán) Island. This unfortunate decision cost Magellan his life on 27 April 1521. See Oviedo, Bk XX, ch. I; *BAE*, vol. 118, pp. 221–3.

[3] Sandinguar, Carraguán spelled Sandingar, Sarragán, in Navarrete, *Colección de los Viajes*, vol. V, p. 55.

[4] Oviedo and Navarrete, ibid., give the toponyms as follows. Ternate: Terrenate; Talao: Talso or Talao. Talao has not been identified but possibly the island containing the crater lake called Taal, however, its location, at 13°58′56″N does not comply with Oviedo's description here.

experienced no hostility but rather much help and welcome. [f. 38v] The lord of the town where they were tried to get the Spaniards to go with him to attack some islands called Gualibú and Lalibú with whom he was at war.[1] He told them there was much gold there, and offered his own sons as hostages but the captain did not accept the offer. The people of that island are not as civilized as those of the aforesaid islands. Talao is at 3 degrees, 35 minutes north of the equator.

In that port, the Spanish refreshed and re-supplied themselves very well and on Saturday, the 27th of the said month of October, they left the island of Talao in search of those of the Maluco, sailing on a course south quarter southeast.[2] The next Monday, the 29th of the said month, they sighted the island of Gilolo.[3] After being becalmed four days, they arrived at a small island two leagues more or less off the tip of Gilolo.[4] This island runs east to west, quarter north-east–south-west with relation to the tip of Gilolo. The Indians of that island came out to speak with the Spaniards, talking to them in Portuguese. Instead of showing them the way to the Maluco, they pointed them in the opposite direction, and the Spaniards followed the route the Indians indicated along the eastern side of Gilolo but along the way they sighted the islands of the Maluco which are very high and turned around to anchor at Camafo on the eastern side of Gilolo.[5] There right away came the governor and lord of Camafo named Quichil Bubacar. (*Quichil* means much the same as *Don* for Castilians and Bubacar is a Moorish name.) So, that lord of Camafo was a Moor. He brought with him an Indian named Sebastián who had been a slave of the Portuguese and spoke very good Portuguese.

This slave told the Spaniards that the place they belonged to was the king of Tidore, one of the Maluco kings. This king was the one who supplied clove to Captains Juan Sebastián del Cano and to Gonzalo Gómez de Espinosa. Also, this Indian told them that there were Portuguese in Maluco and that they had a fortress on Ternate Island and *fustas*, galleons, and other ships. Also he said the Portuguese had seized Espinosa's nao, killed all the people in his [trading] factory and destroyed the island of Tidore and its other lands because they had taken in and befriended the Castilians. Further, the slave said that not forty days ago the Portuguese had burned down the principal town called Tidore, and its king and all his men had taken refuge high up in the sierra. Learning this news, Captain Martín Iñiguez de Carquizano requested from Quichil Bubacar a *parao* equipped to send a message to the king of Tidore and some other kings of the Maluco to inform them of his arrival. The governor indicated his pleasure and right away ordered a *parao* to be made ready.

---

[1] Navarrete, ibid., p. 56, notes that the islands of Aso and Galium were also targets for attack.

[2] Navarrete, ibid., reports that at Talao, Martín Iñiguez de Carquizano promoted Martín García de Carquizano to the position of treasurer general, Diego de Solier to that of factor general, and Francisco de Soto to that of comptroller general.

[3] Gilolo: variously given as Jilolo, Batachina or Halmahera. Oviedo also notes in Ch. XXXIV that the natives called it Aliora. Gilolo can at times also refer to the sultanate and city within it on the western side of the island facing the Spicelands subject to the king of Tidore.

[4] The small island is Rabo, now Rau on the map. Next to it lies another island, then called Maro and now Morotai.

[5] Camafo or Zamafo. Navarrete, ibid., p. 59, locates it at 1°20′N of the equator. The Spanish wished to land on the eastern side of the island in order to reconnoitre the Portuguese on the west where the Spice Islands were located. The high volcanic peaks of Ternate and Tidore could be seen from the eastern side of Gilolo, which is narrow and low-lying at that point.

(And because ahead it will be good <p. 267> for the reader to know what sort of ship a *parao* is, I will say that it is a well-made, light craft with outriggers on both sides [f. 39r] so that it cannot capsize. It is rowed by men seated on six or eight benches in some boats and less in others. In some *paraos*, there are sixty, seventy, or one hundred oarsmen, depending on ship size. They carry fifty to sixty fighting men on top of some frames they make for that purpose. Also, they carry some versos and falconets on their gun cradles but cannot carry heavy artillery. The *paraos* are very swift and are in great use like any well-equipped galley with a sufficient crew. In addition, they can be propelled by sails made of finely woven fibres that are made in those lands.)

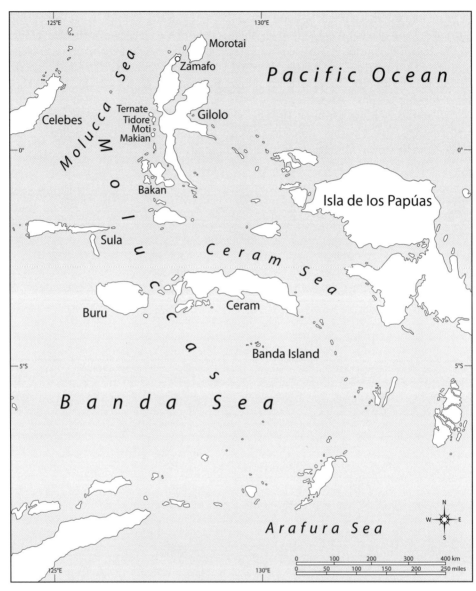

Map 4.   The Moluccas or Spice Islands and the surrounding region.

CHAPTER XIX

Of the embassy that Captain Martín Iñiguez de Carquizano sent to the kings of Tidore and of Gilolo; and of the gracious responses and good will the emissaries received from those kings and how pleased they were at the arrival of those Castilians at their lands; and how the kings sent their ambassadors to the captain and offered themselves as true friends

On Monday, 5 November 1526, Captain Martín Iñiguez de Carquizano sent Captains Andrés de Urdaneta[1] and Alonso de Ríos[2] as his emissaries to the kings of Tidore and Gilolo in the Maluco. They went with four men in the *parao* given him by Bucar, The ambassadors were to inform the kings how the Caesarean Majesty the Emperor-King, our lord, sent a trading fleet of seven heavily-laden ships to the Spicelands and how en route the fleet had been destroyed or dispersed by a violent storm; so that only the flagship had made it to Camafo where it presently was; and that they had learned how there were in Maluco Portuguese who had mistreated the natives because they had declared their friendship for His Majesty. Seeing this, the Captain sent the emissaries to the natives to hear what they thought about the situation and what should be done. Further, that the Spaniards were ready and prepared to favour and help them with their ship, personnel, artillery, munitions, and everything else against the Portuguese as well as against whatever other nations and peoples who were their enemies on sea or on land. For this purpose, the captain sent the emissaries to tell them by his letters what he thought of the matter and that, Our Lord willing, he hoped that very soon the other ships of the armada would arrive so that, with more men, they would be more fully served and their adversaries castigated for their provocations and bad deeds.

The emissaries left Camafo and went south-west along the length of the coast of Gilolo some thirty leagues until they left the *parao* in a small village and sent ahead by land to tell the king of Gilolo that they were coming to him. The next day after they arrived, they crossed [f. 39v] to the western side of the island. There the king sent them an armada of twelve *paraos* with his nephew, Quichiltidore, as captain general, and many other principal gentlemen. He received the emissaries very well and took them to the city of Gilolo about eight leagues from the islands of Ternate and Tidore.

They arrived at Gilolo on Thursday night on the eighth of the month and were joyously received. They were lodged in a good house where the king's envoy greeted them and said

---

[1] This is the first mention of Andrés de Urdaneta in the narrative. Urdaneta (b. 1508) was a protégé of Elcano who enlisted in the armada at age fifteen, and by only three years later had ascended to captain in the Spanish forces and an important figure in Portuguese-Spanish conflict.

[2] Alonso de los Ríos: Navarrete, *Colección de los Viajes*, vol. V, p. 59, states that he was a supernumerary in the armada and got along very well with the king of Gilolo.

that the next morning, God willing, they would meet him. Then they were served an abundant dinner consisting of meat, fish, rice, and the bread of that land called sagú[1] that resembles cassava (although our Spaniards think it better than cassava), much palm wine and diverse fruits. The Indians staged a great fiesta and celebrations upon the arrival of the Castilians that included many singers, dances, and many lanterns.

<p. 268> The next day the king went out to some large shipyards where there were many *paraos* and invited the emissaries to meet him there. When they arrived they found him with few people and on foot. The emissaries bowed, the king embraced them, and then all standing they related their mission through Gonzalo de Vigo who was the *girubasa* that is to say interpreter and knew something of the Malay language that the Indians of those parts spoke as well as their own language. The king allowed that he was pleased with the embassy mission and, after hearing it, he related how the Portuguese had come to those islands and captured Espinosa and the factory with all its personnel remaining on Tidore.[2] The Portuguese had destroyed all those who had been friendly with the Castilians except him, as there were not enough of them to do that. Then he offered to serve the Emperor with all his might and to favour and aid his Castilians and people with all his forces and power if they wished to stay in his land or in Tidore, wherever it seemed best to them. Then he ordered them to be given a *parao* to go to Tidore to present their message to its king.

With the approval of the king of Gilolo, Alonso de Ríos and two companions set out while Captain Urdaneta stayed in Gilolo for the time being. The king of Gilolo said that the two emissaries might run into the Portuguese who would capture or kill them, and there would be no one to return to the ship. If that happened, the Emperor's captain might think that the king of Gilolo had turned them over to the Portuguese. For this reason, he did not consent to Urdaneta's going. So Alonso de Ríos went to carry out his mission to the king of Tidore who, along with his gentlemen, received him very well and fêted him. Like the king of Gilolo, Tidore offered to serve the Emperor and favour and aid his captain and people with all possible power.

Then the king of Tidore sent two principal men, Guzmán [f. 40r] and Bayaño, to accompany envoy Ríos to His Majesty's captain, and they, on the king's behalf, were to order in all his lands that the Emperor's captain and his people be given all they might need. On Ríos's return to Gilolo the two Castilian emissaries had their parley with the king. He said that one of them and two companions were to stay with him, because the king wanted to send Quichiltidore to the Emperor's captain to learn what he desired and to advise him about the Portuguese. Quichiltidore was to beg the captain, on the king's behalf, to come to Gilolo because Tidore was destroyed and there was no better place to repair than in Gilolo.

Seeing the king's desires, they agreed that Ríos and three Castilian companions should stay in Gilolo, and that Urdaneta would return to the captain general's ship taking along with him a gunner for protection because they had some small pieces of artillery. And so, Urdaneta left the king of Gilolo accompanied by Quichiltidore, Guzmán, Bayaño

---

[1] Sagú, *Metroxylon sagu*: the sago palm. A staple of the area, being a starchy pudding-like food made from the interior of the trunk of various palms and cycads.

[2] The factory or trading post, established and left behind by the Magellan expedition in 1522. See above, p. 67, n. 2.

and all the others. They went back to where they first arrived, embarked in three *paraos* and went to Camafo where they found the nao. The Castilians and the Indians were well received by the general, who honoured the Indian emissaries and especially Quichiltidore as he was very valiant, wise, and the leader of the party. The captain, seeing the goodwill and the offer of the kings of Tidore and Gilolo, determined to go to see them.

CHAPTER XX

How the Emperor's captain determined to go to see the kings of Tidore and Gilolo and departed in his ship accompanied by their emissaries in their *paraos*; how on the way he was given a letter from the captain general of the king of Portugal and his response to it; how other demands were made by the Portuguese; how an armada was sent against the imperial ship which dared to pass through it and went to Tidore where the city was rebuilt and fortified

The following Sunday, 18 November 1526, <p. 269> the imperial ship (whose proper name was *Sancta María de la Victoria*) left the port of Camafo, accompanied by three Moluccan *paraos* bearing the emissaries of Gilolo and Tidore. On Monday, the nineteenth, they arrived at the roadstead at the tip of Gilolo, at 2⅓ degrees north of the equator.

I am sure that to some cosmographers it will seem that, with regard to these measures of latitudes of the islands of the Spicelands, I depart from what is indicated in modern charts, and even that I am not much in conformity with the ancient cosmography. And that is true. What I write here is certain and is what has been found by those who in our day have seen and sailed and repeatedly measured on land, astrolabe [f. 40v] in hand.

Returning to the history: while Caesar's ship and his Castilians were anchored off Gilolo point, a fierce storm separated it from the *paraos*. Not being able to return to Camafo, and running where the *nao* could, they rounded a large island called Maro.[1] They sought shelter there for several days in a small bay twelve leagues from the tip of Gilolo. On Friday the thirtieth, the feast of the Apostle Sanct Andrés, a *parao* arrived carrying a Portuguese named Francisco de Castro who was the alguacil mayor[2] of the Portuguese fortress. He brought letters from Don García Anríquez,[3] Captain of the Portuguese, to Martín Iñiguez de Carquizano, our Lord Emperor's captain. The letters Francisco de Castro presented contained certain injunctions from his captain saying that those lands belonged to the King of Portugal, his lord; and that the ship and the Castilians were ordered to proceed to the fortress where they would be received with honour. If they refused to go voluntarily, they would be made to go by force, he said with haughty and unseemly words.

To these demands, our captain responded that he came to those lands by order of his lord, the Caesarean Majesty Emperor-King of Castile; that those lands were his and not those of the Portuguese king; that he would do nothing other than what His Majesty ordered of him; that whoever interfered or presumed to try to interfere in his mission

---

[1] See above, p. 84, n. 4.
[2] Chief justice.
[3] Anríquez: possibly Henríquez or Enríquez.

would suffer the consequences of the appropriate resistance; and that, as to the rest, he did not wish to waste time in conversation. He ordered the Portuguese to leave and not to return with any more nonsense unless he wished to face punishment.[1]

The Portuguese letter was not signed, and when Captain Martín Iñiguez finished writing his response he refused to sign his name. When the Portuguese, Francisco de Castro, saw it unsigned he said –'Sir, why does your grace not sign the response?' – adding that Don García had only neglected to sign his letter because he was pressed to send it right away. To this Captain Martín Iñiguez responded: 'Well, I do not sign because of error or haste; and your Captain Don García was negligent since one must take care how one writes to a captain of His Caesarean Majesty.' He also said that Don García did not merit a response other than one equal to his own, and so it would be with deeds. With this the Portuguese departed. Because of the weather, the *nao* sailed about between those islands almost until the end of December, not being to round the end of Gilolo to go to the Maluco.

While they were anchored off a place called Chiaba, there came some *paraos* with the Portuguese factor and three or four other Portuguese.[2] On board the Spanish ship, they demanded again that the captain and ship go to the Portuguese fortress. The captain replied that he would go to where His Majesty ordered and that was Tidore [f. 41r] which the Portuguese had destroyed for being His Majesty's servants. As for what they said about being taken by force to the fortress, he would not respond to such a vain threat, and that when <p. 270> they attempted it, they would see how mistaken they were. With this, he dismissed them.

This factor was named Fernando de Valdaya. He returned again to make the same demands, and Captain Martín Iñiguez responded appropriately and told him not to come again with the same demands because, without wasting more paper and ink, he would respond in another manner. In spite of this, the captain was very generous with all the Portuguese who came to the ship. He ordered them given woollen, silk, or linen cloth, according to their station.

The following Saturday, 29 December, the ship rounded the tip of Gilolo. Sailing along about six leagues from the cape from behind two islands came out two Portuguese galleons, a *fusta*, some large boats and up to ninety large *paraos* to capture the ship.[3] At this time only one *parao* of Indians from Tidore accompanied the Spanish ship and because of a strong breeze it could not match the ship's speed. When they sighted the Portuguese armada, the ship lowered the topsails to allow the *parao* catch up. After they threw a cable from the stern to tow the *parao*, they resumed their course prepared for battle with anyone in their path. The ship was well armed with very good cannons of bronze and iron, as well as many other arms and munitions. There were guns and

---

[1] Navarrete, *Colección de los Viajes*, vol. V, pp. 62–3, adds that about this time the comptroller general, Francisco de Soto, attempted a mutiny against Carquizano. For this he lost his office to be replaced by Hernando de Bustamante. Urdaneta stepped into Bustamente's old position.

[2] Navarrete, ibid. p. 63, states that the Portuguese came several times to Rabo to encourage the Spaniards to sail on. Later, the Spanish were forced to turn back to Chiaba (Chiava), near Camafo to await better sailing weather.

[3] The island was Doy (or Doi). Navarrete, ibid., p. 64, adds more details. The enemy armada also consisted of 80 *paraos* of Moors of Ternate, Bathán, Aquián, Motil, and with the kings of Ternate and Bathán on board their ships. The king of Gilolo refused to take part. The captain general of the fleet was Manuel Falcón.

91

crossbows for all on board – one hundred and one persons more or less, ninety of them fighting men. As the wind was brisk and favourable, they passed through the enemy armada without them daring to engage the ship. The Spaniards sailed directly to Tidore where they had been and anchored there on 1 January 1526. Within the hour the king, well accompanied by his principal Indians, arrived and came aboard ship. This king's name was Rajamir, who was at that time twelve or thirteen years old, more or less. The king of Gilolo was Sultan Aduluraenjami, who was more than eighty years old.

After the king happily visited with the captain and recounted his misadventures and travails, he and his principals vowed by their law or sect to favour and aid the captain with their lives and treasures and with all their people, vassals, and friends placed entirely at the service of the Emperor and that of Captain Martín Iñiguez de Carquizano with his present and future company and those who might come into the Emperor's service. The same oath was made by the captain. That very day the soldiers began to construct a rampart on land, and the sailors hurried to offload the artillery. The Indian men and even their women helped them with great diligence. So they built a rampart of stone, wood and earth the best they could and afterward two others [f. 41v] for the artillery for when the Portuguese would come. They unloaded everything from the ship except some of the artillery, arms, and ballast. The captain remained on the ship after overseeing the reparations on land and took with him about seventy men.[1] He put the remainder of the men on land under Captain Fe[r]nando de la Torre. The following days they worked on the fortification, expecting the Portuguese to attack at any hour. The Indians began to rebuild their houses previously burned by the Portuguese.

While they awaited the arrival of their adversaries, this Captain Martín Iñiguez, an honourable and spirited man, very diligently supervised the land preparations – the construction of the walls, the rebuilding of the town – and he sent out spies and lookouts to safeguard the ship and the coast. It was a given, according to the demands and letters spoken of above, that the Portuguese would have to come. Especially so considering the captain's letters and statements that he was going to Tidore and then watching him sail defiantly through the enemy armada in spite of their numbers. The captain constantly encouraged the hidalgos and crew saying that even though they were few in numbers, they would count for many in spirit when the time came. Likewise, that they should imagine themselves fighting in Spain since their adversaries were Portuguese. He reminded them that, even though the Portuguese in those parts < p. 271> were powerful, the Spaniards could not shirk battle every time the enemy sought it. This was so, as much for the nation's honour and to serve our lord Emperor, as for the unjust title and the tyranny with which the Portuguese were in those parts belonging to the royal crown of Castile. But in truth, even though the captain was doing his duty, each one who heard him had the same will and desire to demonstrate their fidelity and spirit. And so, in this military operation they awaited the arrival of the Portuguese.

---

[1] According to Navarrete, ibid., p. 65, the ship had arrived at the Moluccas with 105 men on board; about 40 had died between the Strait and the Spicelands.

92

CHAPTER XXI

How the Portuguese went to fight the Castilians at Tidore with many more people than the soldiers of the Emperor; how the ones and the others fared in this encounter; and how the Portuguese returned badly damaged to their fortress of Ternate

On Friday, 18 January 1527, four hours before dawn, the Portuguese came to Tidore with many *paraos*, a *fusta* and some large boats to engage in combat with the Emperor's ship and the Castilians who remained from the armada Commander Loaysa had taken out from Spain.[1] The Spaniards, because of the menace, were well on guard. Right away they detected the enemy and fired a volley of shot that hit the *fusta*, almost sinking it. [f. 42r] The Portuguese were somewhat confounded when they saw that the Spaniards were not taken by surprise, but they began to fire their lombards and artillery. Their first shot struck the middle of the ship's side. On board, as soon as the Castilians felt the impact, some men went below with a light to check the damage. On board the Portuguese galley, they used the light to aim another shot at the ship which entered through the very same hole made by the first shot. This shot killed a ship's-boy holding the candle and wounded three or four other men.[2] All that day until nightfall they fired artillery at each other, and again Saturday until evening when the Portuguese retired to rest on the shore half a league away. Their intention was to return more vigorously to the naval battle the next day. When Captain Martín Iñiguez found out that part of the Portuguese had landed, he sent up to twenty Castilians and two hundred native Indians to attack them. The Portuguese became aware of the Castilian presence and fled in disorder to the ships. But as fast as they were, some Portuguese were stabbed and badly wounded and right away they sailed to their fortress at Ternate.[3]

It is a league from land to land –Ternate to Tidore – and four leagues from the Portuguese fortress to the fortifications of Captain Martín Iñiguez and the Castilians. Before this battle, while the ship and the Castilians were at Camafo, they sighted two sailing ships. Thinking they were ships of the armada, the skiff set out to catch up with them but failed and had to return. Because of that, Captain Martín Iñiguez determined to find out about those ships and he sent out some *paraos* to search for them.

---

[1] Navarrete, *Colección de los Viajes*, vol. V, pp. 69–70, gives a fuller account. Francisco de Castro, servant of Manual Falcón, came with three other Portuguese to demand that the Spanish move to the Portuguese fortress at Ternate. On 5 or 6 January, another Portuguese mission led by Fernando de Valdaya arrived, presenting orders from Captain Don García Hernández that the Spaniards should remove themselves to Ternate. On 13 or 14 January, a fugitive black slave reported to the Spaniards that Manuel Falcón was preparing an attack.

[2] Navarrete, ibid., p. 69, states that the ship's-boy (*grumete*) was named Jorge de Atán.

[3] According to Navarrete, loc. cit., the battle continued until noon the next day.

CHAPTER XXII

How Captain Martín Iñiguez sent a *parao* to determine if the two ships they saw sailing were of the armada or not; and how those who set out on this mission captured two *paraos* at sea and burned a town on the island of Motil that the Portuguese held and killed some people; and of the help that the king of Gilolo requested from the Castilians; and of other things that happened as the war with the Portuguese continued; and how the Castilians took from them several quintals of clove, etc.

As reported above, while the Castilians were at Camafo they thought that two ships <p. 272> they saw sailing by were of their armada, and they sent the skiff after them but it could not catch up to them. Thus, after what happened with the Portuguese armada at Tidore, Captain Martín Iñiguez, desiring to learn the truth about those ships, decided to send out the only *parao* there was in Tidore. On board the *parao* and canoes were Captain Urdaneta, some [f. 42v] Castilians and some Tidore Indians chosen by the general. They went to an island called Motil held by the Portuguese.[1] There our men captured two *paraos* and burned down a good-sized town, killing some people. Afterward, our people withdrew all unharmed. Motil is five leagues from the city of Tidore.

At that time, the king of Gilolo sent five well-armed *paraos* to Tidore to inform Captain Martín Iñiguez and the Castilians that the Portuguese had come out against him while they were searching for the Emperor's ships and had demanded from him the Castilians who were in the city. Because he refused, the Portuguese declared war against him, whereas before that they had been at peace. For that reason, the king asked the Captain to kindly send him twenty Castilians and some artillery and munitions. The Captain complied with the king's request and ordered Martín García de Carquizano, treasurer general at that time, to go with some artillery pieces and some gentlemen of the armada.

While the *paraos* were in Tidore, there was news that a Portuguese ship laden with clove was en route from Maquián to Ternate. Then Captain Martín Iñiguez put fifteen Castilians on the *paraos* of Gilolo and they went in search of the *cempam*[2] or boat. They caught up with it and captured its cargo of clove after a battle with the crew. In the battle, they killed a Portuguese and some twenty Indians and took two hundred and fifty quintals of clove. The captain took the clove for the Emperor and gave some yards of woollen cloth and other things to the Indian captains who fought with the Castilians.

After that, they went on to Gilolo where the king was very content with the Castilians, the artillery, and the munitions. Likewise content was Martín García de Carquizano, charged by the general to build a *fusta*, because the king of Gilolo had offered to contribute everything needed to do so except for the nails.

---

[1] In the 16th century, Europeans defined the Moluccas as consisting of 5 islands, Ternate, Tidore, Motil, Maquián, and Bacan. Motil was reckoned to produce the best clove. Bergreen, *Magellan*, p. 139.

[2] *Sampan*: a shallow wedge-shaped open skiff commonly used in Asian waters.

CHAPTER XXIII

How the general sent Captain Urdaneta to search for the ships they had sighted from Camafo; and how he burned down a town on an island and killed or captured its inhabitants; and how he came upon eight *paraos* with Portuguese on board; and of the ensuing battle and his escape by his courage and resourcefulness

On the fifth or sixth of the month of February in the year 1527, the captain general sent Captain Urdaneta with three *paraos* to search for the ships seen sailing by when the flagship was at Camafo. He was to go to Veda, a town south-east of the Maluco, which seemed to be the destination of those ships.[1] [f. 43r] Because of the ongoing war with the Portuguese, the captain general ordered that he be accompanied by a good Castilian man and an Indian who was an expert gunner. The rest of the crew in the *paraos* were very fit Indian warriors.

After leaving Tidore, they searched for more than twenty days without finding any news of the ships at Veda or any other place, and so they turned back to the Maluco. Because their food supply was very low and all that land was usurped by the Portuguese, Captain Urdaneta and his crew were exhausted. They determined to go to Guacea Island[2] to obtain food either voluntarily or by force. But there the Indians, unmoved by their pleas or offer of payment, refused to give them anything. Faced with their obstinacy, the captain left the *paraos* well-guarded and came ashore armed by swimming on a large shield accompanied by his Indians. Once on land <p. 273>, he deployed his squadron in the best order possible. The island Indians were the ones that began the battle with great fury, but Urdaneta's forces faced them bravely and soon the opponents began to retreat to their houses. The houses were elevated as high as the crow's nests of one hundred and fifty or more ton ships but constructed on four posts. At about a third of the height, there is a floor constructed of cane and there are removable ladders from the ground to the first floor and from the first to the upper floors. As this is a novel type of edifice, I drew one here according to the captain's description.

Taking refuge above in their houses, the Indians let loose such a rain of arrows and stones that was impossible to withstand. Then the captain set fire to the roof of a house that was covered with palm fronds but had no walls, being an open hut. The fire took hold and spread so quickly with a stiff breeze that it was not a quarter of an hour or less before that the entire town was burning. As the Indians saw themselves, their women, and their children menaced, they descended very quickly to be intercepted by our men

---

[1] Veda: not found in Navarrete, *Colección de los Viajes*, vol. V. Urdaneta's destination likely was the town south-east of Gilolo on the eastern side of Gilolo Island, now called Weda.

[2] Guacea Island: not found in Navarrete, ibid. Perhaps present-day Segea, situated on Gilolo slightly to the north-east of Weda, but not on a separate island.

who killed all they wished and captured those who seemed to offer ransom or sales opportunities. Finally, nothing of that place remained that was not burned or captured.

With this victory and booty, Captain Urdaneta and the three *paraos* left that place [f. 43v] and went to a town called Gave where they were received peaceably, given provisions, and where they sold part of the prisoners. There were so many of them that Captain Urdaneta's share alone numbered twenty-five.[1]

From Gave they left for Tidore and en route they came upon eight Portuguese *paraos*, two of them large ones. The Portuguese boldly came alongside and almost took two of our *paraos*, fighting side to side. Then Captain Urdaneta's *parao* turned on the enemy and with a volley of shot destroyed the bow of one of the Portuguese boats, killing some men and sending the ship to the bottom. While the enemy were occupied with saving themselves, Captain Urdaneta had time to gather his *paraos* and row away as fast as they could, firing shots from time to time against their pursuers. Our forces lost all their prisoners – more than one hundred – who, during the fighting, jumped overboard and made for the enemy *paraos*, some drowning in the effort. The majority of our Indians were wounded and some were killed. And so, the three *paraos* made it to Tidore with empty hands although having inflicted much damage on the enemy.

[1] Gave: not found in Navarrete, but likely Pulua Gebe south-east of Segea.

CHAPTER XXIV

How Captain General Martín Iñiguez ordered a galleon built to send to Spain because the flagship was no longer seaworthy; how two *paraos* of Portuguese came and the Spaniards sallied forth against them; and of the barrel of powder that exploded and burned some of our men, among them Captain Urdaneta, who was in danger because of his burns and of being killed or captured by the Portuguese

Captain Martín Iñiguez de Carquizano was anxious to send to Spain to inform our Lord Emperor of the state of things in the Spicelands – of the war with the Portuguese, and the misfortunes concerning the ships and men he had sent to those parts under Commander Fray García de Loaysa. To that end he ordered constructed a galleon to be loaded with clove and other spices. The flagship, the *Santa María de la Victoria*, in which this captain came with the few remaining armada members was no longer seaworthy, its seams having opened up because of <p. 274> the heavy use of the artillery fired from it as well as the damage the ship had sustained. If it were not for the Portuguese threat, they could have careened and repaired it on the western side of Tidore Island. Likewise, the Indians of Tidore at this time were rushing to build *paraos*, because every place there was an island and so without boats it was impossible to carry on the war.

One day in March, 1527, it happened that two [f. 44r] well-provisioned and well-armed Portuguese *paraos* came along the coast of Tidore, chasing some fishermen and then stopping in front of the city.[1] When General Martín Iñiguez saw them, he sent for the island governor named Leveñama and told him to make ready some *paraos* to chase away the Portuguese. The governor said that at the time, he had only one *parao* there in the city, but there were two others belonging to his friend, the king of Gilolo, and with those and his they could engage the enemy. Soon the *parao* was made ready with a crew of good men. The captain of the Indians was Quichilrade,[2] the king's brother, an experienced warrior and good friend of the Castilians. The general ordered Captain Urdaneta and eight Castilians to go with them. With all due diligence, they embarked, left port, and met the *paraos* from Gilolo with the intention of attacking the Portuguese together. But the forces from Gilolo insisted that the fighting be left to them because they wished to test themselves against the men from Ternate as well as the Portuguese, and they could not be persuaded to change their minds. When the Castilians and Captain Quichilrade saw this, they determined to attack the two enemy *paraos* with their one ship, and so they did. When they attempted to come alongside the enemy ships the Portuguese refused to engage and fled. Captain Urdaneta's *parao* pursued them a good league and a half, raining cannon and gunfire on the fleeing ships. The Gilolo *paraos*

---

[1] Navarrete, *Colección de los Viajes*, vol. 5, p. 74, dates this as around 27 March.

[2] See below, pp. 104–5, 107, 117.

followed, although farther off because in them were six Castilians from Gilolo. Likewise, Captain Urdaneta's *parao* and the two enemy *paraos* stopped. As those waters are very hot, our men took off their armour for the return to Tidore. Then they fired off a parting shot at the Portuguese *paraos*, which unfortunately ignited an uncovered barrel of powder in their own boat. The explosion burned some of the Castilians and some fifteen Indians, six of whom died. Captain Urdaneta, seated close to the barrel, was one of those burned. He jumped into the water to escape the fury of the burning powder, but when he sought to get back into the *parao*, he found that the panicked Indians had rowed off leaving him behind in the water. So, the poor Captain wearing only sailor's pants began to swim for shore. Meanwhile, when the Portuguese saw the explosion and fire, they came about to attack the *parao*. In doing, so they saw the captain swimming and turned to capture him. The Gilolo *paraos* that had stopped as well also saw the captain in the water and charged off with great diligence and spirit to put themselves between the swimmer and the Portuguese. While fighting very valiantly, they managed to pick up Captain [f. 44v] Urdaneta in one of their *paraos*.

It was a marvellous thing that this captain escaped. Clearly God wished to save him from the numerous shots fired at him and, moreover, from falling into the hands of those Ternate Indians, because if they had captured him, even if the Portuguese wanted to spare his life, their objections would have done little good. And so the men from Gilolo returned him to Tidore. The captain was badly burned and wounded, and for ten days he could not speak because of smoke inhalation.[1] As for the Portuguese, they retreated when they saw that the captain was rescued.

---

[1] According to Urdaneta's *Relación* cited by Rodríguez and Alvarez in Navarrete, *Colección de los Viajes*, vol. V, p. 74, Urdaneta suffered burns in similar circumstances while in the Strait on his way overland to the wreckage of the *Sancti Spíritus* at Cabo Vírgenes on 23 January 1526: 'as my luck would have it, a flask of powder caught fire and burned me all over making me forget all the past hardships and dangers'.

CHAPTER XXV

Which treats of the arrival of Don Jorge de Meneses in India and of the subsequent differences and wars between the Portuguese and the Castilians; and how the parties agreed to a truce which was broken by the Portuguese when they killed some of the king of Gilolo's Indians; of the king's retaliation; and how the Portuguese poisoned and killed the captain general of the Castilians, etc.

A few days after the events of the preceding chapter, the armada of the king of Gilolo and the Castilians came upon that of the king of Ternate and the Portuguese. Fifty *paraos* of both sides fought for six hours or more until both parties retired without a victory and with no reproach to either.[1] Many Indians of both parties were wounded but no Christians, neither Portuguese nor Castilians, which caused the Indians to marvel not a little. During this battle and afterward many demands were exchanged – the Castilians requiring the Portuguese to leave the land free and clear to his Caesarean Majesty and his royal Castilian sceptre to whom it belongs, according to certain solemn declarations; and the Portuguese requiring that the land be left to them, saying that those islands were the king of Portugal's.

In the middle of the month of May 1527, Don Jorge de Meneses arrived with two ships to command the Portuguese fortress. As soon as he came, he sent messengers to Captain Martín Iñiguez de Carquizano, saying that he was greatly distressed at the differences and war between the Castilians and the Portuguese. He politely asked General Martín Iñiguez to agree to a truce until they could converse about what should be done in all fairness and honesty to both parties.

The Portuguese factor, Fernando de Valdaya, brought these letters and the Castilian captain general responded that he would be pleased with general peace and concord, provided that it not prejudice the rights of the Emperor and his realms. Further, the captaine said that if the Portuguese wished, he would be happy that the two parties consult their princes concerning the state [f. 45r] of things so that they could send orders as to how they were to be served and, while that was happening, they could be at peace, both parties ceasing warlike activities. But, as things later progressed, Captain Martín Iñiguez's equitable response was made in vain because the negotiation did not advance except by trickery, with the aim of treacherous murder under the guise of truce.

That very month of May, two renegade Castilians deserted – one named Soto and the other Palacios. The hidalgo or non-hidalgo, leaving the side and service of his prince

---

[1] After this battle, the *Santa María de la Victoria* was in such bad condition that it needed a complete overhaul. However, as the only place where they could careen it was on the other side of the island where it would be exposed to Portuguese attack, it was decided to salvage as much as possible and then scuttle the ship. The plan was to build another ship in Tidore, to send to Spain via the Cape of Good Hope; Navarrete, *Colección de los Viajes*, vol. V, p. 76.

without legitimate cause and passing over to the enemy without permission and first doing what is required in discharge of duty and honour, not only commits an evil deed and is a traitor, but also is unworthy of being accepted by another prince or captain. No one would trust him after committing such a notorious crime. This act saddened the Castilians on the one hand, but pleased them on the other, because such men left their company before they could cause greater harm.

Before Don Jorge de Meneses arrived, there had been an exchange of letters between Don García Anríquez and Captain Martín Iñiguez concerning the unsigned letter the former had sent (as was reported previously).[1] Both captains disliked each other because Don García, among other things, said that those islands were the king of Portugal's and, as such, it was impossible for the Emperor to send men to the Maluco and so Martín Iñiguez and his company must be thieving pirates. As to that, Martín Iñiguez responded that he lied, and that in single combat against Don García or between groups of Castilians versus Portuguese <p. 276> he would defend how that conquest was the Emperor's and that of his royal Castilian sceptre and not that of any other king or Christian prince; and that the Portuguese intruded like tyrants in what did not belong to them or their king; and that Martín Iñiguez and the other gentlemen, Castilians, and the Emperor's vassals following him had come by His Caesarean Majesty's command and were in his service in those parts. Don García was prepared to accept this challenge, but the king of Portugal's other hidalgos and officials did not consent and so the combat between the two captains did not take place.

So, returning to the main narrative: Heralds and messengers went back and forth with demands between Don Jorge and Martín Iñiguez. With the truce established between the parties, the general sent Captain Urdaneta, who was also comptroller of the flagship, to take to Don Jorge some documents from His Majesty showing that Caesar had sent his armada to the Maluco as his own possession, as it is in fact and of which the Portuguese are well aware, although for their own purposes they dissimulate.

About this time Captain Martín Iñiguez de Carquizano received word that Alonso de Ríos and Martín García de Carquizano in Gilolo were having differences. They were then ordered [f. 45v] to return to Tidore where the general was and so they did. Captain Urdaneta was sent to Gilolo to take charge of the people who were there and with diligence and care finished the *fusta* being constructed. A Levantine had provided the model or form it was to take so that, for the rest, the Indians' carpenters would fabricate it, as they are very clever men.

The king of Gilolo was a very wise and valorous man and a friend and confederate of the Castilians. As for the *fusta* under construction, he ordered work to be done when it pleased him, and at other times stopped the work when he felt like it. Captain Urdaneta asked him one time why he did not order the *fusta* to be finished as quickly as possible to be able to use it. The response was that it was necessary for the work be done in intervals so that the ship would have better fortune. The truth is that, among those people, this king was held as a very great astrologer and wise man, even though the Spaniards thought that the delays also must have been for other reasons.

While Captain Urdaneta was at Gilolo, a truce was established between the captains general. The Emperor's captain general sent via Urdaneta a message for the king of Gilolo

---

[1] See above, p. 90, n. 3.

saying that from then on he could be secure from the Portuguese unless advised otherwise because they had established a truce for everyone. With this news, the king of Gilolo proclaimed throughout all his towns that his Indians could carry on their businesses wherever they wished in his lands without fear of the enemy. Fifteen days later, while many canoes of Gilolo were fishing at sea, there came two large *paraos* from Ternate with some Portuguese on board and they attacked the fishing boats, capturing some of the canoes and killing all the Indians aboard. When this was known in Gilolo, they tried to go out against the Portuguese, but were unable to do so at that time. Captain Urdaneta, angry and incredulous at such unheard of discourtesy, went in a canoe to the two Portuguese *paraos* under a white flag to speak with them and find out who were responsible for that rupture of the truce. Seeing that he wished to talk to them, they awaited him. From a distance, the captain asked if there were any Portuguese among them and was told there were. When they showed themselves, Urdaneta told them he wished to speak with them if they promised safe conduct to approach and leave freely. The Portuguese agreed. But when he attempted it, the Indians rowing his canoe refused to come close to the Portuguese since, during a declared truce they had <p. 277> acted treacherously, and there was now no reason to trust them. In spite of all Urdaneta's urging, he could not get them to approach the *paraos*, so he swam to where the Portuguese were. He came aboard one of their *paraos* [f. 46r] and asked why they had committed such a discourteous act in a time of truce. They responded that they were going to a town called Guamoconora for provisions, and that the Indian captains had captured those canoes against their wishes, among other things.[1]

Urdaneta memorized the names of the Portuguese and Indian captains and wrote them down on a palm leaf and swam back to his canoe. Then he went to Gilolo where he found the king very angry at the captain general, saying that because he had sent Urdaneta to say that his vassals could move about freely, the Portuguese had killed those fourteen or fifteen men. Eight days later, on receiving certain news, the king embarked with Captain Urdaneta and the Castilians with him in Gilolo to intercept certain *paraos* coming from Moro bound for Ternate loaded with provisions. The Gilolo *paraos* found and captured ten or twelve of them with many Indians aboard. The king beheaded all those from Ternate Island and enslaved the rest. And so, the king of Gilolo returned victorious, having avenged the breaking of the truce and with the aforementioned booty.

When the news reached the Portuguese in Ternate they sent to protest to Captain Martín Iñiguez about the king of Gilolo and Captain Urdaneta, recounting what had happened but omitting that they had been the first aggressors to break the truce. The captain general swore that if it had happened as the Portuguese said, and Urdaneta had broken the truce, he would have his head. Urdaneta was warned of this by a letter from a friend in Tidore and left right away to defend himself along with Quichiltidore who was representing the king. In Tidore, they testified in the presence of some Portuguese who were there. Among the many eloquent things that Quichiltidore said to the captain general in defence of the king of Gilolo was the following:

'Consider, Sir, that when the enemy's word, oath or sense of shame is not kept regarding what they promised, for greater security one ought to be at war with such

---

[1] Guamoconora: but spelled Guamuzonora in Chapter XXVI.

persons, accepting no peace, contract or any other pledge they may offer. My lord, the king of Gilolo, trusting in your word, had announced the truce that resulted in the death of his vassals and so with more reason should he complain of you than of the Portuguese. You, captain, were the first the Portuguese offended in breaking the truce. What the king of Gilolo, your Captain Urdaneta and the Castilians in Gilolo did in defence of your king and your men, as at the home of the Emperor's friends and servitors, was to restore His Majesty's and your honour. They did not break the truce; rather, they repaired a shameful offence the Portuguese dared to commit under the king's nose and [f. 46v] at your doorstep, treacherously breaching a promise made to you, to the king, to your nation, and to us. Such an outrage committed by the king of Ternate and the Portuguese would not have happened if you and your truce had not caused it. My king requests that you approve of what was done and that you honour and reward Captain Urdaneta and the other Castilians in Gilolo. Further, the king of Gilolo advises you to be on guard against people that keep their word so badly. Moreover, he notifies you that, however many truces you agree to with the Portuguese, the king of Gilolo will not sleep easy if the king of Ternate does not send him alive those Ternate captains that killed his vassal and broke the truce. And even you, Sir, will do well to ask for satisfaction and the handover of those Portuguese involved in the affair <p. 278> for Urdaneta spoke to them, knows their names and will recognize the ones and the others.'

Captain Martín Iñiguez was very pleased to have learned the truth, and the anger he felt at Captain Urdaneta and the other Castilians disappeared. He embraced the captain and said that he had done well and that, if God gave him the means, he would reward his service to the best of his abilities and would petition his Caesarean Majesty to do so as well. The general sent a gracious reply to the king of Gilolo and ordered Urdaneta to return to the king with Quichiltidore, whom he also embraced and thanked for his advice. But, in truth, the advice was late in coming because, at that time, Martín Iñiguez was very ill, suffering the effects of the poison that the Portuguese factor, Fernando de Valdaya, had given him. It was thought that Don Jorge de Meneses ordered Valdaya to do so as Don Jorge was at the centre of the truces and dealings with the Spanish.

The poison was administered in a glass of wine by Fernando de Valdaya in the following manner: When the Portuguese was dining with the captain general he had the poison on his thumbnail. He said to the captain: 'I drink to you', in the manner of the French and Flemish in their banquets and feasts. The one who says this drinks that cup or glass in front of the person toasted, after which the other person is obliged to drink as much as the person who initiated the toast. So, after the Portuguese drank with gusto, he refilled the cup and handed it to the general but, on so doing, put his thumb in the glass and introduced the venom into the wine. The captain, believing he was dining with a trustworthy Christian man, took the cup and drank the wine and the poison. After the dinner, the Portuguese left for Ternate, and later that very day the evil trick was perpetrated the captain fell ill and died in a few days.[1] Oh, Lord and Redeemer of the world! Who could possibly guard himself from men's evil, the devil's tricks and the dangers of this life without Your protection? As the psalmist well says: *Nisi Dominus custodierit civitatem, frusta vigilat* [f. 47r] *qui custodit eam*:

---

[1] Navarrete, *Colección de los Viajes*, vol. V, p. 83. He died on 11 July 1527.

which is to say: If the Lord does not guard the city, in vain watches he who is on guard.[1]

When I heard of this Portuguese evildoer, I immediately recalled that Egyptian queen of whom it is written that Marc Anthony, in the course of the Attic War and fearing the cunning Cleopatra, refused to eat any dish that had not been tasted. So, the queen donned a chaplet that included poisoned flowers. Later, the banquet increasing in pleasure and gaiety, Cleopatra invited Anthony to drink, from the flowery chaplet. Who would have thought to fear such a trick? Her chaplet was already in a cup bathed in wine and when Anthony started to drink, the queen took the cup from his hand and said: 'I am she, oh beloved Anthony, from whom you so diligently guard yourself. Know that if I could live without you, I would not lack for a place or occasion to kill you.' This said, she had a woman condemned to death brought out of prison and gave her the cup. As soon as she drank, she died.[2]

In my opinion, no kind of treachery can justify such a deceitful way to murder. The greater the confidence that exists between the men, the greater the crime. This trust in an enemy ought not to be held by any individual or by any captain in any situation, so that it not happen to him what happened to Captain Martín Iñiguez de Carquizano who died because of imprudence, failing in service to his king and his men. He was a genteel captain and a very energetic man of good counsel in the matters of war, even though in this instance, he was too careless with his life. Let us pass on to the rest of the history.

---

[1] [*1557 marginal note*: Psal. CXXV] Psalm CXXV in the Vulgate; CXXVII in the King James Bible.
[2] [*1557 marginal note*: Plinio, lib. XXI, cap. III] refers to Pliny the Elder, *Natural History*, Bk XXI, ch. III. See Jones, *Natural History*, vol, VI.

CHAPTER XXVI

How Fernando de la Torre was elected captain general on the death of Martín Iñiguez; how the *fusta* the Castilians were building in Gilolo was destroyed by a fire secretly set by the Portuguese; how a principal gentleman of Tidore was killed for sleeping with the queen; and of some skirmishes with the Portuguese in the continuation of the war; and of other things pertinent to the history

Captain Martín Iñiguez de Carquizano's death was a blow to the Castilians as he was a sagacious and great spirited man, feared by the Portuguese as well as the Indians. In truth, as a choleric man, if annoyed he could be furious, harsh, and given to impetuosity at times, which can be difficult and delay things that require considered attention, not giving in to sheer will as much as to reason and what is needed. But on the other hand, he was a person of good conversation and generous in what had to be done. He was a native of the province of Guipúzcoa from the village of Elgueibar.

At the time of the captain general's death, Captain Urdaneta was in Gilolo where the king and all the Indians were very sorry for this loss. Among the Castilians in Tidore, there was much discord in the election of a new [f. 47v] governor and captain general. Martín García de Carquizano, the treasurer general, and Fernando de Bustamente, the comptroller general, opposed each other for the office, each with some Castilian supporters. But the majority of the men and officers saw that these two were willing to resort to force, and that the election of either could result in much harm to all and disservice to His Majesty. So they met at the fortress and agreed to offer up as captain, Fernando de la Torre, at the time warden of the fortress and the general's lieutenant, and then everyone swore to follow him as captain general. When the treasurer and comptroller saw this, they followed suit together with the factor, then Diego de Cuevasrubias. So, all were at peace. The senior officials who concurred in this election were Alonso de Ríos, Pedro de Montemayor, Gutierre de Otinón, Iñigo de Lorriagua, Martín de Islares, Andrés de Guorastiagua, Pedro Ramos, and Diego de Ayala. Eight days later, Captain Fernando de la Torre sent Alonso de Ríos and some others to Gilolo with a notary to take the oath of allegiance of Captain Urdaneta and the other companions there to the captain general. And so it was done.

Before General Martín Iñiguez died, he gave the captaincy of the *fusta* to Alonso de Ríos and the sea treasury to Urdaneta. Because of this, both men stayed in Gilolo.

A few days later, a Portuguese who spoke fluent Castilian fled to the Castilians. He said he was a Castilian but, as it later turned out, he was nothing but a great traitor. After he was a few days with the Castilians, there came two *paraos* of Portuguese on a certain mission to the captain. By this ruse, they gave to the fugitive some powder grenades to place secretly in the new ship the Castilian had made and to blow it up. The new ship only lacked caulking to be ready. That very night the Portuguese *paraos* left, taking with them the fugitive disguised as a Castilian after he put the grenades on the ship. About midnight, the grenades did their work and our men rushed to the site to put out the flames. The following day they discovered that the evil fugitive was missing. In spite of the explosion and fire, the ship was very little damaged. Later, however, a greater problem was discovered and that was because the Castilians were new in the land and they did not know how to select the correct wood. So, when the time came to caulk the ship, they found the wood almost totally rotten.

About the same time the Indians of Tidore were at odds about an Indian gentleman named Derrota, a servant of the king, who was sleeping with the queen mother.[1] <p. 280> The king's brother, Quichilrade, found out about this situation and was very upset. He reported it to Captain Fernando de la Torre and said that if he did not remedy the situation right away, the Castilians and Indians would be the losers because the queen mother was planning [f. 48r] to move with the king her son to a strong place called Mariecu on the other side of the island facing Ternate. If she went there, it could only be to confederate herself with the Portuguese to destroy the Castilians and those whom she thought were upset with her evil deeds. Learning this, the captain took counsel with His Caesarean Majesty's officers, some others of his choosing, and with Quichilrade. It was agreed that Quichilrade should ready all his friends on a certain date when the captain would have Derota killed. With this agreement, Captain Fernando de la Torre put Martín de Islares and Andrés de Aleche in charge of killing Derota.

The general told these two bold men that the deed was in the Emperor's interest and that of the security of all. Even though they knew that Derota was a high-ranking personage and the queen's confidant, they ambushed him one morning on the river road and stabbed him with a sword. The badly wounded Derota fled to take refuge at the queen's apartments. When the deed was known, Quichilrade came out with all his armed friends as well as the captain and his people and went to the king's palace where the queen and her lover were. They had the wounded man brought down and carried to his house, and the queen went along weeping over her lover. Quichilrade spoke to her quite courteously, informing her of the dishonour she was bringing to the king and to all of them and that she should return to her house. And so, with kind words he made her go back even though against her will. While she was returning, the wounded lover was strangled. The queen's copious tears were of little avail, only serving to mark her as a bad woman, all the worse for her high rank.

That day on orders of the captain general and Quichilrade, all the island's Indians met to learn the cause of Derota's execution as traitor to the king. The majority expressed their pleasure and approval although there were some who were very upset. After this news was delivered, the captain informed the king and all the gentlemen that it would be good if Quichilrade were governor of the kingdom. As he was wise and the king's brother, the position and governorship was due him more than to any other until such time that the king was of an age to govern his state. The captain spoke at length in support

[1] After King Almanzor of Tidore died, his servant Derota (or Derrota) became the favourite and lover of the queen and both had control of the young heir to the throne, much to the dismay of the Indian nobles; Navarrete, *Colección de los Viajes*, vol. V, pp. 83–5. The very complex political rivalries involving the Portuguese, the Spanish, and the sultanates of Ternate and Tidore are elucidated at some length in Abdurachman's most valuable '"Niachile Pokaraga" A Sad Story of a Moluccan Queen'. It appears that the use of poison to remove opponents was frequently practised by natives and Portuguese alike.

of his proposal, so that all would see that it was necessary for the king and kingdom and for the good and benefit of his vassals. Everyone agreed, and so Quichilrade became governor.

While these things were happening, the war between the Portuguese and Castilians was unceasing. When they encountered each other at sea there were fights and skirmishes, each side doing its best to gain advantage. In the month of November of the said year, nineteen *paraos* left Gilolo intending to capture by surprise [f. 48v] an armada from Ternate in which there were many Portuguese. But, as good soldiers, the Portuguese had their spies and so forewarned they discovered the Castilians and went out to meet them en route with some thirty *paraos*. Three leagues off Gilolo the battle lasted from nine in the morning until four in the afternoon. In those seven hours of fighting, many Indians from both sides died. Among the Christians, there were some wounded in both parties. Finally they separated, and the Castilians remained in possession of the field by which they claimed victory.

The Indians hurl canes as long as darts by means of throwing straps.[1] These are discharged in volleys as thick as rain because a *parao* carries fifty throwers (and some *paraos* more), each man armed with no fewer than one hundred canes which they call *calavays*. As they throw them <p. 281> at each other, the majority fall into the water, and after the battle the side that recovers those *calavays* is the victor and the master of the field (or sea). Because the Castilians gathered them that day, they were accorded the victory.

A few days later the Castilians departed Gilolo to attack a place five leagues away called Dondera that was allied with the Portuguese. When they attempted to enter the town, the defenders killed and wounded some people including Captain Urdaneta who sustained a bad leg wound. The war party returned without accomplishing anything useful or capturing the town.

Around that time, Captain Fernando de la Torre sent some *paraos* with Castilians to Camafo and other friendly places for rice and other provisions. On their return, some of the dispersed *paraos* ran into *paraos* of Guamuzonora, who were friends of the Portuguese and enemies of the Castilians. They captured some of our *paraos* and killed two Castilians – the one named Montoya and the other Marquina – but others managed to escape by flight.

---

[1] *Calavays*: Navarrete, *Colección de los Viajes*, vol. V, p. 85, calls them *calabais* and cites this passage in Oviedo as his source.

CHAPTER XXVII

How Quichilhumar, governor of Machián, abandoned the Portuguese and passed over to the Castilian side and how the Portuguese destroyed the city of Machián by means of an Indian traitor; and of the intervention of the Portuguese and Castilians in support of their allies; and of the memorable deed of a Javanese Indian who killed his wife and children so that they would not be subject to the Portuguese, and after he killed them he fought against and killed one Portuguese and wounded another and ultimately died fighting valiantly

In the month of December around Christmas of the year 1527, the Castilian *fusta* was launched and sailed from Gilolo, where it was built, to Tidore.[1] Around this time Quichilhumar, governor of Machián, passed over to the side of the Castilians, having been until then a friend of the Portuguese. When the Portuguese found this out, they [f. 49r] made ready to attack Machián. Quichilhumar sent for help from the Castilians and the general sent six Castilians and with them Martín de Islares. They took along some cannon and munitions. A few days later, the Portuguese came with a great armada of Indians, a galley, a *fusta* they had built[2] and some skiffs and attacked Machián (the city and the island sharing the same name). The battle continued for three and a half days during which time our men mounted a spirited defence. However, on the fourth day, by the treachery of a native of that town, the Portuguese entered a certain part of the city and took it. They killed many people and stole everything they came upon. They killed Martín de Somorrostro, a Castilian, and captured another named Pablo. Martín de Islares and the rest of the Castilians took refuge in the sierra along with Governor Quichilhumar. A few days later, Martín de Islares and Quichilhumar went to Tidore.[3]

More or less a month after the above happened, Quichilrade and some Castilians went to Gilolo with an armada of thirteen *paraos* to join the king of Gilolo'a fleet in an attack on the armada of Ternate that was besieging a place friendly to the Castilians called Zalo. In the battle between the two armadas, both sides fought valiantly resulting in many Indians killed or wounded on each side. Quichilrade himself was gravely wounded by a

---

[1] Oviedo does not record that in December of 1527 there was discord in the Portuguese camp. The former captain, García Henríquez/Anríquez, seized the fortress at Terenate and arrested the new captain, Jorge de Meneses, supposedly outraged by the latter's underhanded attempt to destroy the Spanish ship being constructed; see above, pp. 104–5. It is more likely that Don García was retaliating for having been arrested by Meneses, when he resisted giving up his very lucrative governorship. Don Jorge's party retreated to the mountains and sought help from the Spaniards, but while negotiations were in progress the two Portuguese factions came to an agreement. See Navarrete, ibid., pp. 86–7.

[2] Ch. XXVI records that the *fusta* was destroyed by Portuguese treachery and poor construction. This would have been in July 1527. Evidently, another more seaworthy *fusta* was constructed to replace the first.

[3] According to Navarrete, ibid., p. 88, before the Spaniards left Machián, they destroyed 500 quintals of clove belonging to the Portuguese.

107

cannon shot. Also wounded were some Portuguese and Castilians and one Portuguese was killed. After they had exhausted all the ammunitions, each army retreated to its home base. Never before in the Maluco were there so many lamentations as there were from this battle, because all those who could bear arms fought in it.

In the battle of Machián, reported above, there occurred a deed by an Indian that I cannot reasonably fail to record for being notable and famous as I will now relate. This Indian, a native of Java but married in Machián, found himself <p. 282> in that city when the Portuguese captured it. What happened was this. When the Javanese saw that the city was entered by the enemy, he went to his house and told his wife and children that the Portuguese were already in the city and they could not escape being killed or taken as slaves. He said he preferred to die fighting rather than be a Portuguese slave or see his wife and children in their power. He told them he had decided to kill his wife and children first, and then die fighting the Portuguese and avenging all their deaths. His wife replied that she was content and that he should do it. Not wasting any time, he killed the wife and his children and went to where he saw the Portuguese squadron. He grabbed the Portuguese leader and cut his throat with his dagger. Then he fiercely slashed the face of another Portuguese before they shot and killed him. It seems there could not be more courage in a human being than his, and that this is one of the things that histories celebrate as very rare and notable and admirable as, in truth, they are.

CHAPTER XXVIII

How, at the Emperor's command, the governor of New Spain sent a galleon and crew to the Spicelands to learn of Captain Fray García de Loaysa's armada, and found things in the state that has been related, and of what happened on the galleon's arrival; and how the Castilians with their *fusta* captured the Portuguese galley in hand-to-hand fighting, and of other skirmishes and things concerning the discourse of the history; and of the death of the traitor Fernando de Valdaya who administered the poison to Captain Martín Iñiguez de Carquizano

In February of 1528, the king of Gilolo sent to request of Captain Fernando de la Torre some more Castilians than what he had to attack Tuguabe, three leagues from Gilolo and allied with the Portuguese. The captain sent the king twelve Castilians and the force went by land from Gilolo to attack Tuguabe. They failed to take it but they did capture four other small towns. During the attack on Tuguabe, the enemy killed one of our men; a youthful gentleman of gracious spirit named Paniagua and, by a musket shot, gravely wounded another named Fibes.

While they were besieging Tuguabe they sighted the sail of an approaching galleon. Right away they sent to find out whose ship it was and discovered that it came from New Spain, sent by Captain Hernando Cortés on His Majesty's orders, to learn of the armada commanded by Commander Fray García de Loaysa.[1] Two Castilians went aboard the galleon to inform the captain, Alvaro de Saavedra, of the state of war with the Portuguese and all that had happened until then. Later that same day, a Portuguese *fusta* came up to identify the galleon. In the parley, the Portuguese tried to mislead Captain Saavedra with false statements, telling him that presently there were no Castilians whatsoever in the Maluco and that the Castilian ship that had been there had gone to the Portuguese fortress where it had been given everything necessary and sailed off for Spain. Captain Saavedra told them that he knew for certain that there were Castilians in the Maluco and that they were on Tidore Island. When the Portuguese saw that he was on to them, they determined to sink the galleon but it pleased God that their large lombard misfired allowing time for the galleon to move off somewhat from the *fusta*. Then both parties began to fire at each other, but the galleon, taking advantage of a favourable wind, entered Gilolo.

---

[1] This ship with a crew of 45 was the *Florida* commanded by Alvaro de Saavedra Cerón. A fleet of three ships sailed from Zihuatanejo on 31 October 1527, but became separated before arriving at the Ladrones Islands. The *Florida*'s pilot died 200 leagues from Tidore and only by sheer luck did they make it to the Moluccas. Along the way, stopping at Bizaya/Vizaya Island, the *Florida* rescued three survivors of the wreck of the caravel *Santa María del Parral*, which had become separated from the flagship on the Pacific crossing. The unfortunate voyage of this fleet is detailed by Navarrete, *Colección de los Viajes*, vol. V, pp. 94–114.

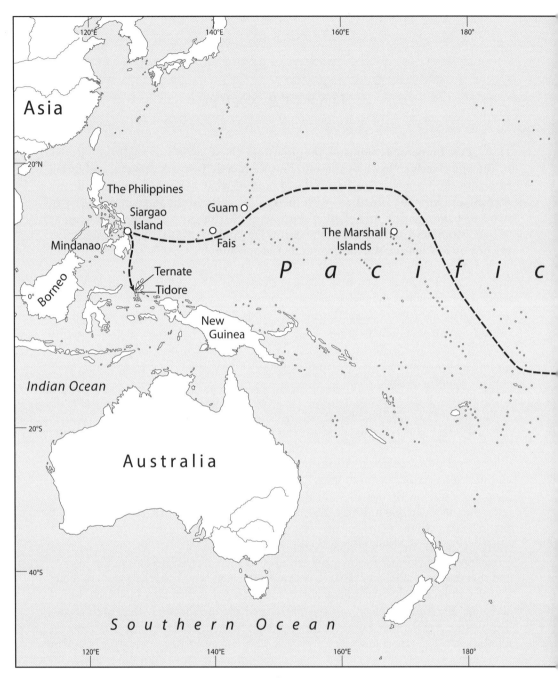

Map 5.   Saavedra's voyage across the Pacific.

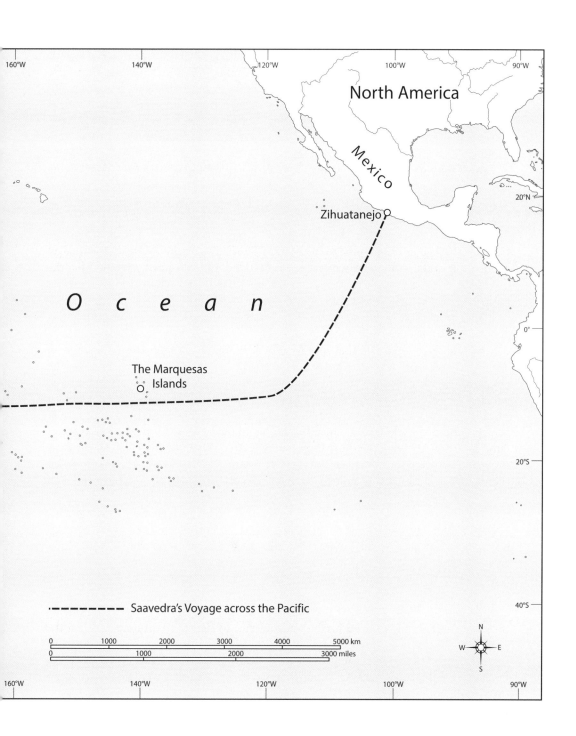

North America

Mexico

Zihuatanejo

20°N

$O \quad c \quad e \quad a \quad n$

0°

The Marquesas
Islands

20°S

40°S

- - - - - - Saavedra's Voyage across the Pacific

| 0 | 1000 | 2000 | 3000 | 4000 | 5000 km |
| 0 | 1000 | | 2000 | | 3000 miles |

160°W   140°W   120°W   100°W   90°W

Right away, the king of Gilolo informed the Castilian general that a galleon had arrived and the captain general ordered made ready <p. 283> the *fusta* to go to Gilolo. That night a Portuguese skiff arrived to join their *fusta*, and the following morning both vessels began to bombard [f. 50r] our galleon. While that was happening, our *fusta* appeared and, as the Portuguese recognized it, they left off their barrage and sailed away. So, the galleon, accompanied by our *fusta*, went to Tidore where the Castilians received them very happily.[1]

Two or three days later, the Castilians in Zalo besieging Taguabe left for Gilolo leaving behind up to five hundred Indians and four swivel-mounted muskets. From Gilolo they went to Tidore. Five or six days afterwards, the Portuguese with their galley and *fusta* attacked and took Zalo killing many people. That day they burned Zalo and the fire signalling its destruction by the Portuguese could be seen from Tidore. Then the Castilians in their *fusta* and some *paraos* went to Ternate where they burned a town called Toloco, one of the strongest places in the whole island, and killed many people. That the Castilians dared to attack that place was a celebrated deed whose audacity greatly impressed the Portuguese and the Indians.

Preparations were begun to send the galleon back to New Spain. Up to thirty-five persons had come to the Spicelands on that ship.

On the last day of April in that year, Martín de Islares took a *parao* to an island fifteen leagues from Tidore where he burned a town and took prisoner its inhabitants. The people of the other islands sounded the alarm, sending word to Ternate where fourteen *paraos* were launched and on the way to the beleaguered island intercepted Captain Martín de Islares. The enemy chased him, firing artillery at him until they forced him to run aground on Gilolo Island where he and his Indians escaped into the forests. That same day news arrived of the fourteen *paraos* sent after Martín de Islares, and right away the captain ordered the *fusta* prepared to go to his rescue. When the Castilians arrived at the island called Mare, they found out that those of Ternate had taken our *parao* and returned to their island. Then our *fusta* also returned home.

The following day, which was 4 May 1528, while the Castilians were hearing mass, Governor Quichilrrade arrived to relate how fourteen Portuguese *paraos* were on their way to burn down a town in Tidore called Saconora,[2] a league away from Tidore. Right away the general ordered the *fusta* to be made ready to go there. Thirty-seven well-armed men embarked in it under Captain Alonso de Ríos. They stationed the *fusta* behind a promontory so that if the Portuguese were to land, the Castilians *fusta* could attack the armada. But while our men were waiting there, a small Portuguese *parao* reconnoitring the coast spotted the *fusta* and fired a warning shot to alert the Portuguese. When the Castilians saw they were discovered, they came out from behind the promontory to take the measure of the enemy armada. To their dismay, they saw fourteen *paraos* and a Portuguese galley and, in view of the obvious danger [f. 50v] they were in, they thought they would not be able to escape death or imprisonment.

Then Captain Alonso de Ríos said to the principal Castilian hidalgos and the others on the *fusta*: 'Gentlemen, what do you think we should do?' They responded that, since

---

[1] The *Florida* arrived on 30 March 1528 with a cargo of much-needed medical supplies and arms, Navarrete, *Colección de los Viajes*, vol. V, p. 114.

[2] Spelled Zoconora, in Navarrete, ibid., p. 115.

they had left Tidore by the general's order in search of the enemy and now had them so close by, even though they were many, they could not return without dishonour if they refused the battle, even at such a disadvantage, and moreover, the Indians would think the less of them. Furthermore: being men as they were so far away from help, it was necessary to risk their lives since it was better to lose them fighting and not fleeing; and that they should commend themselves to God and attack the enemy. The captain, noting the gallant spirit with which they spoke, said: 'Gentlemen, I am <p. 284> grateful for your advice. One would not expect anything less than your reply from such valiant and loyal men!' And, praising their response, he said: 'Gentlemen, let us pray to God, to whom I commend you and offer myself with you, and let what needs to be done be done.' They fell on their knees and with brief words they wholeheartedly commended themselves to the True Defender and Powerful Determiner of victories. Then they armed themselves and began the battle, calling on God and the Apostle Sanctiago to aid them.

At the same time, Quichilderebas, captain general of the Indians *paraos* and governor of Ternate, a valiant and spirited man, on his own account (or better, moved by God) wished to observe what sort of skill the Castilians possessed and what would be the results of their efforts. It seemed to him an unworthy thing that, with a large galley and so many *paraos* and there being such inequality in the numbers of the enemy, they all fight against the Castilian *fusta*. He also desired to see how Christians fared against each other, since the Portuguese were much more numerous and given the great difference between the galley and the *fusta*. Quichilderebas said to the galley's captain, Fernando de Valdaya (the man who poisoned Captain Martín Iñiguez de Carquizano), that since the Castilians had only one *fusta* and the Portuguese a galley, giving them a great advantage, he wished to withdraw to observe how Christians fought against each other and how quickly the Portuguese would capture the Castilians on their own. The captain of the galley responded that he spoke as a true gentleman and should do as he proposed. Then Quichilderebas withdrew the *paraos* a distance, and the galley and the *fusta* came up side by side and with great impetus and spirit the two parties fought a good two hours long until at last the galley was taken.

After the surrender, the Castilians with the galley and the *fusta* turned to face the *paraos* who were coming to the galley's aid. But the Castilians gave them a sprinkling of artillery shots, and the *paraos* fled as fast as they could. So, the Castilians remained the victors and took [f. 51r] possession of the galley.

Four Castilians died and some others were wounded. Of the Portuguese, eight were killed, among them Captain Fernando de Valdaya. He was only able to say a few words making his confession before he gave up the ghost, but among them he confessed to having given poison by his thumbnail to Captain Martín Iñiguez, as reported in Chapter XXV of this book. Many Portuguese were wounded and made prisoners and were well secured.

CHAPTER XXIX

How Hernando Cortés's galleon, captained by Alvaro de Saavedra, departed the Maluco carrying some Portuguese prisoners and the despicable thing they did to the captain in stealing the ship's boat; and how the ship returned to Tidore where two of the said Portuguese were imprisoned and then publicly executed

A few days before the Portuguese galley was captured, two Portuguese fled from Ternate and passed over to the Castilian forces – one was a hidalgo named Simón de Brito and the other Bernaldino Cordero.[2] Their eventual fate will be told here.

It is unnecessary to recount the many forays made by those few Castilians sent by the general in which they burned and destroyed many towns. Wherever some of our men went out, the general singled out one man from the most esteemed to be obeyed as captain by those who accompanied him. <p. 285> Under this man's command and decisions the Indians and the Christians made war in the prosecution of which much blood was spilt on both sides. But I will not trouble to relate everything, rather only the most outstanding things to bring to an end the report of the arduous and infelicitous story of this armada that left Spain bound for the Spicelands under Commander Loaysa.

The cleric Don Juan and Captain Santiago, who came to New Spain with the pinnace *Sanctiago*, one of the ships of this armada, gave a complete report of all that happened up to when the said commander passed through the Strait of Magallanes. This report Governor Hernando Cortés sent to His Caesarean Majesty, who then ordered the governor to send with all diligence to the Spicelands to obtain news of the armada. The galleon captained by Captain Alvaro de Saavedra was sent out with this mission, as previously stated. The galleon was repaired and made ready to return to New Spain, which was the shortest route to inform His Majesty of the events happening in the Maluco.

The galleon departed Tidore in August of 1528, piloted by Macías del Poyo.[1] Captain Fernando de la Torre sent a certain Asturian, Gutierre de Tañón, with the reports and dispatches. Also, Captain de la Torre sent along five or six of the Portuguese prisoners in verification of the war carried on with them. Among these Portuguese was that [f. 51v] Simón de Brito mentioned previously who travelled not as a prisoner, but a friend who had voluntarily passed over to our side.[3] Likewise went Brito's companion, Bernaldino Cordero, because these two requested that the captain general allow them the favour of going with the galleon. The general granted the request and these two went along very well treated, for the reason stated.

---

[1] Navarrete, *Colección de los Viajes*, vol. V, p. 124 gives the departure date as June 1528, and the given name of the pilot as Matías, the spelling also adopted in *BAE*, vol. 118, p. 285.

[2] Urdaneta, whose report is most to be relied upon, gives this name as Romero. This was also accepted by Navarrete. See below, pp. 115, 152–3.

[3] In addition, according to Navarrete, ibid., Brito took the position as pilot, perhaps because Macías had died.

As their deeds later showed, Simón de Brito's purpose in going was not for good because, in October of the same year, the captain general learned that on the eastern side of Gilolo Island at a place called Bicholli, two Christians calling themselves Castilians and an Indian had landed in a canoe. Right away the captain ordered Urdaneta to go there. Suspecting they were probably Portuguese, Urdaneta went directly to Camafo where he had ten *paraos* made ready. He went on to Guayamellín, learning before he got there that they were, in fact, Portuguese. So that they would not flee, Urdaneta arrived at night and conferred with the Guayamellín Indians, vassals of the king of Tidore. Then Urdaneta went up the coast and had them arrested. The Portuguese turned out to be Simón de Brito and the owner of the galley taken by our men.[1] Asked about the galleon, he said that it had sailed and by then was probably in New Spain. Brito said that he and the galley owner had gotten off the galleon on an island two hundred leagues from there because Captain Saavedra had ill-treated him. But Urdaneta, not believing him, brought them closely guarded back to Tidore. There, the galleon having returned, Captain Saavedra was only too pleased to get his hands on Simón de Brito because he and four or five other Portuguese had run off with the skiff in the Papúas Islands, leaving Captain Saavedra and the rest on land.[2] Simón de Brito and his companions became lost and put in at some islands where the companions stayed with the skiff while Brito and the galley owner determined to pass over to the Portuguese in the Maluco in a canoe. On their way there they found themselves in Guayamellín where Urdaneta captured them.

Captain Saavedra lodged a criminal complaint against Simón de Brito and the galley owner. With Captain Saavedra's testimony and the confession of the two, Captain Fernando de la Torre sentenced Simón de Brito to be beheaded and the ship owner to be hanged. Then the well-deserved sentences were carried out as their punishment and as an example to others.

[1] According to Navarrete, ibid., p. 125, the name of the galley owner was Fernán Romero.

[2] After six months, Captain Saavedra was forced to return on 19 November 1528, mainly because he could not find favourable winds to return to Mexico, and for lack of the ship's skiff that Brito had stolen. It was only years later that Urdaneta, on a voyage to the Philippines, would discover the proper latitudes for catching the winds back to the New World; see above, pp. 22–3.

CHAPTER XXX

How it was learned of the loss of the galleon *Sancta María del Parral* whose captain in the armada of Commander Loaysa was Don Jorge Manrique and who was treacherously and cruelly murdered; how the truth was known and one of the evildoers executed; how Captain Saavedra's galleon returned to the Maluco to be cleared to return to New Spain; how the king of Gilolo and special friend of the Castilians died; how Tidore was lost as well as our fortress by the treason and mutiny of Fernando de Bustamante [f. 52r]; and of the terms under which Captain Fernando de la Torre abandoned the fortress; and of other particulars pertinent to the history

When Captain Alvaro de Saavedra returned through the Célebes Islands, the Indians brought him two Christians to see if he wished to ransom them. They were two Galicians from the galleon *Sancta María del Parral*, captained by Don Jorge Manrique. This ship was one of the armada that was bringing Fray García de Loaysa to the Spicelands. The galleon was wrecked on Senguín Island, some seventy leagues from the Maluco.[1] The captain rescued them with gold and took them to the Maluco. One was named Romay and the other Sánchez. A few days after they were rescued they gave away how they had been lost and when Captain Fernando de la Torre found out he had Romay arrested. Sánchez fled to the Portuguese. About the same time a Fleming named Guillermo wrote from the Célebes Islands where they had been wrecked. In his letter, he condemned these two Galicians and because of that and other indications, Romay was subjected to several sessions on the rack. Finally, he confessed how they had arrived at Vizaya and sent a skiff ashore that was captured by the Indians who killed all aboard. The survivors on the galleon left to anchor at another island. There these Galicians and others conspired to kill the captain and other persons. Captain Don Jorge Manrique, his brother Don Diego, and Francisco de Benavides, the ship's treasurer, were thrown overboard alive and were murdered with spears alongside the ship. From there, sailing without a captain or a pilot (who had died), they wrecked the ship off Sanguín Island. The Indians there attacked and killed the majority of the crew and sold the rest around those islands. On the basis of his confession, Romay was sentenced to death and was drawn and quartered.

The galleon was again prepared and again set sail for New Spain. The previous time Captain Saavedra sailed north seeking favourable winds for New Spain but did not find them. He was advised many times that he should sail south to twenty-five or thirty degrees where he could probably find the winds he needed but Saavedra refused to listen. The ship departed in January of 1529.[2]

---

[1] Senguín, Sanguín Island: Sangín in Navarrete, *Colección de los Viajes*, vol. V, p. 128. Now Sarangani.

[2] Saavedra was also advised to go via the Cape of Good Hope but he refused that route. According to Navarrete, ibid., p. 129, he set sail in May of 1529.

At that time, what with the continual war and the terrible hardships that constantly afflicted the Castilians, part of them died in battle, part from sicknesses, and every day their numbers dwindled. As for the Portuguese, each year they received reinforcements and supplies and hostilities increased. At this time, our forces constructed a twelve-bank brigantine to accompany the galley and the *fusta* but all of the raids were made with the Indians' *paraos*. [f. 52v] Few weeks passed that they did not encounter each other and do battle. Many Indians were killed as well in this war, and the survivors were exhausted. Around that island there were very few villages not burned and destroyed with great loss of life.

Nevertheless, the king of Gilolo's <p. 287> friendship with the Castilians remained firm, and he favoured them with all his might and the Castilians returned the favour. In Gilolo, there were constantly stationed twelve Castilians captained by Fernando de Añasco. As the king of Gilolo was very old he soon died. At the end of his life, Captain Andrés de Urdaneta, representing the captain general, came to visit and console him. The king strongly commended a five- or six-year-old son of his to the captain general and the Castilians, saying that he expected the son to find in our men the favour and friendship they had with his father while he was alive, as they had seen. And so, everyone swore they would gladly do his will. Then he ordered certain principal Indians to go with these captains to the captain general and to the king of Tidore to commend to them his son and entire kingdom.

Upon his death, the king left as governors two of his nephews, the one named Quichilbumi had long been exiled from the kingdom because he had tried to kill the king, proclaiming himself the rightful ruler. According to the Indians, there was some validity to his claim. On his deathbed, the king pardoned Quichilbumi and urged him to look out for his son. In fact, Quichilbumi would have quickly made the son disappear if he had gotten his hands on the boy.

In the month of October of that year 1529, Quichilrade, governor of Tidore, prepared an armada to go against Moro. He requested twenty Castilians from Captain Fernando de la Torre who granted them, although much against his better judgment as he had few soldiers at hand and the enemy was close by. Four days after leaving Tidore, they came upon a Portuguese armada in the late afternoon. The ships grappled with each other and fought until it was too dark. Still, our men captured a *parao* with two bronze cannons and a crew of almost one hundred. They killed almost all the captured Indians. At the same time, an armada from Gilolo with all the Castilian residents there was cruising those waters.

As those who want to avenge their injuries await a suitable time for it, it seemed to the queen of Tidore that this was the moment to avenge the death of that Derota, her lover discussed in Chapter XXVI. Likewise, there was a bad Spaniard named Fernando de Bustamante who was highly offended because the Castilians had not elected him captain general after Martín Iñiguez's death. Because of this, it appears the loyalty he ought to have had was lacking in him. He was one of those first members of the voyage of discovery of Magallanes to the great and famous southern Strait, and had returned to Spain on the *Victoria* that sailed around the world with Captain Juan Sebastián del Cano. [f. 53r] The Emperor had honoured and rewarded Bustamante, making him an officer in Commander Fray García de Loaysa's armada. Thus, Bustamante's disloyalty and wickedness was even worse.

117

So, that shameless, evil queen; the said Fernando de Bustamante; and a Portuguese named Master Fernando wrote to Don Jorge de Meneses, the Portuguese captain, informing him that the best and greater part of the Indians and the Castilians of the armada were away, and that Don Jorge could easily take the city of Tidore, its fortress and everything else because there were very few people on the island and no one to offer resistance. With this information, Don Jorge prepared his armada, attacked Tidore and took control of it. Our forces defended themselves as best they could, but at the city's entrance a Castilian was killed and some Indians wounded and killed. Captain Fernando de la Torre took refuge in the large bastion with those who were able to accompany him. The remainder of the Castilians forces was not able to join him because of the rapidity of the Portuguese attack.

Don Jorge de Meneses then sent to demand the surrender of the fortress, promising the captain to respect the persons and possessions of him and all his company. The captain responded that there was no way he would <p. 288> surrender; rather, he was determined to defend himself and die as God would decide. The Portuguese made the same offer two more times. As the captain did not wish to give in, Bustamante told him to negotiate the best terms possible because they were running out of time, and neither Bustamante nor many others there would fight the Portuguese. Faced with this situation there was much discussion.

Finally, seeing that only very few people backed him and that he had the enemy or part of them within the fortress, Fernando de la Torre agreed to make the best arrangement he could. If Bustamante had not encouraged the men to mutiny, Torre would have been able to defend against the Portuguese and the Indians, because the fortress with its magazine was strong and held much artillery and munitions.

In conclusion, the terms were that Captain Fernando de la Torre would depart in the brigantine with the men who wished to follow him to Camafo;[1] that the brigantine would carry one Lombard cannon, four or five versos, all their possessions and arms as well as all the materials from the imperial Factory that they could accommodate. With these conditions, they were given the whole of the next day to leave the island. Once in Camafo, no Castilian could enter the Maluco without Portuguese permission until there might come some ship of one party or the other and if that were to happened they would determine what would be done then.

With that agreed to, Captain Fernando de la Torre departed in the brigantine with those who wished to follow him. They were: Pedro de Montemayor, his lieutenant; Martín García de Carquizano, general treasurer; Diego de Salinas, factor; Martín de Islares, Pedro Ramos, Diego de Ayala and others [f. 53v] – in all, probably nineteen or twenty men. Another twenty passed over to the Portuguese with Bustamante to share in his disloyalty and infamy.[2]

---

[1] See above, p. 84.

[2] Navarrete, ibid., pp. 132–3, records that the Flemish gunners, Masters Ans and Artus, the cleric Juan de Torres, and the supernumerary Francisco de Godoy departed with Bustamante. The latter took with him all the written records and accounts of the expedition. The Portuguese plundered the factory, took all the personal items left behind in the fortress, confiscated many pieces of ordnance and all slaves belonging to the Spaniards, and burned a *fusta*.

CHAPTER XXXI

How some of the Castilians opposed what their Captain, Fernando de la Torre, had agreed to with the Portuguese because they were not consulted in the matter and because they believed that consenting to the agreement was a disservice to the Emperor; and how the galleon of Governor Hernando Cortés returned a second time, coming to Camafo; and how Captain Fernando de la Torre joined the Castilians and renewed the war because the Portuguese did not live up to the agreement; and how the Indians on both sides made peace among themselves and agreed to kill the Castilians and the Portuguese, and how this wickedness was discovered; and of other things pertinent to the history

After Captain Fernando de la Torre and the Castilians lost the island and fortress of Tidore in the manner related in the previous chapter, our men in Quichilrrade's armada were dispersed in Camafo, some in one part and others in another. Captain Urdaneta returned to Tidore with Governor Quichilrrade and six Castilians the night after the Portuguese took the fortress. Abandoned and dispirited, Urdaneta begged the loan of a *parao* from Quichilrrade to take them to Gilolo. The governor ordered a principal Indian named Machá, a very valiant man, to take them. And so Urdaneta left for Gilolo with two other companions and two bronze versos, the other companions having passed over to the Portuguese. The Indians who crewed the *parao* were so tired and recalcitrant that they could not be made to row, and it was now daylight and they were not a league and a half away from the Portuguese. Urdaneta, faced with their refusal to row, told Machá, the *parao*'s captain, that, for the love of God, if he did not compel them, the Portuguese would come out to capture them all. Machá, recognizing he was right, talked to the Indians, telling them to <p. 289> start rowing so that the Portuguese would not capture them. Some of them responded that they did not want to go to Gilolo but rather wished to return to Tidore to find out about their wives and children. Urdaneta, hearing this, threw a spear at one of those who wanted to return and ran him through. Machá, likewise, rose against the Indians threatening to punish them severely if they did not row. Duly frightened, they all began to row so vigorously that in less than an hour and a half they came to Gilolo. Captain Fernando de Añasco and twelve companions there were greatly pleased with Urdaneta's arrival.

Fifteen days later they had news that four companions of the same armada were [f. 54r] hiding from the Portuguese in a small place.[1] Right away Urdaneta went there in a well-armed *parao* and brought them to Gilolo. And so, nineteen Castilians were gathered

---

[1] These men were Alonso de los Ríos and the remnants of his expedition to Moro, the others having gone over to the Portuguese; Navarrete, *Colección de los Viajes*, vol. V, p. 133.

there. The king of Gilolo offered to give them everything they needed if they consented to remain in his territory. And so he did since those who had been in the armada had no other possession than their arms.

Sometime later, the governors of Gilolo decided to send Alonso de Ríos and Urdaneta to Camafo to bring back Captain Fernando de la Torre and those few Castilians who were with him perforce. These men insisted that they were not in favour of what the captain had agreed to with the Portuguese, as much as it was a disservice to Our Lord Emperor, as that they had not been consulted, had not consented and did not intend to agree. Alonso de Ríos and Urdaneta went in three *paraos* from Gilolo to Camafo. Once there, after they made known their mission, Captain Fernando de la Torre told them to leave him behind as he would not break his word concerning what he had agreed and sworn to with the Portuguese unless they first breached the agreement.

Learning his will, because he was a well-respected and valiant person, Ríos and Urdaneta did not wish to anger him with returning to Gilolo. So they left, accompanied by Treasurer General Martín García de Carquizano and four others. At the time of the agreement and oath between Captain Fernando de la Torre and the Portuguese, this Martín García was not involved in it and, as such, he said he was not bound by it, especially as the agreement was so prejudicial to His Majesty and to Castile.

Three or four days after they arrived in Gilolo, the Portuguese armada appeared. The Castilians there were enjoined to give themselves up or go to where their captain, Fernando de la Torre, was. Neither choice was acceptable to the Castilians. Instead, they planned an early morning attack to affirm the Caesarean Emperor's rights and to show that what was agreed to with Fernando de la Torre was null, void, and did not pertain to them, nor were they in favour of it even if it cost the lives of all those who remained behind. But it seemed that the Portuguese were informed of their plan, because they sailed off without further ado.

The following December of that year 1529, Captain Saavedra's galleon from New Spain returned to Camafo where he found Captain Fernando de la Torre. Because, at that time, the Portuguese still had not observed some of the terms they had agreed to, the captain of the Castilians decided to go to Gilolo with the galleon, the brigantine, and all those men with him. And so it was done and almost sixty-five Castilians gathered together, although some of those who returned to Camafo on the galleon went over to the Portuguese.[1]

With this, the war with the Portuguese was rekindled and lasted a good five months more. During that time, Don Jorge de Meneses secretly tried his best [f. 54v] to induce the Indians to kill the Castilians, promising them some lombards and however much money they wished. Along with these proposals, Don Jorge told the Indians that he had received word <p. 290> from India that the Emperor had pledged the Maluco to the

---

[1] The *Florida* returned again on 8 December 1529 with 22 on board. They had sailed to 31°N without finding winds to return them to New Spain. At that point, they were 1,200 leagues from the Moluccas and 1,000 from New Spain. Captain Saavedra had died on the journey. After their return, some of the crew were captured by the Portuguese and sent to Malacca, where 10–12 died and the remainder were sent on to Goa. At least 1 crew member, Vicente de Nápoles, made it to Lisbon in 1534; see below, Appendix 2, and Navarrete, ibid., pp. 136–9.

King of Portugal and consequently the Castilians no longer had reason to be there.[1] Upon hearing this the Indians were greatly offended and said to each other that neither the Emperor nor any other king or prince had the power to sell them and that the Emperor and the King of Portugal could make whatever arrangements among themselves they liked but they, the Indians, also would do what was best for themselves, which was to kill the Portuguese and the Castilians so that none of them remained.

This plan decided and agreed to, Don Jorge de Meneses was approached by his Indian friends who said that if he wished to capture or kill the Castilians, it was necessary to make peace with all the Indians of the Maluco as well as with the Castilians. Being at peace, Don Jorge would then better be able to carry out what he desired because they would come to an understanding with Quichilbumi, one of the governors of Gilolo.[2] This governor was unhappy with the Castilians essentially because they supported the child-king. (That was true because Quichilbumi wished to seize the kingdom but the Castilians would not allow it and, together with the other governor, Quichiltidore, took the side of the child-king in remembrance of the friendship and good treatment by the king, his father, who had entrusted the boy to the Castilians when he died.) So that once peace was established among all the Indians of the Maluco, it would be easy to expel the Castilians from those parts. Don Jorge was delighted to hear this plan, thinking that the Indians proposed it only to hurt the Castilians and to increase Portuguese power. So he agreed and said that it should be carried out as they proposed.

Now all the Indians of the Maluco were in contact and spoke with one another and agreed to kill all the Christians. They could very well have done so, but it was God's will to protect the Christians from such great treachery. A very important Indian, who was Captain Urdaneta's friend, secretly revealed to him the agreement that all the Indians had devised to kill all the Christians. Right away Urdaneta warned Captain Fernando de la Torre of the plot. Soon after, Don Jorge Meneses approached the Castilians with a peace offer that the Gilolo Indians said they ought to accept, because they were very hard pressed and worn out by the constant warfare. Our side strongly desired to reject the peace because, knowing what the Indians had planned, that peace would be more perilous than war. But as much as they tried to scuttle the peace offer, they were not successful and were forced to agree to it. Captain Fernando de la Torre and the governors of Gilolo sent Urdaneta and two Indian gentlemen [f. 55r] named Quichilliaza and Quichilatimor to the Portuguese along with Quichilderebes, the governor of Ternate, to negotiate the peace terms.[3] Together these ambassadors discussed the various conditions and terms and agreed to the peace treaty.

During the negotiations, Urdaneta secretly informed Don Jorge de Meneses of the treachery the Indians were planning but he refused to believe the captain. Instead, Don Jorge cultivated the Gilolo Indians as much as he was able, offering them rewards if they would kill the Castilians. But while the peace agreement was being worked out, the

---

[1] Although the Castilians naturally suspected a Portuguese trick, it was true that Emperor Charles V, perennially short of money, had agreed, not to sell, but to pawn his supposed rights to the Moluccas for 350,000 ducats for a period of 30 years, in Zaragoza some 9 months previously, 22 April 1529. See above, p. 21.

[2] Named Quichil-Catarabumi in Navarrete, ibid., p. 142.

[3] Named Quichil de Revés in, ibid., p. 145.

Indians were secretly preparing to effect their treachery and news of it became so public that it came to the attention of the Portuguese. Then Don Jorge realized that Urdaneta had told him the truth. He called to the fortress the boy-king, Quichilderebes[1] the governor of Ternate and other Indian gentlemen, saying that he wanted to discuss with them a certain matter of importance. Once there, Don Jorge had Quichilderrebes beheaded and the others thrown into the sea with stones tied to their necks. After that all the Indians rose up against the Portuguese.

When the Gilolo Indians found out that Don Jorge and the Portuguese had killed those principal Indians, they took up arms. As hard as Captain Fernando de la Torre tried to persuade them, he could not get them <p. 291> to send a *parao* to Ternate with some Castilians to verify what had happened there. Rather, Governor Quichilbumi and other confederates began to stir up the people against our men. This governor feared that what the Portuguese had done to Quichilderrebes would happen to him because these two were the principal authors of the treacherous plan.

The Castilian captain was very upset by all this. Because he could not learn the truth of the situation in Ternate, Urdaneta told him that he would go there secretly that night in a canoe to find out what was happening. The captain was very grateful to him, and wrote a short letter accrediting Urdaneta's mission. That night he left in one canoe with five slave rowers and a sailor to steer. No matter how they hurried along they were not able to reach Ternate before dawn because there were a good eight leagues from Gilolo to the Portuguese fortress. The Ternate Indians recognized Urdaneta and signalled him to come to land, calling him by name, but he did not dare to approach them and went on to the fortress where the Portuguese received him with much pleasure, thinking that he was fleeing from the Castilians.

Urdaneta delivered the letter to Don Jorge, who read it and asked him what he wanted. Urdaneta said that, on behalf of Captain Fernando de la Torre and all the Castilians in Gilolo, if Don Jorge saw that in some way they could help and favour him, without regard to past wars and vexations, the Castilians would do all possible even to the point of death. Don Jorge and the other Portuguese responded with many thanks, and said the [f. 55v] aid he and the Portuguese requested of Captain Fernando de la Torre and all the gentlemen and hidalgos with him was not to help the Indians against them. Further, if the Castilians wished to pass over to the Portuguese, he promised to favour and help them and send them very rich to India. Don Jorge advised the Castilians to accept the offer since they saw that the Indians wished to kill them, and they did not have enough forces to resist. Also, he informed them that the Emperor had pledged that conquest of the East Indies to the King of Portugal. Urdaneta responded that, speaking for the captain and the Castilians, he gave his word that at the present they would not be aiding the Indians against the Portuguese.

After Urdaneta had thanked Don Jorge for the offer, with regard to the information concerning the Emperor's pledge, he said to him: 'Don Jorge, Sir, it would be a great favour to me and to all the Castilians if you would show us some command from his Caesarean Majesty via Portugal ordering us to leave this land free and unoccupied. For if His Majesty so orders it, immediately we will pass over to your side because the Castilians and vassals of the Emperor are not in the Maluco suffering so many hardships, deaths,

---

[1] The Portuguese fortress at Ternate was then besieged by the Indians.

and dangers except to serve His Majesty. When we receive some order of His Majesty to abandon the land and lay down our arms, we will comply with the letter as loyal vassals and will be pleased to pass over to you to then go to Spain to account for our actions, as we are obligated and we will praise God for it. But, otherwise, it is useless to speak of this.' And so, Urdaneta returned that very day to Gilolo, coming back at night so as not to upset the Indians more than they were already.

CHAPTER XXXII

How Gonzalo Pereyra came to the Maluco as the king of Portugal's captain and arrested Don Jorge de Meneses; and how Gonzalo Pereyra and the Castilians reestablished the peace between the parties as before they had with Don Jorge and the Portuguese; and how the Indians of Ternate rose up against the Portuguese, took the fortress and killed Captain Gonzalo Pereyra; and how the Portuguese recovered their fortress and <p. 292> and appointed Vicente de Fonseca their new captain; and of the help the Castilians gave to the Portuguese captain without which he and the Portuguese would have been lost; and how the Castilians sent to India to request passage to Spain because after so many years His Majesty had not sent any armada or aid; and how the king of Portugal's captain in India sent the dispatch and money to enable the Castilians to go to India

Urdaneta returned at night to Gilolo, as was recounted above, to find the captain and the Castilians on the alert, prepared for war, [f. 56r] with their artillery at the ready, and guns shouldered. The Indians were likewise armed and ready. The captain and everyone were delighted with Urdaneta's arrival and with the news he brought. He reported everything he had said and done on his mission as messenger.

The Indian revolt against the Castilians was not backed by all the indigenous because the boy-king's supporters feared that if they killed the Castilians then right away Quichilbumi would take over the kingdom. As a result, some of the Indians made known to Captain Fernando de la Torre that they favoured the Castilians against Quichilbumi, the author of the disturbances. The principal Indians favouring the Castilians were Quichiltidore, Bongal, Quichilbaidua, the chief justice and uncle of the boy-king and uncle of Quichilbumi himself; and another Indian who was lord of a town called Cebubut.[1] But when it came to punishing Quichilbumi the last two refused to do so.

Captain Fernando de la Torre told Urdaneta that those two gentlemen had offered themselves as supporters of the king the day of the uprising, but it appeared to Captain de la Torre that they were also arming themselves against the Castilians. Hearing this, Urdaneta went to the king's dwelling where Quichilbumi and all the other Indians were armed and ready to fall on the Castilians. As the Indians saw that he was going there, they signalled for him to turn back. But he refused and went up to the door where the governor sent to ask him what he wanted. Urdaneta replied that he wished to speak with Quichilbaidua, the chief justice. When he came out, Urdaneta took him aside and asked him what was going on and why did he want to kill without cause or reason the Castilians, his friends, having always received from them good deeds and loyal company? The chief justice responded that the governor feared that Captain Fernando de la Torre would kill

---

[1] Spelled Cebubu in 1557 edition; Cebubut in *BAE*, vol. 118, p. 292.

him, and for that reason had gathered all the Indians. Urdaneta replied that the captain bore no ill will against the governor; to the contrary, he was a very good friend of his. Moreover, if they wished, he, Urdaneta, would have the captain and the other Castilians swear by their religion not to cause the slightest vexation to the governor or to any other if the governor and his men would do likewise, swearing by their religion. So, with these and other words, Urdaneta brought him around and the chief justice said he would work to that effect. After returning to the palace he arranged to put the peace into effect. That afternoon they all got together to take the oath. Captain Fernando de la Torre, Pedro de Montemayor, Alonso de Ríos, Fernando de Añasco, Factor Diego de Salinas, and Urdaneta swore for the Castilians and on the other side the governor and many principal Indians. So, peace was renewed and all remained great friends.

At that time, the Ternate Indians came to the Castilians with great offerings to beg for help against the Portuguese and with the same intent they approached the Gilolo Indians. But neither [f. 56v] the ones nor the others wished to hear or aid them. Instead, they responded that they had only recently established peace and that the Castilians customarily did not break peace treaties unless the opposite side gave them cause to do so. Even though the Ternate Indians continued to push for their proposal, the Castilians never agreed to it because it was clear <p. 293> that if they killed or took the Portuguese prisoners, then the Indians would kill the Castilians. At that time, there were only about forty Castilians, the others were either dead or had fled to the Portuguese.

Two and a half months later, which would be the month of October 1530, some ships and a galley of Portuguese arrived from Malaca bringing Gonzalo Pereyra as the new captain of the fortress.[1] In order to calm and pacify the region, as soon as he took charge of the fortress, he arrested Captain Don Jorge de Meneses for the murder of Quichilderebes. The Ternate Indians came around to peace when they found this out, and also because their king, a boy of twelve or thirteen years, was being held in the fortress by the Portuguese.

That captain, Gonzalo Pereyra, was more than sixty years old and very arrogant. He began to mistreat the Indians by word and deed, for which they began again to plot against him.

In January of 1531, Gonzalo Pereyra sent Don Jorge de Meneses under arrest to India. On board that ship was a Portuguese gentleman who was a confidant of Captain Fernando de la Torre.[2] By means of this man, the captain sent the Emperor a very lengthy and detailed report of Castilian activity in the Maluco. This Portuguese gentleman and Urdaneta worked out the details by which Urdaneta gave him the report signed by Fernando de la Torre and the Portuguese gentleman swore on a consecrated altar to carry it to His Majesty or die in the effort. For his part, Urdaneta swore on the same altar that he would tell no other person except his captain, who would likewise take an oath not to tell any other person of the mission for eighteen months. But, as they later found out, that Portuguese made it to Lisbon only to die a few days later.

In April 1531, because the Ternate Indians were greatly affronted, they decided to rise up against the Portuguese and take the fortress. One day, leaving behind all the others

---

[1] Gonzalo de Pereira/Pereyra arrived in October 1530 according to Urdaneta. Navarrete, *Colección de los Viajes*, vol. V, p. 145, gives 3 November 1530, attested by Hernando de la Torre

[2] Navarrete, ibid., p. 147, identifies him as Aníbal Cernichi.

hidden and prepared to attack the fortress at the opportune moment, eight principal Indians entered as if to speak to their king who was detained there. By this audacious ruse, they killed [f. 57r] Gonzalo Pereyra and certain others and took control of the fortress. They then signalled the Indians in hiding who rushed out to loot the houses of the Portuguese. Those Portuguese who were able went to the fortress where they killed or captured all the Indians inside. That day the Indians killed many Portuguese and burned or destroyed their entire settlement.

Among the Portuguese who regained control of the fortress there were some differences as to whom would replace their dead captain. But finally, they chose Vicente de Fonseca, a hidalgo and good friend of the Castilians whom he honoured and took into his house when they came to the fort. Fonseca, being a friend of many of them, determined to send a galley to the Castilians to ask them not to aid the Indians against the Portuguese, and to send some supplies for which he sent money. Captain Fernando de la Torre was pleased to help as much as he was able and had the Gilolo Indians sell the Portuguese everything they needed.[1] <p. 294> The galley returned to the fort fully loaded and later the process was repeated. If it were not for this aid, the fort could not have held out for a month because when it was surrounded the Portuguese did not have food for more than twenty-five or thirty days. The Ternate Indians sued for peace when they saw the aid the Christians and Gilolo Indians were giving them. In return for the Castilian aid, Captain Vicente de Fonseca offered to do anything they wished.

In the year 1532, seeing that no armada of our Lord Emperor had come to their rescue after so long a time, Captain Fernando de la Torre and the Castilians with him agreed to send an emissary to the Portuguese governor in India to ask him for passage to Spain with a loan of some money to defray their expenses. Pedro de Montemayor went as their emissary with instructions from Fernando de la Torre as to what he was to do. Captain Vicente de Fonseca, on hearing this, was pleased to provide a ship to take Pedro de Montemayor to India, recognizing that it was in the king of Portugal's interest that the Castilians leave the Maluco, and for Fonseca and the Portuguese the conflict with the Indians was enough, without having to contend with the Castilians. This messenger departed in January of 1532 and returned in October of 1533 with Tristán de Atayde, the incoming captain of the fortress of Ternate.[2] Pedro de Montemayor fully accomplished his mission. Nuño de Acuña, the governor of India, sent Jordán de Fretes with a ship to carry back to India those few Castilians.[3] [f. 57v] In addition, the governor sent with Tristán de Atayde two thousand gold ducats and an order that no Portuguese captain of any fortress or ship or territory was to have any jurisdiction over the Castilians except their captain, Fernando de la Torre, until they came to where the governor was.

---

[1] The queen mother of Ternate tried to dissuade the Castilians from helping the Portuguese by promising to become a vassal of Emperor Charles V. Fernando de la Torre, however, declined in the face of the strength and manpower of the Portuguese, and because if the Indians did prevail over the Portuguese, then they would turn against the Spaniards who were so few in number; see Navarrete, *Colección de los Viajes*, vol. V, p. 147.

[2] Navarrete, ibid., p. 149, states that Tristán de Atayde or de Taide arrived on 26 November 1530.

[3] Navarrete, ibid., notes that by then the Spaniards were reduced to 27 or 28 men.

CHAPTER XXXIII

How the Portuguese took the city of Gilolo where the Castilians were and how the Castilians and their captain passed over to the Portuguese and went with them to their fortress in Ternate where Captain Tristán de Atayde gave them the two thousand ducats that the Portuguese governor of India granted them for their journey; and of other particulars relative to the course of this history

When Pedro de Montemayor returned from India where Captain Fernando de la Torre and the Castilians had sent him, they discussed how they would pass over to the Portuguese. Having then informed Tristán de Atayde how they would go to where he was, by some unknown way the Gilolo Indians found out the Castilians' plan and were so angry that they were moved to kill them. The Indians then started a war with the Portuguese so that the Castilians would not have an opportunity to join them. The Castilians, recognizing the Indians' evil intent, told them that they did not want to go over to the Portuguese; rather they wanted to help the Indians in their war (though telling them the opposite of what they had in mind was painful but necessary).

When Tristán de Atayde learned that the Gilolo Indians were on the warpath he thought that it was a Castilian stratagem not to join them or leave their territory. He then called together a great number of Indians and, with a large armada went after the Spaniards intending to finish them all off. On the arrival of the Portuguese at Gilolo our men endeavoured to inform Tristán de Atayde of their true intention <p. 295> which was to pass over to them. But there was not enough time to make them understand fully the plan. Nevertheless, the Portuguese captain recognized the Castilians' desires by signs and that night he ordered throughout his armada that no Portuguese or Indian was to dare to harm any Castilian nor disturb their belongings. And so, before dawn the next day the Portuguese began their attack on the city with heavy artillery. Tristán de Atayde himself with the main body of his troops landed at a previously designated spot half a league from Gilolo City. The Castilian captain with ten men and the majority of his Indians came out to where the Portuguese had landed and Captain Urdaneta with four Castilians and a certain number of Indians remained behind where the ships were outside of the city.

[f. 58r] On a path through the woods Captain Fernando de la Torre came upon the Portuguese and our men acted as though they were going to attack them but the Gilolo Indians refused and ran away and with them these few Castilians returned to the city. From that first encounter Factor Diego de Cuevasrubias was wounded by a stray musket shot to his elbow.[1] He died ten days later of this wound. Captain Fernando de la Torre and the Castilians took refuge in the city to await there the Portuguese. The Indians fled

---

[1] Navarrete, ibid., p. 153, records that the factor was Diego de Salinas.

to the woods and the interior of the Island abandoning the city. And so the Portuguese captured the city without resistance. There was little of value to loot in the city because the Indians had previously removed the best of their possessions and their wives.

Captain Tristán de Atayde received Captain Fernando de la Torre and the Castilians very well and no Portuguese or Indian mistreated them by word or deed. The Portuguese urged them to identify the king's treasure places and the properties of the Indians, offering to share equally or better in the booty. But there was no Castilian who wished to accept the offer even though the majority of them knew where the Indians stored what they had, which was a sizeable amount. It seemed to the Castilians that the looting was wrong and they felt that it was not the time to enrage the Gilolo Indians who had kindly taken them in and treated them well. In spite of the few times they had decided to kill the Castilians, in the end, they desisted because, although some hated the Castilians, others liked and favoured them the entire time they were in Gilolo. The king gave food rations to all in general and to some in particular he secretly gave more to help with their expenses.

The day the Portuguese captured Gilolo, there were a total of seventeen Castilians in all, the rest having died of illnesses and others, to their shame and ignorance, having deserted to the Portuguese.[1] So, these few loyal survivors from the armada of Commander Loaysa went to the Portuguese fortress. There Captain Tristán de Atayde gave two thousand gold ducats to Captain Fernando de la Torre who distributed one thousand five hundred among the Castilians as he saw fit. The money was not in settlement of their merits, which greatly deserved larger rewards, but rather for their travel. Their trials and tribulations were constant while they were in Gilolo and Tidore, as much for the many illnesses as for the wars with the Portuguese and for the suspect company of the Indians who many times conspired to kill them. Miraculously God saved them! Because their poverty was great and they had nothing other than that ration the king of Gilolo gave them they wandered about ill-clothed and shoeless through those wild and rugged lands hunting wild pigs. That activity was a great help to them because they always had something to eat and feed their friends and families, each one having his little Indian woman and some having sons and daughters.

---

[1] This out of some 450 men in 7 ships that had set out in 1525.

CHAPTER XXXIV

A description of the clove islands called the Maluco, and an account of the clove gathered in each island one year to the next; and of their customs, marriages, conduct and merchandise exchanged between those people; and likewise of the Célebes Islands, the Banthán Islands where nutmeg is gathered and of the islands of Burro, Bandán and Ambón; and of the common money circulating in the islands of the Maluco[1]

The five Moluccan islands where clove is found are the following:

Ternate (where the Portuguese have their fortress) has a king. This is the most northerly of the islands at 1 degree, more or less, north of the equator. Its terrain is high and mountainous. The clove trees are found in the middle of the sierra on the northern side. The trees are very large and produce each year three thousand quintals of clove. The king is also lord of many other islands. Ternate is probably eight leagues in circumference.

Tidore is the island where the Castilians built their fortress and is likewise mountainous, its peaks or summits being more rugged than those of Ternate. There is a king who is lord of many other islands and lands. Tidore is a ⅓ of a degree north of the equator. Its circumference is about eight leagues. Each year three thousand quintals of clove are harvested. The distance between Ternate and Tidore is one small league.

Motil produces clove. Its landscape is not as high as the preceding two islands. There is no king as it is subject to that of Ternate or Tidore. Its circumference is about five leagues. It lies three leagues from the coast of Tidore on the equator.

Machián is less high than Ternate but higher than Motil. Its circumference is seven leagues and is located three leagues from Motil. Each year the harvest produces three thousand quintals of the best clove of any of the other islands. There is no king but many lords, one of them called *Zangagi*, which is the equivalent of duke or marquis, and is a title higher than others but less than king. Likewise, the greatest lord of Motil is called *Zangagi*.

Bathán is wide and mountainous with many surrounding islands that seem part of it. It lacks the high grounds that the others have. There is a king who always favoured the Portuguese. Bathán is ten leagues from Machián. Machián is 1 degree south of the equator; Bathán is at 2 south.[2] This island produces one thousand eight hundred quintals of clove yearly but the quality is not as good as that of the other islands. All these islands are oriented north–south.

---

[1] Banthán Islands: in both the 1557 and *BAE*, vol. 118 edns, and then later Bathán (now Bacan). This island is the fifth island of the Moluccas, as Oviedo notes in the first pages of this chapter. Here Oviedo is confusing Banthán with the much farther south Bandán (Banda) Islands, 4°31′34″S, 129°54′37″E, where the nutmeg grows. Later, to add to the confusion, we find references to the islands of Bahán, Burney, Bangay.

[2] Bacan: variants, Bachán, Bathan, 0°33′56″S, 127°30′22″E.

Map 6.   The Moluccas in the maritime trade world of Asia.

Even though there are many islands not named here, some of which produce a little clove, no other island produces it in such quantities [f. 59r] except for the five aforementioned.

Gilolo Island is large, with a circumference of some two hundred leagues. The Indians call the island Aliora, Gilolo being a province of it where the king is. The island is close to Tidore towards the east about two leagues. The king of Gilolo only rules a small part of Aliora. The principal town of Gilolo is eight leagues from the city of Tidore toward the north-east. The kings of Ternate and Tidore rule parts of Aliora.[1]

These islanders are very intelligent. They have weights and measures, and if someone is delinquent they punish him with exile or death, according to the gravity of the crime, but usually the punishment is a fine. The people are of medium height like the Spaniards, and are very nimble, agile and well-proportioned. They go about shorn <p. 297> normally, clothed in cotton or silk and wearing cloth headdresses. They are Moors and also there are some pagans. They take as many wives as they wish, the men paying bride money to her family; they also divorce whenever they feel like it. The wealth they prize and hold in greatest esteem is gold that, although it does not occur in these islands, comes each year from the Célebes Islands in exchange for merchandise. They also prize silver, even though they do not get much of it. All brightly coloured velvet is highly desired, as well as coloured cloth to make short garments of mid-thigh length or longer. Large quantities of silk and cotton cloth are brought to them from Portuguese India. From China comes porcelains that in the Maluco are prized more than any other part of the world – a medium-sized hand basin there is worth twenty, thirty, even fifty ducats and a vessel with a three-palm-wide mouth goes for three hundred and more. They have musical instruments played at parties and when they go off to fight. The sound is that of bells and they are highly prized and worth a good deal of money. The largest bell seen in the time period referred to was of four palms wide. The bells are circular, and in the middle have a crown like that of a hat. They are made like a sieve.

They also have other instruments and many drums. When they row about they always sing, even when they are at sea for two or three months. They prize greatly things of brass, glass and those Flemish products, as well as knives, mirrors, scissors, ivory items, beads, and corals.

In the Célebes, the majority of the population are idolaters with a few Moors mixed in, as the sect of Mohammed has reached even these islands. All these Indians are warriors and paint themselves from head to toe with [f. 59v] diverse designs. They paint themselves before commencing courageous deeds in wartime. The paint is permanent as long as they live, rather like that of the painted Moors of Barbary, which is to say like that of black ink over blood red that never ever comes off.[2]

These Indians wear their hair long but gathered into a knot at the back of the head. In the Célebes, they value the same things listed above for the Maluco but, much more than that, iron to make their arms and hatchets to cut wood. In some of these towns of the Célebes (and even in the Maluco) they obtain some bronze pieces of ordnance made in Java which is south-west a quarter west, three hundred leagues from the Maluco, at 8 degrees south of the equator.

[1] Aliora: variant, Halmahera; see above, p. 1.
[2] A description of the practice of tattooing.

The islands of Bandán are 4 degrees south of the equator. They are seven small islands in which they harvest nutmeg. At the present time it is not known if nutmeg is found in any other part of the world. Every year in these islands they gather three thousand *bahares* of nutmeg, the equivalent of twelve thousand quintals at four quintals to the *bahar*. To go to Bandán from Tidore (where the Castilians have their fortress), you head south-west about ninety leagues as far as Burro[1] and Ambón, and from the latitude of Burro you turn east for sixty leagues to reach the Bandán Islands. The people of these islands are not as attractive or as cultivated as those of the Maluco. They have no king only lords. The population is dedicated to trading and they are wealthy.

Between the islands of Bandán and the Maluco are the Ambón Islands, also called Java.[2] There are so many of them one cannot go from Maluco to Bandán by a direct route. Although within their lands the people of Bandán are bellicose, outside them they are much less so. They possess much artillery of bronze cannons and other ordnance, and also employ muskets for which reason they are not subject to anyone and no one can subjugate them. Every year the Portuguese go there from Malaca and take away all the nutmeg. The islands <p. 298> of Ambón are, for the most part, ruled by the kings of the Maluco. In Ambón there are no worthwhile products save many types of provisions, especially bread like cassava which, made into hardtack, is taken on many junks to other places. That hardtack can last three years without ever being infected by weevils or any other nastiness or corruption.

In all these islands of the Maluco, there circulates a certain copper coin pierced by a small square hole in the centre. Some call it *picis* and others *caz* with the form as illustrated here in actual size with certain letters or characters in a language unknown to me on one side and on the other [f. 60r] there are no letters or figures.[3] Martín de Islares gave me four of these to record them in this account, and I include here drawings of both sides of the shape of this money.

The island of Burney is a rich place ruled by a king.[4] Much cinnamon is gathered there. The island is at 3 degrees south of the equator and something more than sixty leagues from the fortress of Tidore on a north-easterly route although Bahán and many other islands are in between.

Almost sixty leagues west of Bahán Island is the small, low-lying island of Bangay of probably eight to ten leagues circumference.[5] I learned from Captain Urdaneta, who was there, that there is a king and his people are all idolaters of a bellicose disposition unequalled in any other nation of those parts. That king is lord of many islands and provinces. A league and a half away is another large island whose circumference the captain was unable to provide as he only sailed about part of it. That island is called Tobucu (or at least one province of it was so named) and was about sixty leagues from

---

[1] Burro: now Buru.

[2] Obviously, not the much larger Java that Oviedo mentions previously and describes more fully in Chapter XXXV, which is 300 leagues from the Moluccas.

[3] The coins were Chinese *cash*, usually strung in large numbers on cords and used throughout the region. It is strange that Oviedo could not identify the country of origin or the meaning of the characters as the Pigafetta narrative, which he consulted, clearly explains 'on only one side of it are four characters, which are letters of the great king of China; and they call that money *picis*'; see Pigafetta, *First Voyage*, 2007, p. 72.

[4] Burney: not to be confused with Brunei, and perhaps now known as Pulau Taliabu or Mangole.

[5] Bangay, or Gapí: now Banggi.

Bangay.[1] In that island they forge the iron from which are made all the arms of the Célebes archipelago, Maluco, Ambón, Bandán, and many other parts. It is astonishing and has to be seen to be believed, the huge quantity of weapons made in that island – scimitars, daggers, javelins, harpoons, many other types of arms and hatchets and large knives to cut down groves of trees and woodlands. Urdaneta was there and swears that in Tobucu in 1533, together with some Gilolo Indians, they loaded a cargo of those arms to take to other parts to sell. There they greatly prize, among other better things, all sorts of glass beads.

The people of that big island are idolaters. In 1532, Captain Urdaneta was sent to Bangay, also known as Gapí, by Captain Fernando de la Torre and the king of Gilolo in response to a previous emissary sent by the king of Bangay. Captain Urdaneta arrived a little after the queen died and found all the Indians there grieving her death. There was a great massacre of Indians because they believe that, after death, souls go to another world where they need food and people to serve it. So, when the queen of Bangay died, they killed many principal men and women who were the friendliest and closest to her. Later, each week they killed a certain number of persons during the entire forty days Captain Urdaneta was there. Those dedicated to the queen's service (or better said, the devil's service) were strangled with a rope or cord and their bodies hung about the king's dwellings. After a while they threw the bodies into the sea with heavy weights tied to their feet. When Urdaneta [f. 60v] asked them the reason for that great cruelty, they responded that they were killed to accompany and serve the queen in the other world. Those killings were to last fourteen weeks or until three full moons passed and the fourth was entered, counting from the day the queen died.

<p. 299> This diabolical belief is present in some parts of our Indies, islands and Tierra Firme. The reader could observe it in Cueva province and other parts in the regions of Castilla del Oro where I have seen some of this.

Returning to Urdaneta's report: He says that in that island of Bangay it happened that a relative of the king stole from the king's house some gold earrings weighing about four pesos.[2] Theft is so abhorrent there that, as soon as the king found out, he ordered the thief killed as well as the others who knew and did not report it. Likewise, that king ordered executed one of his principal vassals, along with his wife and children, saying they were sorcerers.

Ambassador Urdaneta could never manage to obtain an audience with the king, who maintained he was in mourning and unable to see any stranger whatsoever. The king informed him that he was to relate his mission to certain gentlemen he sent but Urdaneta refused, saying that an emissary of the captain general of the Emperor's could only deal with the king himself. There were great altercations over this matter, to the point that the king was determined to have Urdaneta and the Gilolo Indians killed. They, being advised of this, took to their *paraos* to depart. But when the king found out they were leaving, he sent certain principal Indians to beg Urdaneta not to go and that he would meet with the captain soon to hear his message. Because of such profuse protestations and oaths made according to their practices (including the one about the chest blood which will be related further on), Urdaneta disembarked and went to the king's dwelling

---

[1] Tobucu: Tubuzu in Navarrete, *Colección des los Viajes*, vol. V, p. 165; now Tataba.

[2] *Pesos*: one *peso* was 1/100 of a Spanish pound of 480 grams, or 4.6 grams.

to present his mission. He took with him some principal Gilolo Indians to whom the king sent to say that if they would eat pork, they should come with the Christian ambassador, and if not they should go back. Since the Gilolos are Moors, when they heard what the king sent to tell them, they responded that the king of Gilolo did not send them to break the law of their faith, but rather as his messengers and ambassadors to inform him of king Gilolo's wishes which Captain Urdaneta knew and could relate. And so they returned to the *paraos* and Urdaneta went on alone.

Arriving at the palace, the king sent to beg pardon because he could not see him in person, and that Urdaneta should impart his message to certain gentlemen who would relay it to the king. Then Urdaneta saw how blatantly the king and his messengers had lied, and that the king's will was not to see him and that to insist would be dangerous. Urdaneta in fact no longer desired to meet the king [f. 61r], and so he reported to the king's gentlemen what he was sent to say. The captain relayed to the king some gifts that did not impress him very much (and in truth were of little value). Nevertheless, the king took some German-style cloths, and returned the rest to Urdaneta who distributed them among the king's gentlemen who were pleased with them. After that the captain received the king's response to the embassy mission which consisted of entirely empty promises. Then the captain was ordered to be fed and given some middling gifts.

So, the mission retired with the king's licence. They bought a quantity of iron goods and then left the island because they were carrying much silk and cotton textiles and other goods, and wanted to go to Tobucu to load a cargo of iron. They travelled fifteen days against unfavourable winds which eventually forced them to return to Bangay. When the king learned of their return and that they had attempted to go to Tobucu for iron, he was very upset, asking why they had not traded for iron on his island. As a result, he ordered that they were not to be sold anything, nor given food, nor allowed to land. So, they had to leave there without water or food.

Because their proposed route took them through hostile lands, they put out to open water to sail directly to the Maluco, hoping to find fish along the way as they had brought along fishing equipment. They sailed five <p. 300> days to the Maluco. The little water they had lasted only two days, but they caught many fish that they ate raw, not having any firewood. They ate shark liver along with the other flesh and, as they say that shark liver is cold or cooling by nature, they did not suffer from thirst.

Above I mentioned the oath or protestation on breast or chest blood without specifying what that ceremony or security is, and so it seems to me that here is the best place to describe it. I learned from Captain Urdaneta and from Martín de Islares that in the islands of the Célebes, Bangay, and Tobucu, the ceremony to make peace with foreigners is this: the parties take blood from their arms and mix it together in a cup of palm wine. Sometimes this oath is broken, but there is another stronger and more solemn one that is inviolable, broken only with very just cause; it involves taking blood from the chest or breast and drunk in the same manner as above. That was done when they brought Urdaneta to the king of Bangay and the king's men drank on his behalf and he theirs so that each party would feel secure. Captain Urdaneta told me that he had participated in this ceremony some other times in those parts, and it was customary among the most high-ranking men and ambassadors.

CHAPTER XXXV

Of some customs, ceremonies, and rites of the Indians of the Spicelands; and of how the [f. 61v] Castilians left Maluco for India, passing by way of Java; and especially of Captain Urdaneta, the one who most travelled and saw things of those parts; and of where pepper is obtained and of the commerce between the Levant and the Malacca; and how Urdaneta came to Lisbon, Portugal, and from there went to Castile to report to His Majesty's Royal Council of the Indies all that happened in the Spicelands (His Caesarean Majesty being absent from Spain); and how later he passed through this city of Santo Domingo on the island of Hispaniola with Adelantado Don Pedro de Alvarado where he and Martín de Islares informed me of what was previously reported and of what will be told in this chapter

In some parts of the Célebes, the Indians are more inclined to the libidinous than in others. The Indians there insert small round stones beneath the skin of their genital members, and the man with the greatest number of these stones is most sought after by the women for their bestial gratification. Other men, when they engage women in coitus, insert into their members a silver or tin tube (depending on their status) on which are small silver or gold studs.[1]

Some of the Célebes Indians have their teeth drilled and the holes filled with gold so that when they open their mouths, the gold sparkles. They say that it is a special remedy against bad breath, and that the tooth so adorned never decays and they never have toothache. Moreover, among them the practice is a sign of great gentility.

High-ranking men also wear gold ear ornaments and beautifully worked gold anklets and wrist bracelets and some, especially the gentlemen and men who follow the military profession, wear gold bands on their upper arms. Captain Urdaneta observed many other particulars of those people, but when he was here, he did not have time to report more than what I have set down in this chapter.

Returning to his departure from the Maluco: He says that in 1534 Captain Fernando de la Torre left for India.[2] Captain Urdaneta left the following year, 1535, passing through Java where he stayed in Panaruca.[3] Java is a very good land, rich in gold. In it are horses, buffalos, cows, swine and chickens, just as in Spain. <p. 301> The king of Panaruca is a pagan. There they worship oxen. The people are very bellicose and very sagacious. They

---

[1] Pigafetta was quite interested in the sexual practices of the South East Asian peoples called *palang*, which involves male genital piercing. Here Oviedo mentions two types which are described in much greater detail in some of the four manuscripts of Pigafetta's journal, although in some cases omitted from later editions; as is the case in *First Voyage Around the World by Magellan*, edited by Lord Henry Edward John Stanley, Hakluyt Society, 1st ser., 52, London, 1874.

[2] Navarrete, *Colección de los Viajes*, vol. V, p. 152, reports that Torre left on 15 January or 16 February.

[3] Ibid., pp. 157–8.

fabricate much bronze artillery there. The city of Panaruca is large and surrounded by brick walls with watchtowers at intervals. There are many large ships called junks, some of great cargo capacity. In Java, much pepper is produced in Zunda, and those who own it are very great enemies of the Portuguese. A large quantity of the pepper is taken to China where it is very valuable. If the Castilian trading presence in the Maluco were to endure, it would be easy to make money on the Javanese [f. 62r] pepper trade.

In Java there are four kings who are continually at war with each other. Of all the Indians in the Indies, those Javanese are the most accomplished in treachery and evil deeds. In some parts, they trade with the Portuguese where it frequently happens that some of their young men go to the Portuguese ships to look them over and attempt to see if they can deceive the Portuguese. If they fail, one of them might give the Portuguese to understand that his companions are his servants and slaves and induce the ship's captain to buy them. Thus, the poor victims are duped and sold and the rogue returns to land with the price of his companions. At other times it happens that the Javanese sell each other by rounding up as many Indian men and women as they come upon at night and taking them at dawn to the Portuguese ships to sell for the best price they can get.

In Panaruca City, the abovementioned swindles are not practised because there there is law and order and such conduct is strictly punished. In addition, the king of Panaruca is a great friend of the Portuguese and, as such, favours them.

From Panaruca, Urdaneta passed on to Malaca where he stayed three and a half months. The Portuguese have a fort in Malacca where five hundred of them are continually stationed but outside the fort they have no dominion. At that time, the Portuguese were at peace with all the surrounding Indian territories. In the short time Urdaneta was there, he says that more than three hundred junks arrived, some with food stuffs and others with diverse items of merchandise. The ships come from Java, Timor, Bandán, Maluco, Bruney, Pahán, Patane, Pegú, Malabar, Bengala, China, as well as the Guzarates and many other provinces.[1] Among those many nationalities there was likewise a variety of merchandise – spices and drugs, musk, sandalwood, marble, silk and cotton cloth, gold, silver and precious stones, among many other things. From Zamatra, which Urdaneta says is twenty leagues away, they came with much fine gold.[2] One day, two small boats came with more than seven quintals of gold. The Portuguese buy very little of the gold, the majority is purchased by merchants they call *Quillines*.[3]

The city of Malacca is world famous for its commerce in various luxury items. Huge quantities of items are bought, sold and traded in that city yearly. The equator passes through the island of Zamatra, mentioned above as the source of so much gold, so that part of the island lies in the northern hemisphere, and the rest in the southern. [f. 62v] In the opinion of many, Zamatra is that famous, large, and rich island that the ancient cosmographers such as Pliny and others called Taprobana.[4]

Urdaneta left Malaca on 15 November 1535, for what we call East India. Eight days before Christ Our Reedemer's nativity, he came to the kingdom of Cochín, where

---

[1] Los Guzarates: Gujarat.

[2] Zamatra: the large island of Sumatra.

[3] *Quillines*: possibly referring to traders from Quilon (Kûlan), India.

[4] [*1557 marginal note*: Plinio, lib. VI, cap. XII] Oviedo's note refers to Pliny the Elder, *Natural History*, Bk VI, ch. XXII. Taprobana was the fabled source of Solomon's gold, according to some, and identified with Ofir and the Aurea Chersonesus (Malay Peninsula). Others identify Taprobana with the island of Ceylon.

he found Fernando de la Torre and the other <p. 302> Castilians who were about to leave for Portugal. Urdaneta remained in Cochín until 12 January 1536, when he sailed for Portugal on board the *San Roque*, which was part of a convoy of five vessels commanded by the captain general.[1] Captain Fernando de la Torre remained in Cochín, leaving some seven or eight day later because the Castilians feared that the Portuguese would throw them overboard or poison them en route. The Portuguese have taken great care to cloak with secrecy the things of the East Indies to prevent the Emperor from being fully informed of them. To this end, they endeavour that no Castilian who passes through there returns to Spain, especially men of credit and intelligence. Fearing this, Fernando de la Torre gave Urdaneta a letter of introduction to His Caesarean Majesty in case the captain arrived in Spain before him.

Urdaneta arrived in Lisbon on 25 June 1536 after undergoing many hardships. On disembarking, the commander of the guard, seeing he was Castilian and returning from the Maluco, searched his sea chest and his person and found the letter to His Majesty which he confiscated along with all other papers and written accounts that detailed at length everything he had experienced in the Maluco. Urdaneta protested the guard's actions to the royal officials in Lisbon to no avail. So he went to where the king's court was to complain in person of the confiscation.

On arrival at court in Evora, Urdaneta went to the Emperor's ambassador, Don Diego Sarmiento, to inform him of what had happened.[2] He asked the ambassador's aid as to what he should do to recover his papers. Don Diego told him that under no circumstances should he appear before the Portuguese king; rather, he should go immediately to Castile. A person very close to the king had informed the ambassador that the king knew Urdaneta was in Portugal. Don Diego firmly believed that the king would be very displeased if our Lord Emperor would be entirely and truthfully told about what had passed between the Castilians and the Portuguese in the Maluco, and so it would not take much for the king to order Urdaneta be secretly killed. Even though the captain [f. 63r] strongly desired to speak to the king, he desisted taking the advice of Caesar's ambassador, and set out for Spain as quietly and secretly as he could.[3]

In August 1536, the captain arrived in Valladolid where the Empress (of glorious memory) was in residence.[4] He went before the Royal Council of the Indies to make his report to the council members who were very pleased to learn the things Urdaneta related. In addition to being very useful to His Majesty's service that his Royal Council be entirely assured of the truth, Urdaneta was intelligent and knew how to deliver well, step by step, his eyewitness account. The gentlemen of the council advanced him sixty gold ducats until our lord emperor returned to Castile, at which time they said they would help

[1] Amador de los Ríos notes in *BAE*, vol. 118, p. 302, n. 17, that the commander was unnamed in the original codex he consulted, as well as other sources including the 1557 edition.

[2] Don Diego Sarmiento: Luís de Sarmiento, according to Navarrete, *Colección de los Viajes*, vol. V, p. 162.

[3] According to Urdaneta's own account, he left behind in Lisbon 'a daughter he brought from the Moluccas and other things', ibid. Like others marooned in the islands, he had taken up with a native woman who bore a daughter named Gracia. Kelsey, 'Finding the Way Home', states that she went to live with Urdaneta's brother's family. Navarrete, ibid., p. 162, states that Macías del Poyo likewise fled to Spain to avoid being detained or worse.

[4] The Empress: Isabella of Portugal, beloved wife of Charles V. She died three years later in 1539, the same year that Oviedo interviewed Urdaneta in Santo Domingo and presumably composed this section of the *History General and Natural*.

Urdaneta obtain rewards from His Majesty. The year before, the Emperor had gone to Africa where he captured Tunis and from there passed on to Italy, and had not yet returned to Castile.

By chance, a little later Adelantado Don Pedro de Alvarado, governor <p. 303> of Guatemala came to Castile. Don Pedro learned about Urdaneta's qualities, and spoke with him a few times, strongly encouraging the captain to accompany him to Guatimala. Don Pedro told Urdaneta that, by His Majesty's command, he was to outfit ships in the Southern Sea to sail for China, or toward those parts. Captain Urdaneta accepted the offer to serve his king on account of his great knowledge of those parts of the Maluco he had travelled through. In addition, he was a man very well versed in the things of the sea and land. Also accepting Don Pedro's offer was that other hidalgo, Martín de Islares who was spoken of earlier. Last year, 1539, both Urdaneta and Islares were here in this fortress of my command in the city of Sancto Domingo on the island of Española. At that time, they spoke to me and gave me a written statement of what I have reported.

From here they and the adelantado continued their journey to Tierra Firme directly to the Port of Honduras. From there they were going to Guatimala where the adelantado himself informed me he had already built ships to send to the Spicelands. Don Pedro further said he held in high esteem the person and experience of both Captain Urdaneta and Martín de Islares as men of action and men of fine abilities.

After Urdaneta came to Court in Castile, there arrived Captain Fernando de la Torre and some of the hidalgos who were in the Maluco. They confirmed what is reported above to our lord Emperor and to his Royal Council. The Emperor was well pleased with their service and ordered them rewarded.

At that time, 1539, another armada was being prepared. It was to be led by Captain Camargo, brother of the bishop of Palencia, Don Gutierre de Vargas. The armada was well outfitted with good people, artillery and munitions, and everything necessary to go via the Strait of Magallanes to the [f. 63v] Spicelands and others say to China. Time will tell of this voyage. God grant it better fortune than that of the ones up to now.[1]

The reader will recollect that of the armada of seven ships that set out under Captain Fray García de Loaysa for the Spicelands, we know the fates of four of them:

The ship *Sancti Spíritus* was lost in the mouth of the Strait on Cabo Vírgenes.
Another ship, the *Sanctiago*, captained by Santiago de Guevara, made port in New Spain, aboard which was the cleric Don Juan.

---

[1] The proposed expedition to China of Alvarado which brought Urdaneta and Islares to Guatemala never materialized because of Alvarado's death on an expedition against rebellious natives in Mexico. Of Captain Camargo's 1539 armada to the Spice Islands or to China, Javier Oyarzun Iñarra, *Expediciones españoles*, p. 81, writes: 'We know very little about this expedition since, although there is abundant documentation on its preparation, the reports that we have of the voyage are meagre and very brief.' Don Gutierre de Vargas Carvajal, Bishop of Plasencia, advised by his brother-in-law the viceroy of Mexico, Don Antonio de Mendoza, to mount an expedition to New Spain through the Strait, sent out four ships under the command of his brother, Francisco de Camargo. Oyarzun Iñarra, p. 84, summarizes the fate of the venture as follows: 'Of the four ships, the flagship was wrecked at the entrance to the Strait; another ship made it through the Strait and reached Peru; the third tried and failed to rescue those shipwrecked on the flagship and blown about by storms returned to Spain or perhaps the Antilles; the fourth ship disappeared without a trace.'

Another ship of which something is known was the armada's flagship, the *Sancta María de la Victoria*. This ship arrived alone at the Maluco and Tidore Island where the Castilians built their fortress.

The fourth ship, the *Sancta María del Parral* captained by Don Jorge Manrique was lost near the Maluco.

It is not known exactly where or how the other ships were lost, although one could deduce or imagine their fates from the misfortunes of the ships that have been discussed briefly.[1] In truth, the blame for the loss of those ships may not be entirely the fault of the Portuguese (even though they are trespassers in the demarcation and conquest areas belonging to Castile and its kings). The interminable voyage can cause disproportionate good and evil desires among men aboard ship, not always in conformity with respect to good conscience or to the loyalty due to the king and to their fellow men. This is born out by what happened to poor Don Jorge Manrique with those Galicians. How many times has it happened to many others who, under the guise of confidence, have killed their very companions? Consider Simón de Alcazaba's sad end,[2] and that of Captain Martín Iñiguez de Carquizano. That well-known saying expresses it well:

> The loyal man lives no longer
> than what the traitor wishes.[3]

<p. 304> Only God can preserve the life of a man, for, on his own, there is no one that can or knows how to protect himself without God's special grace.

---

[1] Of the three other lost ships: The *San Gabriel* deserted the fleet at the Strait to return to Spain, but ran into diffiulties off the Brazilian coast. The *Anunciada* was separated from the fleet by a storm at the Strait, and was never heard from again; see Morison, *Southern Voyages*, p. 480. Navarrete, ibid., p. 185, states the *San Lesmes* was wrecked on Tepujoé Island in the Marquesas group, because of a cross found there in 1772.

[2] Oviedo's account of Simón de Alcazaba's murder by mutineers, at Puerto de los leones in Bahia Gil, Argentina follows.

[3] "*No vive más el leal / de cuanto quiere el traidor*".

CHAPTER XXXVI

Of a remarkable case of a fruit resembling almonds, and how many of them are found on a small islet without there being an almond tree or any tree that bears such a fruit on that island nor is that fruit produced where it is found; rather it comes by air[1]

A half-league to a league from Gilolo in the Maluco, a bit more than 1 degree north of the equator, there is a small islet heavily covered with woods that grow there *a natura*. But there is no almond tree or any tree that produces a similar fruit nor any tree useful to man, nor have any ships or men taken almonds there and, notwithstanding that, on that islet one can gather almonds by the bushel or sack-full. [f. 64r] And note another marvellous thing, that if today you gather them all, tomorrow you will find as many or more. They are so abundant that you can not exhaust them during the season when they naturally grow and ripen.

What I say here is not a fabulous tale, but something seen and touched by many of our Spaniards. I have it from Captain Urdaneta and Martín de Islares, mentioned above, who many times were on the very islet and ate those almonds which, although very similar in appearance and taste to our Spanish almonds, are larger than the ones in Castile. But, once known how those almonds arrive through the air to that islet, it becomes plausible and credible.

As the aforementioned authors said, on that islet almond trees do not grow. But what happens is that innumerable ringdoves eat those almonds on Gilolo when they ripen. Over the shell there is a green covering which the birds digest in their craws, but the shell surrounding the nut is hard and not digestible. At night the birds pass over to the islet from Gilolo to roost in huge flocks, and there they defecate the undigested nuts in the shell. Because there are so many of these birds, these hidalgos assured me that every day they could gather many sacks of them. As soon as it becomes light, the birds return to feed on the large island of Gilolo where they spend the day, returning to roost at nightfall on the islet with their craws filled with almonds.

With all the grief and privations the Castilians suffered from the war with the Portuguese in the Maluco (especially those few who remained from the armada of Commander Fray García de Loaysa), many times these almonds I have described were, for them, a welcome addition to their rations.

No more of this work was printed because the author died.

Here ends Book XX of the second part of the *General History of the Indies* written by Captain Gonzalo Hernández de Oviedo.[2]

---

[1] Oviedo previously included the contents of this chapter with very little variation in Bk VI, ch. XIV, *BAE*, vol. 117, pp. 174–5.

[2] Hernández/Fernández: the interchangeability of H and F is a common feature of the Spanish of Oviedo's day, as seen previously with Cortés variously referred to as Fernán/Hernán or Fernando/Hernando, and as witnessed in the colophon to Book XX where we find Francisco Fernández de Córdova.

APPENDIX 1

THE narrative which Andrés de Urdaneta submits to your Majesty of the fleet which your Majesty despatched to the Spice Islands under the Comendador Loaysa, in the year 1525, is as follows:[1]

We sailed from the city of Coruña with seven ships, on the eve of the blessed Lord St James,[2] and shaped a course for the Canary Islands. We anchored off the island of Gomera on the seventh or eighth day after leaving Coruña, where we were taking on board things necessary for the fleet until the 14th of August.

On the 14th of August, the Eve of our Lady, we departed from the island of Gomera and after a month and a half, a little more or less,[3] we met with a Portuguese ship on the equinoctial line. The Captain General sent Santiago de Guevara, Captain of the pinnace, to see what vessel she was. Guevara obeyed the order and the Portuguese shortened sail. In returning with the pinnace, Don Rodrigo de Acuña, in the ship *San Gabriel,* ordered a shot to be fired. This seemed to the Captain of the pinnace to be wrong, and there were words between him and Don Rodrigo. The Portuguese ship came to our *capitana* and the Captain General did much honour to the Portuguese, sending letters by their vessel to Spain. So we parted with the Portuguese and continued our voyage, encountering foul winds and calms until nearly the middle of October. We had sighted one island called San Mateo,[4] which is about 3°S of the equinoctial line. At this island we took in water, and killed many birds, called boobies, with sticks. There was good fishing. The Captain General and other captains and officers partook of a large and excellent fish. The others, who ate the fish, had very bad attacks of diarrhœa so that we thought they would not recover, but after many days they were well again.

At this island the Captain General ordered an enquiry into what had passed between Don Rodrigo, Captain of the ship *San Gabriel*, and Santiago de Guevara, Captain of the pinnace. After the investigation Don Rodrigo was ordered to come on board the

---

[1] AGI, Patronato, L. 37, R. 3, 'Relación hecha por Andrés de Urdanete contador en la armada que partio a la Especiera el año 1525 al mando del Comendador frey Garcia Jofre de Loaysa', 26 Feb., 1537. Translated and published by Sir Clements Markham in *Early Spanish Voyages*, pp. 41–89.

[2] 24 July 1525.

[3] Following the track of Magellan, they kept near the African coast and were delayed by calms.

[4] Markham notes that St Matthew Island is mentioned as having been discovered by the Portuguese in George Peckham's *A true Reporte of the Late Discoveries, and possession taken in the right of the Crowne of Englande, of the Newfound Landes*, London 1583. Its position is given in the *Index Geographicus*, 21°10′ W and 1°50′S. It was still on the charts in 1803 in Admiral Burney's time in 1°24′S. In 1817 Sir James Yeo and Captain Jenkin Jones, R.N. searched for it and went over the position given to it. There was no land. St Matthew was removed from the charts in 1820. For discussion that it may have been Annobón Island, Equatorial Guinea, see above, p. 39, n. 7.

Capitana, and Martin de Valencia was appointed Captain of the *San Gabriel.* We were at this island for about ten days.

The seven vessels sailed from St Matthew Island in company, crossed to the coast of Brazil, and sailed along it. At the end of many days, and after we had passed the River Plate, there was such a storm that the fleet was scattered. In a few days six had again joined company, but the *capitana* was not in sight, and we steered in one direction, then in another, but we were never able to get a sight of her. We went on our way to the Strait, and at the end of four or five days Martin de Valencia, with the ship *San Gabriel,* was out of sight. The other five vessels were still together. On reaching the entrance to the river of Santa Cruz,[1] the Captain Juan Sebastian del Cano[2] spoke with the captains of the other ships, and told them that it would be well to enter the river and wait there for the Captain General and Martin de Valencia. Pedro de Vera[3] Francisco de Hozes[4] and Jorge Manrique[5] captains, and Diego de Covarrubias, general agent, answered that it would be advisable for all the captains and officers, as well those of His Majesty as those of the ships, to meet on board the ship of Juan Sebastian to decide what should be done. Accordingly they all met. They concluded that it would be late for passing through the Strait, if they waited in Santa Cruz, and that it would be better for the pinnace only to enter the river, and deposit a letter under a cross, on a small island near the mouth. If the Captain General should come, he would learn from the letter that the ships had gone up the Strait to the port of Sardinas,[6] to refit and get in wood and water, and there to wait until his arrival. According to this agreement the pinnace entered the river of Santa Cruz, and the other four ships made for the Strait.

On Sunday morning, thinking we were entering the Strait, the ships found themselves at the entrance of a river 5 or 6 leagues from the Strait, where we were all in danger of being lost. As we were being embayed, Juan Sebastian sent his skiff, with some men to see if it was the Strait; and before these men could return, the tide rose and the ships went out to sea. As we found that the skiff delayed, we sailed along the coast, and recognized the Cape of 11,000 Virgins which is in the Strait.[7] It was late before we anchored within that cape. Being there, such a violent storm arose that all the ships dragged their anchors until they were near the shore. The wind continued to increase in violence, and the ship of Juan Sebastian del Cano, where I was, drove broadside on to the beach. In reaching the land nine men lost their lives, and the rest were half drowned.

Next day there was such a furious gale that the ship was broken up, many casks of wine and bales of merchandise being lost, as well as all the bread.

---

[1] See above, p. 41, n. 2.

[2] See above, p. 9, n. 3. Markham held this to be the correct spelling of the name as attested by a family member that he had consulted. Navarrete, *Colección de los Viajes,* vol. V, uses del Cano.

[3] Captain of the *Anunciada.*

[4] Captain of the *Lesmes.*

[5] Captain of the *Parrel.*

[6] Now Bahía Andrés.

[7] Admiral Burney held that Cabo Buon Tiempo, the north cape of the mouth of the Gallego river, might well be taken for Cape Vírgenes, without any impeachment of the ability of Elcano. Seixas y Lovera, p. 60, notes 'The coast of the Rio de Gallegos seen from the sea matches that of Cabo Vírgenes.'

When the wind went down, about the middle of January, Juan Sebastian went on board the ship of Pedro de Vera[1] to look after the ships which remained within the Strait, I and others going with him. Before we could take shelter a furious contrary wind sprang up. It was on the following Thursday. We thought we should be wrecked; all three ships lost their boats, and the ship of Pedro de Vera got out to sea.

On the following Friday the weather was finer, the wind went down, and we again entered the Strait, passing further up than on the first occasion, and found an anchorage with a length equal to a cannon shot's flight, and a width equal to two stone's throws. To the NE we saw the caravels anchored in a bay in that direction. It gave us great pleasure to see the caravels, as we had given them up for lost. On shore we saw people who were Patagonians. When we arrived where the caravels were at anchor, they sent the skiff of the ship of Pedro de Vera on shore, and they brought back a Patagonian. He was given food and wine, and presented with some small things which pleased him much, especially a looking-glass. When he saw his reflection he was so astonished that the things he did were worth seeing. They also showed him gold and silver, but such things did not surprise him at all. He was a large man and ugly, wearing the skin of a zebra[2] and a plume of ostrich feathers[3] on his head, a bow in his hand, and sandals on his feet. When he saw that it was nightfall, he made signs to be taken on shore.

Next day they sent me on shore with five companions to where Diego de Covarrubias, the general agent, was, with the crew of the lost ship. They were to collect all the merchandise, wine, munitions, artillery and rigging, to have it ready when the caravels should send for it and for the crew. When we landed, presently the Patagonians came to us and asked, by signs, for something to eat and drink. We gave them some of what we had in our knapsacks, and then went to see their settlement. It consisted of huts made of the skins of zebras where they had their wives and children. When they want to go somewhere else, they take up their huts and put them on the backs of their women, while they march only with bows and arrows. About ten of them followed us for a day and a half, but when they saw that our knapsacks were getting empty, they turned back. We remained at the place where the ship was wrecked for four days, though we were nearly dying of thirst on the third day.

On the same day that I arrived at the place where the people of the wrecked ship were, there entered round the Cape of 11,000 Virgins the *Capitana*, the *San Gabriel* and the pinnace. God knows what pleasure we received from the sight of them, for we thought that all were lost, except the pinnace.

When the Captain General saw the wreck on the beach, he sent the pinnace to find out what it was. When he knew that the ship was lost, he did not wish to be detained, and proceeded up the Strait, to where the other ships were. Having arrived there, he sent Juan Sebastian del Cano with the two caravels, the pinnace, and the boat of the *San Gabriel* to where we were, to pick up the crew and all that had been saved from the wreck.

Directly Juan Sebastian arrived with those vessels, we began to get things on board, but when we had nearly finished it began to blow so hard that the caravels had to put to

[1] The *Anunciada*.
[2] Guanaco.
[3] See above, p. 52, n. 2.

sea, leaving the pinnace and the boat in a creek. We came out into the Strait with the caravel of Don Jorge Manrique,[1] and the other caravel of Francisco de Hozes[2] was driven out of the Strait to the south as far as 55°S. They said, when they returned, that what they saw appeared to be the end of the land.[3]

In this same gale the *Capitana* was nearly lost, the Captain General and all the people landing, except the master and sailors. We, being anchored near the mouth of the Strait, saw the ship of Pedro de Vera but in spite of our signals he did not wish to come to us, sailing out of the Strait and never seen by us again.[4] The *San Gabriel* also sailed out, with Don Rodrigo on board, for the Captain General had reinstated him in his command. As he saw our signals he came and anchored where we were, in a good little port.

Next day the *Capitana* followed into the channel. Much heavy cargo had been thrown overboard, and most of the people landed, which lightened the ship and enabled her to float again. In this way the master and his sailors brought the ship out, and the Captain General embarked again with his people. The ship was anchored outside, and it was resolved to return to the river of Santa Cruz to repair and refit the *Capitana*; for she had been much injured by bumping on shore, and she made much water. We, therefore, sailed past the Cape of 11,000 Virgins, leaving the *San Gabriel*'s boat, the pinnace and another boat inside.

When 15 leagues from the Cape of 11,000 Virgins on our way to the river of Santa Cruz, the Captain ordered Don Rodrigo de Acuña to go back to where the pinnace was, and to recover his boat, for it was fine weather. He was to tell the captain of the pinnace that we were going to Santa Cruz, and to go for the boat with as much despatch as possible. Don Rodrigo answered the Captain General that if he returned in such weather he would be lost. The Captain General replied that it was necessary to return and recover the boat, because boats were much needed. Don Rodrigo then asked the Captain General why he was ordered to go where he did not want to go. However he went and took the boat, which was handed over to him by the captain of the pinnace. He then went where he chose, for we never saw him again.[5]

[1] The *Parral*.

[2] The *Lesmes*.

[3] The eastern end of Staten Island, in 54°50′S. Brouwer was the first to sail round the east end of Staten Island. Previously it was believed to be part of the imaginary Antarctic Continent.

[4] Markham states that Pedro de Vera tried, for many days, to rejoin at Puerto Santa Cruz, but the wind prevented him. He then resolved to try and reach the Malucos by the Cape of Good Hope. The *Anunciada* was never heard of again. Markham provided no source for this information. An order from the Consejo de Indias, 19 February 1532, ordered Cristóbal Haro, factor of the Contratación de la Especieria, to provide the sister of Pedro Vera with a copy of the agreement made between the Crown and Pedro de Vera that his sister might collect the 275,000 maravedís that he was owed; AGI, Indiferente General 422, L. 15, F. 121v (2).

[5] Markham states that Rodrigo de Acuña also tried for several days to rejoin the fleet in Puerto Santa Cruz. He then went north for water and provisions, and fell in with some French cruisers. He went to them in a boat for news, and found that there was war with France. They would not let him return to his ship. but his crew refused to surrender and eventually returned to Spain. Acuña reached Pernambuco in an open boat where he was badly treated by the Portuguese, but at length he also returned to Spain. Markham did not provide a source for this information. It is likely that he referred to AGI, Patronato 37, R. 27, 'Información de Rodrigo de Acuña: expedición al Maluco', made in Cadiz, 10 May 1529, and Patronato 38, R. 7, 'Autos del fiscal contra Rodrigo de Acuña'. 1537.

The pinnace came to the river of Santa Cruz after twenty days. We had very hard work in repairing the *Capitana* as it was winter. We were working in the water, and we found three fathoms of her keel broken. We applied a remedy in the best way we could, first with boards, and then with sheets of lead. We had very convenient tides, rising five fathoms, so that we could repair the caravels and the pinnace, and we got in our wood and water. We also caught quantities of fish in this river with a net we had. Every day, when the tide began to ebb, many fish remained on land, and we took them.

There is an island in this river on which the seals[1] came every day to bask in the sun. When we saw them, 36 men, divided into six parties, six men for each seal, went to the island. On the beach along which we went to the seals, we found so many ducks without wings[2] that we could not break through them. Yet we got at the seals which were on the land, with hooks, clubs and lances to kill them. But we never were able to kill more than one which was above all the others asleep, and we broke all the weapons we brought with us. We opened the seal that we had killed, and we found several large stones in the stomach, as big as a fist and very smooth. This seal had as much meat as a bullock in the fore quarters, and very little in the hind parts. The hunters ate the liver, and most of us who ate it suffered from the head to the feet.

We departed from this river of Santa Cruz as soon as the ships were repaired, making for the Strait, and entering as far as some islands which were beyond the place where the *capitana* got on shore. Being at anchor off an island, a cauldron of pitch caught fire and began to burn the ship, and in a little time we should have been burnt with it. But with the help of God, and by our own diligence, we put out the fire. Beyond this island we got amongst a bed of seaweed, for we had mistaken the channel, but we soon recovered it again, the sea being quite smooth. From this point forward we found very good ports on the north side of the Strait, and good anchorages. There are many very high mountains covered with snow. There are many trees, and among them there is one with a leaf like a laurel[3] and its bark has the same smell as cinnamon. There are also mussels in great quantity containing pearls.[4] In this Strait the agent Diego de Covarrubias died.

We got out of the Strait in the month of May 1526, the fleet now consisting of the *capitana Santa Maria de la Victoria*, the two caravels *Parral*[5] and *Lesmes*[6] and the pinnaces.[7] After a few days we encountered a great storm, in which we were all scattered, and never saw each other again. With the heavy seas that struck her, the ship became leaky in many places and we were distressed by the quantity of water which we could not keep down with two pumps constantly going. Each day we expected the end to come. On the other hand we had to reduce the rations by reason of the number of

---

[1] Urdaneta's report to Oviedo refers to these as sea lions; see above, p. 54.

[2] Penguins.

[3] The Winter's bark tree (*Drimys winteri*).

[4] Seed pearls known by the Portuguese as *aljofar*.

[5] The *Sancti Spiritus* wrecked, and the *Anunciada* and *San Gabriel* left the fleet. The *Parral* crossed the Pacific. Her fate is described by Urdaneta below, p. 165. See above also, p. 18, n. 3.

[6] The *Lesmes* was never heard of again. But the Spaniards of the Quiros expedition saw an old cross on Chain Island in 1606, which may have been put up by the shipwrecked crew of the *Lesmes*. See above, p. 18.

[7] Urdaneta refers here to the *Santiago* and the tender.

additional men who had come on board from the ship that was wrecked. Thus while on the one side we worked hard, on the other we were insufficiently fed. We passed through much misery, and some perished.

On the 30th of July the Captain General died. On the production of a secret order of His Majesty, Juan Sebastian del Cano was sworn as Captain General. He appointed a nephew of the late Captain General Loaysa to be Accountant General, which post had become vacant, Martin Perez del Cano to be pilot, and Hernando de Bustamante to be Accountant of the ship, a post which had become vacant through the death of Iñigo Cortes de Perez.

On the 4th of August 1526 the Captain General Juan Sebastian del Cano died, and the nephew of the Comendador Loaysa, who had been appointed Accountant General, also died. We elected Toribio Alonso de Salazar to the command, by votes, and he appointed Martin Iñiguez de Carquizano to be Accountant General, and in his place, as chief Alguazil, Gonzalo de Campo was appointed. At the same time the Treasurer died, Gutierrez de Tunion being appointed in his place.

At this time we were sadly overworked and worn out, being in 14° or 15°N, seeking for Cipango. As the people were so worn out from much work at the pumps, the violence of the sea, the insufficiency of food, and illness, some died every day. We, therefore, agreed to make the best of our way to Maluco.

Being on this course, we discovered an island in 14°N, which we named San Bartholome. It appeared to be large, but we could not reach it, and continued our route to Maluco.[1]

In about twelve days from having sighted this island, we came in sight of the Ladrone[s] Islands[2] in 12°N. where we anchored the ship. Here we found a Galician named Gonzalo de Vigo, who had remained on these islands with two companions, from the ship of Espinosa.[3] The other two died, but he remained alive. He came on board, and was of great use to us, as he knew the language of the islands. According to Gonzalo de Vigo the group consists of thirteen islands, extending from 12 to 19 N. There are no sheep, nor fowls, nor other animals fit for food; but rice in great quantities, fish, coconuts, oil and salt. The natives of these islands go naked, not wearing anything. They are well made men wearing their hair and beards long. They have no iron tools, and work with stones. They have no other arms than slings, clubs hardened in fire, and a sort of knife made of shin bones of dead men, and fish bones. At these islands we took eleven natives to work at the pumps, because there were many sick on board. Having taken our water on board we sailed for Maluco, the Galician coming with us, of his own accord.

We were eleven or twelve days at the Ladrone[s] Islands, and before the eighth day the Captain Salazar died. We elected the Captain Martin Iñiguez of Carquizano to

---

[1] See above, pp. 75–6.

[2] See above, pp. 75–7.

[3] Gonzalo de Vigo had left San Lucar with Magellan's fleet as a *grumete*, or first-class cabin boy, on board the *Concepcion*, and transferred to the *Trinidad* after his former ship had to be burned. Gaspar Gomez de Espinosa was Magellan's alguazil or master-at-arms, who assisted in suppressing the mutiny at Port San Julian and eventually succeeded to the command of the expedition after Magellan's death. Sebastian del Cano became Captain of the *Victoria* and completed the circumnavigation of the globe. Espinosa had intended to find his way back by way of Mexico, but he failed, and eventually surrendered to the Portuguese. He and other survivors of his crew were transferred to prison in Portugal, 1525–6.

succeed him, who was then Accountant General. There also died Juan de Huelva, Master of the ship, Iñigo de Loriaga succeeding him.

About fifteen days after we left the Ladrone[s] Islands we sighted a large island called Bendenao,[1] and anchored in a port called Bizaya.[2] Presently we went to the shore in a boat, to hold converse with the natives, for the Galician knew a little Malay and could talk with them. We bargained for a pig and some fowls if they would trade, but they refused to sell any. The people of this island are well clothed. They go about dressed in clothes of cotton and silk, and also wear dresses of Chinese satin. They all go armed, their lances in their hands and their hangers, like daggers, in their belts. They also have *paveses*.[3] They are a treacherous people, and intended to seize the ship by treachery. But we were on our guard, and their plan did not succeed. They often came at night in their very light row boats to cut our cables, but we kept a good watch and they never were able to do any harm. We were in this port ten days, but never succeeded in buying any fresh provisions.

In this island of Bendenao there is much gold, and they brought it for sale. But the Captain ordered that no one was to buy, so that we bought nothing; and thus we had to continue our voyage without refreshment. We here took a native and brought him to Maluco. He told us that two junks came from China every year, which are a kind of ship which the Chinese use. They come to buy gold and pearls, which they have in great quantity. More vessels come to the other islands to trade. In this same island there is cinnamon in the western part.

We departed from this port of Bizaya and anchored off another island called Talao,[4] about 40 leagues from it, where we found the natives more friendly. They sold us many pigs, goats, fowls, fish, rice, and palm wine, besides other provisions, so that the people were very well refreshed. The ship was refitted, the guns properly mounted, and our arms furbished up, for we were near Maluco. The Indians of this island said that there were some islands to the eastward where there was much gold, and they wanted to take us there. But as the ship was large and drew much water, we did not care to navigate amongst islands, and so we did not go there. When we arrived in this archipelago of Célebes, Martin Iñiguez de Carquizano made some appointments. Martin Garcia de Carquizano became General Treasurer, Diego de Solier Agent General, and Francisco de Soto Accountant General.

After a stay of fifteen days at Talao we sailed for Maluco. We were 105 people, 40 men having died during the voyage from the Strait.

On the third day after leaving Talao we anchored on the east side of the island of Batachina,[5] in a port called Zamafo.[6] The natives of this place are vassals of the king of Tidore. When they knew we were Spaniards they received us very well, including the Governor named Bubacar. In this place we found a fugitive slave of the Portuguese, who spoke Portuguese very well. He told us that there were Portuguese in the islands of

---

[1] Mindanao, variant Bendenao.

[2] The eastern coast of Mindanao was called Bizaya.

[3] Large shields.

[4] See above, p. 83, n. 4.

[5] Another name for Gilolo.

[6] Camafo on the east coast of Gilolo. Markham, as do some other sources, stated that it was located on Morotai Island. See above, p. 84, n. 5.

Maluco, and that they had a fort on the island of Terrenate.[1] He said that it was not many days since they had defeated the king of Tidore who was always at war with them, by reason of the two ships which had been laden with clove at his island, being those of Juan Sebastian del Cano and Espinosa. When he heard this, Martin Iñiguez asked the Governor of Zamafo to give him *praos* or vessels with oars, to send secretly to the kings of Tidore and Gilolo, who were said to be very good friends of the Spaniards. The Governor at once ordered the *praos* to be got ready.

The same afternoon the Captain sent me, with five companions, in a row[ing] vessel, to the kings of Tidore and Gilolo, to let them know that seven ships had been sent to Maluco, that we only had arrived in the port of Zamafo, and that the others were coming behind. We had found that the Portuguese were in these islands, who made war on the king of Tidore for selling clove to the captains Juan Sebastian del Cano and Espinosa. The captain sought that the kings would say what it was that they wished to order, for that he was there with all his people and ship and artillery to help them, as loyal friends of His Majesty, against any that were against them, and that he was ready to join with them against whosoever might make war, whether Portuguese or natives of the islands. Thus we went secretly to the town of the king of Gilolo and made it known to him that we were there. We sent to ask permission to go to his city where he was, which is in the same island of Batachina on the west side. As soon as he received the news he sent his nephew with ten armed row boats for us, and so we came to the place where the king was.[2] He received us very cordially, and showed much pleasure at our arrival, and consequently all the chiefs and people of the land felt the same. The king ordered all the people of the neighbourhood to assemble for the reception of our embassy, and in this way we were received on the following day. As we said that we wanted to go to the king of Tidore, he ordered a very light rowing boat to be got ready, and sent two of his chiefs with us. So we went to the island of Tidore, which is about six leagues from the city of Gilolo. We found the king of Tidore retired in the mountains. When he knew that Castilians had come to Maluco, though the king was a boy,[3] the chiefs showed so much joy that it was a thing worth seeing, and all the people followed their example. Having received our embassy, they offered to help us in every way in their power, even to die for us. They asked us that we should not fail to come with the ship for that we had no reason to refrain from fear of the Portuguese. The king of Tidore sent two chiefs with us to wait on the Captain. So we returned to Gilolo, where the king offered to help us in every way that was possible, though he was then at peace with the Portuguese. He sent his nephew with three rowing vessels in my company, and so we returned to where the ship was. Three Spaniards of my company, with two large arquebuses, remained with the king of Gilolo, in case the Portuguese should come, on learning that we had been with the king.

Having arrived at Zamafo, where the ship was, Captain Martin Iñiguez received the ambassadors of the kings of Tidore and Gilolo very well, and presented them with some gifts. On learning the desire of the kings, we made sail for Tidore, but those of Gilolo

---

[1] Ternate.

[2] In Década III, Herrera y Tordesillas, gives his name as Abderahman-Jami, aged 80.

[3] Herrera y Tordesillas, ibid., gives his name as Rajamir, son of Almanzor recently deceased. See below, pp. 149, 174.

wanted us to go to their town, because Tidore has been entirely destroyed and all its towns were burnt.

Being at anchor, by reason of a contrary wind, off an islet called Rao, a row boat arrived from the island of Terrenate, with a Portuguese named Francisco de Castro, bringing letters from the captain of the fort whose name was Don Garcia Enriguez. He demanded that we should not enter the islands of Maluco, except where he had his fort, for those lands belonged to the king of Portugal. If we complied, we should receive all honour and courtesy; if not he would send the ship to the bottom, with all on board.

The Captain Martin Iñiguez replied to the letter and the demand, not conceding what was required, but stating that those lands and islands belonged to His Catholic Majesty, and that he would go to any island he thought fit. With this answer the Portuguese returned, and we worked for two months, unable to double the cape of the island of Batachina. The row boats of Gilolo went back. During this interval a Portuguese named Hernando de Baldaya came twice with the same demand. He was factor of the fortress held by the Portuguese. He required that we should either come at once to their fort, or else that we should depart from those parts and not touch at any of the Maluco islands. If we refused, a great fleet would come and either take us by force, or send us to the bottom. Our answers were always contrary to what they wanted, and so that Portuguese went back, after threatening us many times.

At the same island of Rao we heard that the Portuguese were coming against us with a great fleet. The Captain seeing this, took the opinion of the crew, which was that under no circumstances should we desist from going to the islands of Maluco in spite of any risk we might run. When the Captain saw the goodwill and resolution of the people, he made sail with a fair wind for the island of Tidore, and we began to navigate with a good fresh wind, all our artillery ready and the men well armed, and willing to die in the service of His Majesty.

On the 29th of December 1526, on our way to Tidore with a strong wind, the Portuguese fleet came out from between two islands, called the isles of Doy, where they were waiting for us. We were determined, the wind was fresh, and we were well armed, so they did not dare to come within range, and we passed on our course. The fleet which the Portuguese brought against us consisted of two caravels, a lateen rigged vessel, large boats, and other gun vessels, with about 80 row boats belonging to the Moors of Terrenate, Bachan, Traquian and Motil. The kings of Terrenate and Bachan came in person. They also summoned the king of Gilolo, but he did not want to come, saying that he was a friend of the Spaniards and would not go against them. The Captain General of this Portuguese fleet was named Manuel Falcon.

We anchored off the island of Tidore, in front of where the city used to be, on the 1st of January 1527, and presently the king, named Rajamir, arrived with all his chiefs. They swore, according to their law, to be our loyal friends, to favour, and to do all in their power against our enemies; and we swore to the same effect. On the same day we began to construct three earthworks to plant artillery for a defence against our enemies, and all the natives helped us, even the women. Next day we got some of the artillery on shore, and, as a consequence, all the merchandise and things of value on board, in case the Portuguese should come, and send our ship to the bottom. We also landed half our people.

After we had been four or five days at Tidore, the Portuguese Hernando de Baldaya came with a demand from his captain that we should depart from the island where we were, and if not the Portuguese would come with a great fleet, taking and killing us all. Our Captain replied, as on former occasions, refusing to concede to their demand.

On the 12th of January of the said year, before daylight, the Portuguese arrived with a great fleet intending a surprise. But as we kept a good watch, we heard the noise of their oars and fired, for they came with the intention of boarding us. But when they saw we were prepared, they did not dare to board, and began to fire at us from outside. With their second shot they killed one, and wounded three or four of our men. Thus we began to blaze away one at the other until the following Saturday, both sides wounding several, and with that they returned to their fort. Although many of their shots struck our ship they did not injure her seriously, and we passed a band round her that she might not go to the bottom. Nevertheless the ship received serious shocks by reason of the number of shots we fired from her, which had the effect of opening her seams worse than before, and she leaked badly. We worked hard without being able to keep the water under. We wished to ground her, but could not find a suitable place in the port, though there was one in another part of the island. But we did not dare to take her there from fear of the Portuguese. At last we burnt her, and so, after three months a little more or less,[1] the said ship went to the bottom.

At the end of three or four days after the Portuguese attacked us, there arrived five of the king's vessels from Gilolo, and, being still in the same port, the news came that a Portuguese bark was coming from the island of Maguian to their fort, laden with clove. As soon as he knew of this the Captain sent five native vessels, with nine Spaniards, to attack the said bark. They fought her and captured her with the cargo of clove. One Portuguese was killed. With the five rowing vessels the king of Gilolo sent to ask the Captain for twenty men and some artillery to defend himself against the Portuguese, a request with which the Captain complied.

With the same rowing vessels officers went to Gilolo to build a ship with all the necessary furniture, as well nails as other requisites such as timber for the planks, the same king of Gilolo ordering all to be provided at his cost.

At the same time we began to build a ship at Tidore to send by the Cape of Good Hope. The natives were also building war vessels, and they already had some with which we were able to annoy the enemy.

As the king of Gilolo had the Spaniards with him, he carried on warlike operations against the enemy, and he did us all the honour in his power and showed us favour. If it had not been for his help we should have been in a much more difficult position.

In the month of May two Portuguese ships arrived, bringing one Don Jorge de Meneses as captain of their fortress.[2] Soon after he arrived he began to make the same demands as the former captain. We replied in the same way, saying that the islands of Maluco, Banda, and other lands, which were all round us, were within the line of demarcation of your Majesty. As this was the case we demanded that the Portuguese should evacuate those islands and leave the land free. Nevertheless this demand of ours profited nothing, for they said that the islands were within the demarcation of the king

---

[1] Since they arrived at Tidore.

[2] On his voyage from Malacca, he had steered a course north of Borneo, instead of south as was the usual route. Carried to the eastward by the current, he sighted New Guinea, and is usually credited with having been the first European to do so. He wintered on the north coast of the same, reaching Ternate in May 1527.

of Portugal. As the said Don Jorge de Meneses saw that we were so well established in the country, he proposed to the kings of Gilolo and Tidore that they should kill us by treachery, promising them great rewards. But they never wished to do such a thing, and they told us what the Portuguese had proposed to them. When they saw that neither could they attain their object in this way, Don Jorge de Meneses determined to kill us by poison, ordering it to be put into a fountain from which we drank. This plot was divulged by a Portuguese priest, who wrote to our chaplain to tell him that the next time his countrymen came to Tidore they intended to put poison into the well from which we drank. So we were on our guard for that time, closing the well, and thus being in no danger whatever.

At this time Captain Martin Iñiguez sent me to Gilolo to take command of the Spaniards who were there, and to push forward the building of the vessel. While I was there some Portuguese came to Tidore, pretending to want to make peace with us, and they gave some poison to Captain Iñiguez in a cup of wine, of which he presently died. The Captain Hernando de la Torre, who was Lieutenant in the time of Martin Iñiguez de Carquizano, was chosen to succeed him by votes. Before the Captain died he appointed Diego de Solinas to be Agent General, taking the place of Diego de Solier. While we were at Rao it was reported that Francisco de Soto was plotting against Captain Martin Iñiguez, for which he was deprived of the office of Accountant General, Hernando de Bustamante being appointed in his place, and I became Accountant of the ship.

At the time when Martin Iñiguez de Carquizano died, there came to us the chiefs of certain towns in the island of Maguian, which is one of the Clove Islands, whose name was Quichil Umar. He said that the Portuguese destroyed all his towns and killed many Indians. They also killed one Spaniard, and took another prisoner, out of the six who were with Quichil Umar, sent to him by the Captain Hernando de la Torre. Quichil Umar came as a fugitive to the island where we were.

In the month of July a Portuguese deserter arrived, who was a spy. At the end of several days that he was with us, he put certain grenades of gun powder into the ship we were building, one night. At the noise of the explosion, the people were aroused, and put out the fire, which might have done much harm. The planks of the ship's sides were blown out, and she could not be kept above water. Thus all our labour was lost and in vain. We were new to the country, and did not know the kinds of wood to use.

At about the same time some boats of Tidore were coming laden with provisions, having five or six Spaniards on board. They fought with some of the boats of the enemy who captured two of our boats, and killed two Spaniards.

In the month of December we brought the finished vessel of 17 banks of oars to Tidore, where Alonso de Rios became her Captain, and I was appointed Treasurer.

In March we were with the king of Gilolo, twenty of us, acting against a position of the enemy which was in Batachina. Being there we saw a ship sailing over the sea, and presently we sent two Spaniards in a boat of the king of Gilolo to learn what ship she was. She turned out to have been sent by Hernan Cortes from New Spain, by order of His Majesty, to obtain news of us. Don Alvaro de Sayavedra came as Captain. When they recognized us, we went on board, and the boat returned with the news, at which we rejoiced. We sent the news to our Captain at Tidore, that he might send some help, if it should be necessary.

Next morning, the ship being becalmed, a boat of the Portuguese came alongside, and finding that the ship was Spanish, the Portuguese in the boat tried to deceive the Captain. But Sayavedra had correct intelligence from the two Spaniards who were on board. However, he asked the Portuguese to tell him in which island of Maluco the Spaniards were settled. They replied that there were no Spaniards in Maluco, though it was true that a large ship had come in a condition so that she could scarcely keep above water, that the Portuguese had helped them to build a ship, which they had done, and that the Portuguese had supplied them with provisions and many other things that they wanted. They added that if he would come to their fortress he would be received with all honour and courtesy. Sayavedra answered that it was no use making such a statement, because he knew that there were Spaniards in Maluco. There was some further talk, but when the Portuguese saw that they could not deceive him with words, they opened fire on his ship which he returned. The wind then freshened and the Spanish ship went on, anchoring at Gilolo.

That night a vessel of the Portuguese and some Moorish row boats arrived, and began to fire at the ship towards dawn. The Spaniards defended themselves as well as they could. While this attack was proceeding, our vessel with some Tidore boats arrived, which were sent by Fernando de la Torre when he heard of the arrival of the Spanish ship. As soon as the Portuguese saw this reinforcement they departed and returned to their fortress.

When our fleet came to where the ship was at anchor, she got underway and came to Tidore. From that time the war proceeded with much greater heat. On Monday, the 4th of May, 1528, a Portuguese galley, with fourteen row boats of the Moors, attacked us. We embarked 37 men on board our vessel under Alonso de Rios, her captain, and went along the land whence they came, thinking the enemy only consisted of row boats, but then we descried the Portuguese galley which had recently been built. We consulted among ourselves and put it to the vote, resolving that, being so near to each other, it would be a great mistake to turn in flight, and that it would appear to the natives like cowardice. So we commended ourselves to God, and to the Lord St James, and advanced to grapple with them, for they had great superiority in long shots, by reason of the quantity of artillery carried by the Portuguese galley. We were fighting hard for full three hours, and at last we captured the galley, but it was very hard work. They killed four of our men, and most of us were wounded. We killed eight of their men and the rest were badly wounded. Thus we brought the galley to the city of Tidore, with all her people, where the prisoners were well secured.

Having been provided with all that was required, in June 1528 the ship of Sayavedra left Tidore on her return voyage to New Spain. She took Macias de Payo as her pilot and she also embarked some Portuguese who had deserted to us, one a gentleman named Simon de Brito, the other Bernardin Cordero. Some of the prisoners were also sent on board, including the captain of the galley, that they might inform His Majesty respecting what had happened. Being on the voyage, the ship was anchored near some islands inhabited by negroes called Papuas to the east of Maluco, about 200 leagues.[1]

---

[1] 'Papuas' and 'Isla de Papuas': Markham noted that 'Papuas' referred to the so-called 'frizzy hair' of the people encountered at New Guinea. This commonly held explanation is no longer generally accepted although still found in dictionaries. Detailed research by Sollewijn Gelpke, 'On the Origin', finds that it was a commonly used Asian toponym for the region of the Moluccas meaning 'land below the sunset'.

Simon de Brito and Fernan Romero, the captain of the galley, with the other Portuguese, seized the boat and went back in her to Maluco, leaving the ship without a boat. For a long time they were lost, owing to the currents which prevented them from reaching Maluco, and drove them to some other islands. There they left the boat, and some of the Portuguese remained there. But Simon de Brito and the captain of the galley got a canoe to take them to Maluco. They came to Batachina, on the east side, 40 leagues from where we were.

One day the news came that there were in Batachina, at a place called Guayamelia, certain Portuguese who had lost their way. The Captain ordered me to go, with two companions, to see how the story originated, and, if they were Portuguese, to make them prisoners. I went to Guayamelia, and found that they were Simon de Brito and Fernan Romero, Portuguese who had fled from the caravel of Sayavedra. I arrested them and brought them, well guarded, to Tidore, where I found Sayavedra, who had returned owing to the contrary winds, and also because he had no boat. He wanted to wait for better weather, also to fill up with wood and water. So he came back, over 700 leagues, six months after he had left Tidore. Those of the ship did not dare to go on without a boat.

On examination, without torture, Simon de Brito and Fernan Romero confessed how they had escaped and, as it appeared to me, with the object of doing a service to the king of Portugal, thinking it would be a great service if they prevented the ship from returning to New Spain, because it would prevent His Majesty from knowing what was going on at Maluco, and how the Portuguese had taken possession of the lands of His Majesty. Having taken their depositions our Captain, in consideration of the evil things they did, sentenced Simon de Brito to be beheaded and quartered, and Fernan Romero to be hanged, which sentences were pronounced by Fernando de la Torre, and executed on the same day.

When the ship returned, the work of building another boat for her was proceeded with. As the ship herself was leaky and worm eaten, we made a sheathing of planks for her sides, with a kind of bitumen which they are accustomed to use here for ships. Supplied with all necessaries, as well provisions as all other things, we were ready to despatch her. Fernando de la Torre, our Captain, and all who remained in his company, were of opinion that she ought to go back by the Cape of Good Hope, as she would meet with contrary winds in returning to New Spain, but Sayavedra was resolved to return the way he came, and so he departed in May 1529.

In this campaign we had great wars with the Portuguese, and conquered all the island of Maguian by force of arms. We restored all his lands to Quichil Umar, and captured four vessels of the enemy, with all their crews and artillery, and we burnt and robbed many towns.

The said Don Jorge de Meneses, Captain of the Portuguese, sought what plans he could arrange to do us harm. One day, our chaplain was at the fortress of the Portuguese to confess, after having sought security. The said Don Jorge sent a Portuguese, a principal man, who landed and went to the fortress. Then the Captain Don Jorge de Meneses ordered our chaplain and a youth who came with him to be seized and secured in a prison under the tower, where he kept them more than seven months. At the end of that time we gave four Portuguese in exchange for the chaplain and his companion, from among the prisoners we held, giving Don Jorge de Meneses his choice, because we had no other clergyman, and those who died went without confession.

On the 10th of October 1529 we went with a fleet of the Moors of Gilolo and Tidore, and thirty men, to destroy some towns of the enemy, about 50 leagues from Maluco, to the eastward of Batachina. On the fourth day, after leaving Tidore, we encountered seven row boats off the island of Terrenate with many Portuguese on board. We fought them and captured one boat with all the crew, but the others fled and escaped.

As we departed from Tidore, the Portuguese were informed that we had set out with the largest force we could muster, including the greater part of the Moors of the island. According to public report, he who gave the information was Fernando de Bustamante, the Accountant General.

On the day of St Simon and St Jude, when the Portuguese knew that the greater part of the Spaniards and Moors were away from the island of Tidore, that not more than forty men remained there with Fernando de la Torre, and that the said Fernando de Bustamante was on their side, for he had already corresponded with them, they came with a great fleet against the city of Tidore, landed and entered by force of arms. At the entrance they killed one Spaniard and captured two others badly wounded. They killed many natives, wounded more Spaniards, and sacked the town.

Our Captain, Fernando de la Torre, seeing that he was unable to resist the Portuguese, retreated to the principal earth work we had constructed, and from thence he ordered fire to be opened on the enemy. Then Fernando de Bustamante, the Accountant General, said to Fernando de la Torre that it was no use to fight any more against the Portuguese, that they should all be united, and consequently the Constable of the gunners said that no shot was to be fired, because he had now spoken with the said Bustamante. Seeing this, Fernando de la Torre and other Spaniards began to fire off the guns themselves and fight the Portuguese, for although there was another Flemish artillery man in the fort, he would not fire a shot, but went out with the *mecheros*[1] in his hand. Other Spaniards also said that they ought to join with the Portuguese and not fight any more. In spite of this the Captain and those who remained loyal did not desist from fighting. At this juncture the Portuguese sent a man to the Spaniards with a white flag, as is the custom, and called upon them to surrender. The Captain Fernando de la Torre and other Spaniards declared that they would not surrender, but rather defend themselves ; for they had artillery, munitions, and powder, and they did not doubt that all the people of the island would join them, and give them victory, with the help of God. With this reply the Portuguese returned. Meanwhile Fernando de Bustamante went about, stirring up a mutiny, saying that they were now at the end of the year 1529, and had been five years away from Spain, and that no fleet of His Majesty had come, or was likely to come, so that it would be better to go over to the Portuguese. Don Jorge de Meneses, Captain of the Portuguese, as he had already corresponded with Fernando de Bustamante, sent a Portuguese once more to our fort, to require us to surrender. When the Captain Fernando de la Torre saw that Bustamante was trying to induce the men to mutiny, he agreed to make a proposal to the Portuguese. He offered to restore the island of Maguian, the galley we had captured, all the guns we had taken, and to liberate the prisoners. But the Portuguese would only consent to a surrender and submission to them. The Spaniards would not agree, and Fernando de la Torre, with those who wished to follow him, determined to go on board a small

---

[1] Lighters, meaning matches.

brigantine and sail away to Zamafo, where we were first with the ship, remaining there until we received orders from home. In the event of receiving no orders, we bound ourselves to settle among ourselves what we should do. Fernando de la Torre was not to take more in the brigantine than one bronze gun, his arms and property. This agreement was made with the Portuguese, and we surrendered the earth work to them, with all the artillery and public property. The Portuguese seized everything, including the private property of those who were away with the fleet, and many other things. Fernando de la Torre went away to Zamafo in the brigantine, with twenty men who stood by him. Bubacar, the Governor of Zamafo, received him very well.

Fernando de Bustamante, the Accountant General, went over to the Portuguese with all the other Spaniards, taking with him the account books, inventories, wills of the men who had died both on the voyage and after the arrival at Maluco, with all other writings of living and dead. Some of the Spaniards who went over with Bustamante to the Portuguese, were Maestre Ans, Constable of the gunners, Artus the Flemish artillery man, Francisco de Godoy a supernumerary, our chaplain named Juan de Torres, and others whose names I forget.

After the Portuguese had got possession of everything they burnt a very good vessel we had, with a public proclamation, as a rebel and insurgent in the lands of the King of Portugal.

On the 3rd of November I returned with the Governor of Tidore, who was a brother of the king, named Quichil Rade, with six Spaniards and three boats, leaving the rest of the fleet at Moro, on the east side of Batachina. On the way we received news that the Portuguese had taken and burnt the city of Tidore, and that the Spaniards were shut up and besieged in the fort. When we arrived at the island of Tidore we went to a very strong place called Tomolou, to learn what had happened. We were then informed that the Portuguese had taken the town and fort. So I asked the Governor, Quichil Rade, to give me an armed boat that I might go to Gilolo where there were twelve Spaniards. It was not my wish to join the Portuguese. For we had been sent in arms to Maluco by your Majesty. As Gilolo is very strong we could very well defend ourselves there, against the Portuguese. Quichil Rade had a very good will to serve your Majesty. He gave me a well-armed boat in which I went with two companions, taking with me two small bronze guns. I agreed with Quichil Rade that, in. four days, I would come with the Gilolo fleet to the island of Tidore at night, for him to embark for Gilolo, and be in our company, bringing his wife and children. This Quichil Rade was always our firm friend and a good servant of your Majesty. So I went to the city of Gilolo, and was well received by the king, the chiefs, and the Spaniards who were there. The king of Gilolo offered that, until we were armed by your Majesty, he would give all that we required, as well food as clothes, for all Spaniards were in your Majesty's service, and he undertook to give us all possible help, as he did.

On the fourth day we left Gilolo and went with a fleet to Tidore for Quichil Rade, who came with his wife and children, and the other principal chiefs, with their wives and children, abandoning their estates and property.

After ten or twelve days we had news that the fleet of Tidore, which I had left at Moro had returned, and that the rest of the Spaniards had gone over to the Portuguese, except Alonso de Rios who had taken refuge on a mountain in Batachina, with three companions, armed with two small pieces and their muskets. I at once started, with a swift and well-armed boat, to where the four Spaniards were. I found them and brought them safely to the city of Gilolo. Altogether we were now nineteen companions.

At the end of four or five days we armed four boats to go to where our Captain Fernando de la Torre was, at Zamafo. I and Alonso de Rios went with the idea of bringing Fernando de la Torre and his companions to Gilolo, where we could build forts, and wait for the fleet which your Majesty might send to Maluco, better than anywhere else. Having arrived at Zamafo, we consulted with Fernando de la Torre. We represented to him that it would be for the service of His Majesty to be in a position to help any Spanish vessel that might arrive, in defiance of the Portuguese. This could not be done at Zamafo, but easily at Gilolo. The answer of Fernando de la Torre was to excuse himself, saying that, by the capitulation, he was bound to keep the peace with the Portuguese, and not to enter the Maluco islands unless a fleet should arrive. When we saw that it was not his will to comply, we asked some of his companions to return with us to Gilolo, for we had certain news that the Portuguese and all those of Maluco were preparing to go and destroy Gilolo. Five Spaniards came back with us to Gilolo.

Two days after we had returned to Gilolo, the Portuguese came against us, with a fleet. We defended the landing so that they could not disembark, and they retreated without doing us any harm.

In the month of December 1529 the caravel of Sayavedra came back, not having been able to return to New Spain. She anchored in the port of Zamafo. This time Sayavedra himself had died at sea, as well as three or four of the crew.

Finding that the said caravel had not returned to New Spain, and the advice we had given now appearing good to him, Fernando de la Torre resolved to go to Gilolo where we were. Accordingly he came with the caravel and brigantine, so that altogether we numbered 60 men, and the king of Gilolo supplied us all with food. We began to renew our war with the Portuguese, continuing it until 1530, though many Spaniards went over to the enemy, and others died of diseases contracted by the hard work and the unhealthy lives they had to lead. Neither had we any resources, except what was given to us by the king of Gilolo, although the Captain helped us so far as he was able.

At this time the Portuguese inflicted certain injuries on the natives of Terrenate and they were ready to rebel, although for a time they dissimulated, advising that there should be peace between the Spaniards and Portuguese, and consequently with them. Then all the people of Maluco conspired both against the Portuguese and against us, and to kill us all. It pleased our Lord God that, as I had much friendship and conversation with many principal natives, and knew the language of the country very well, I should come to know of the conspiracy against us, and presently I informed our Captain.

In the month of May 1530 we began to entertain the idea of establishing peace with all, as well Christians as natives of the islands. I went to the Portuguese fortress with certain chiefs of Gilolo, and made peace with the Portuguese and the king of Terrenate, advising the Portuguese Captain of the conspiracy to arm the natives. He did not believe me, and conversed secretly with the chiefs of Gilolo, promising them great rewards if they would kill all the Spaniards in the land. At the end of eight days he sent to Quichil Catarabumy, who was Governor of Gilolo, and had been at peace with us, promising great rewards if he would kill us all. This Catarabumy was, at that time, on bad terms with us because he had a scheme to seize the kingdom for himself, while we

156

supported the king who was a child, and who had been commended to our protection by the late king when he died. Catarabumy did not dare to act although there were many on his side. But he agreed to what the Captain of the Portuguese had proposed, and promised that he would do it. This became known to a very near relation of the king named Quichil Tidore, who at once informed us, so that we went about armed and kept a very good watch at night. The natives did us many injuries, though not all, only those who were of the party of Quichil Catarabumy. The consequence was that we suffered much misery and anxiety, all for the service of your Majesty, for if we had chosen to go over to the Portuguese we should have been very well off. But we believed that your Majesty would not fail to send a fleet to Maluco, and that we, being there, could be of use to the fleet and of service to your Majesty. We never thought of joining the Portuguese, but resolved to wait in spite of all risks and hardships, holding it to be our duty to be ready to sacrifice our lives in the service of your Majesty.

In August 1530 Don Jorge de Meneses came to know that the natives of Terrenate, in concert with all those of Maluco, had agreed to rise against the Portuguese and us. When he became convinced of this, he one day sent for the King, Governor, and other principal men of Terrenate to come to the fortress, concealing his real object. Presently they came. As soon as he had them within the fortress, he ordered them to be made prisoners, and tortured some of them. They confessed that they had given orders for the natives to rise in arms against the Portuguese. The Captain, therefore, ordered Quichil de Reves, the Governor of Terrenate, to be beheaded. He was the most feared man that there was in those parts. Meneses then killed four or five other principal chiefs, and kept the king a prisoner in the fortress.

When the death of Quichil de Reves, the deaths of the other chiefs, and imprisonment of the king, became known to the people they rose in arms against the Portuguese, who could not venture an arquebuse shot outside the fort.

When the news of the deaths of the chiefs of Terrenate arrived at Gilolo, the natives took to their arms, and we did the same. As some of the relations of the king were friendly to us, they assured us that if the Governor chose to attack us, they would be on our side, so that in reliance on their help we had no fear.

On the same night I went secretly to the fortress of the Portuguese, in a small canoe with only five rowers. My object was to put aside what was past, and to offer to the Portuguese, on the part of the Captain and ourselves all the assistance in our power, if they needed our help. In truth we offered more than they could if they had made a similar offer, because the will we had to assist them was not owing to necessity. So the Captain and all the Portuguese gave me thanks and offered the same help. It was agreed between us that, if the necessity should arise, we would help each other and remain very good friends, forgetting what was past. In the same hour I returned to the city of Gilolo, running great risks, for the natives of the land attempted to seize me.

When I returned to Gilolo, I found a serious state of affairs. The Captain, with about forty men who had remained with him, was armed and entrenched in some large buildings, with his artillery placed and ready.

Seeing this I went straight to the house of the king, where I found the Governor with a large body of armed men. I made a speech in their language before all, saying that the Governor knew very well that, from the time that we arrived at Maluco in the ship, the people of Gilolo and ourselves had always been friends even unto death. We had received great favours from the king of Gilolo, and he had always had from us all the service we could possibly give him. Besides this, our Lord being pleased that it should be, when the fleet of your Majesty arrived, the king of Gilolo would be made Chief King of all Maluco in reward for the favour he had shown us. Until then we had always been friends, and had been as one. Let us then continue the same friendship for the time to come, without intervening in the quarrel between the Portuguese and the people of Terrenate. This speech had such an effect that before evening we had sworn eternal friendship.

In the month of October 1530 a Portuguese Captain arrived with troops, as Governor of the fortress of Maluco. His name was Gonzalo Pereyra. We renewed with him the peace we had arranged with the Captain Don Jorge de Meneses. When Gonzalo Pereyra arrived, he examined the acts[1] of Don Jorge de Meneses, and arrested him for the execution of Quichil de Reyes. Thus under arrest, he was sent, by way of India, to Portugal. When the natives saw that Gonzalo Pereyra had arrived with more troops they made peace, though it did not last long. At the end of six months that Captain Pereyra was in Maluco, the Indians of Terrenate were poniarded within the fortress, many Portuguese were killed, their town was burnt, and the fortress itself was nearly taken. All the Maluco islands rose against the Portuguese except the people of Gilolo, who took neither one side nor the other, for love of us, although the natives of Terrenate offered great rewards both to us and to the Gilolo people, if we would help them. But we excused ourselves with good reasons, for we reflected that we were few Spaniards and that if the natives captured the fort of the Portuguese, at the same hour they would fall upon us, being so few in number.

At the end of a month, Gonzalo Pereyra being dead, the Portuguese sent a well-armed galley to Gilolo, where we were, asking us to give them provisions in exchange for their money, as they were in great need. Seeing their necessity, we used such persuasion with the Governor and chiefs of the land that they supplied plenty of provisions for money, indeed as much as the galley could carry. Seeing this the natives of Terrenate presently raised the siege of the fortress.

Further we negotiated between the Portuguese and the people of Terrenate to make peace, with success, on which account the Portuguese and the natives became our very good friends. In the year 1531 I gave the narrative by Fernando de la Torre of all that had happened for His Majesty's information to one Anibal Cernichi in Maluco, who swore on a consecrated altar to deliver it, unless he died on the road.

In 1532, by reason of the great friendship that had arisen between us and the Portuguese, we asked Don Vicente de Fonseca, the Captain of the Portuguese that, as we desired to send an ambassador to the Portuguese Governor of India, he would order a vessel to be provided. Vicente de Fonseca replied that he was much pleased at the determination we had come to.

We sent Pedro de Montemayor to the Governor of Portuguese India, informing him that we had been a long time in Maluco, and had never received any orders from His Majesty. We had heard that His Majesty had ceded Maluco to the King of Portugal for 300,000 ducats. We, therefore, had resolved to return to Spain, leaving the land to the Portuguese, but we had no vessel. We, therefore, requested him to send us a vessel in

---

[1] Urdaneta means that Meneses's replacement conducted an official investigation or *residencia* into the latter's conduct of his office.

which to return to Spain, and to apply 1,000 ducats, on His Majesty's account, for our expenses.

In October 1533 Pedro de Montemayor returned from Portuguese India to Maluco, accompanied by a Captain of the King of Portugal named Tristan de Taide who came as Captain General and Governor of Maluco. The Governor of India sent us a ship with a captain named Jordan de Fretes, a native of the island of Madeira. The Governor also sent us the 1,000 ducats we asked for, although Tristan de Taide was unwilling to pay it until we had come over to him. The Governor also sent a decree for which we had asked, that no Captain of the King of Portugal was to detain us in any of the forts we might pass, nor to have jurisdiction over us.

When the people of Gilolo realized that we were going to pass over to the Portuguese, they felt great sorrow and besought us not to do so. To ensure this they declared war on the Portuguese, although we did not wish it. But the Portuguese thought that we were causing the trouble, and sent many threats that they would come against us with a great fleet, and not leave one of us alive. On the other side the natives wanted to kill us, because we would not help them against the Portuguese. So that we were in danger from both. When we saw our predicament, we gave the natives to understand that we wanted to side with them, although we did not want to do so.

The Portuguese came against the city of Gilolo and the Captain of them had himself rowed along the coast in a canoe, to find a good place for landing. On seeing him a Spaniard got into the water with his musket, and fired a shot from behind a mangrove, at very short range. In firing he said in a loud voice, so that the Portuguese Captain should understand, that we did not desire war with him. The Portuguese Captain, therefore, gave an order through the fleet that no Portuguese nor native allies were to do any harm to a Spaniard. On the following day the Portuguese and their native allies landed and took the city of Gilolo. For when the people of Gilolo saw that we would not fight, they fled. At the entrance they killed the factor Diego de Salinas with a small gun. We went with the Portuguese to the fortress, without receiving any ill treatment from them. At this time we had not more than 17 men, all the rest being dead.

Having joined the Portuguese the Captain gave our Captain the 1,000 ducats, which he divided amongst us, after having taken what was just for himself. Then we all embarked for India with Jordan de Fretes. We departed on the 15th of February 1534, but I remained in Maluco, with authority from Fernando de la Torre, to recover certain *bahares* of clove which the natives owed to His Majesty and also to Fernando de la Torre and other persons of his company. I was using diligence to recover some of this, when it came to the ears of Tristan de Taide, Captain of the Portuguese. He sent for me and ordered me not to seek for anything from any native, for if it came to his knowledge he would punish me severely. He also sent orders to some kings of Maluco and other chief persons among the natives who owed clove to His Majesty, that they were to pay nothing. I, therefore, did not dare to seek anything from any native. Also, before Fernando de la Torre left Maluco, Tristan de Taide gave orders to all the Spaniards that all who had taken part in the past wars with the Portuguese might return, and that those who had been with us might not return.

In the year 1528, when Sayavedra came from New Spain, three Spaniards of our company were on one of the islands of Célebes called Sarragan. Of these three men two were Galicians and the third a Portuguese. They had been in the caravel *Santa*

Maria del Parral, and were rescued by Sayavedra. For the Indians had sold them as slaves, and he brought them with him to Maluco. These three men told us that the first island which the caravel reached, whence they came to the archipelago of Célebes, was Mindanao, in the port of Bizaya. When they sent their boat on shore for provisions, the natives seized it and killed all the crew. When the people in the caravel saw this they made sail for Maluco, but when passing an island called Sanguin, a sudden squall drove her on shore, and she was lost. The natives came down to the wreck, killing or making prisoners of all who were on board. They sold their prisoners as slaves, and the men said that there were seven or eight more in the other islands of Célebes. When Fernando de la Torre heard that there were other Christians kept as prisoners in those islands of Célebes, he ordered five or six boats to be sent to redeem any Christians who might be found in those islands. At the time when the boats were starting, one of the Galicians told another Galician who belonged to our ship that it was true that the Indians of Bizaya had taken the boat of the caravel with all on board. Afterwards there was a mutiny in the caravel, and the mutineers had thrown the Captain Don Jorge Manrique, his brother Don Diego, and one Benavides, alive into the sea, and then killed them with lances. These two Galicians had been among the mutineers, and they, therefore, wanted to join the Portuguese, where they would not be known.

When the boats went to those islands of Célebes the two Galicians and the Portuguese went in them with some Spaniards, because they knew the language. After they had been gone two or three days, that other Galician belonging to our crew told what the other had divulged to him. When Fernando de la Torre heard it, he sent off a swift boat with orders to bring back the three men. The swift boat overhauled the others at Zamafo. When one of the Galicians saw her coming he got on shore, and ran away to, join the Portuguese. The other two were taken and brought to Tidore, though the Portuguese was not culpable. The Galician was subjected to the torture of the cord, and when he confessed he was hung and quartered. Nothing more was done to rescue the other Christians, who remained where they were.

I and the pilot Macias de Payo, who had remained with me, were in Maluco until February 1535. The Captain of the Portuguese wanted to detain us, because he wished to send a caravel to Célebes, and us to go in her. For he had received tidings from some natives of Célebes that there was much gold in one of the islands of the Célebes archipelago, as well as much sandalwood, and they brought some to show the Captain of the Portuguese. The sandalwood is an important article of merchandise in Portuguese India, for if it is large and thick it is worth 40 ducats the *bahar in* Malacca. At the time when Fernando de la Torre left Maluco I remained behind, on condition that in the next year, 1535, I should leave for Portuguese India in company with a merchant named Lisuarte Cairo in his junk, and that Tristan de Taide, Captain of the fortress, should not detain me nor my companion the pilot, against our wills; but that he should let us go, and give leave for us to depart to Malacca with Lisuarte Cairo.

On the 15th of February 1535 we left the Maluco islands in company with Lisuarte Cairo, arriving at Banda on the 5th of March. Here we found two Portuguese ships laden with mace and nutmegs.

These islands of Banda are seven in number. They yield mace and nutmegs, found nowhere else in the world. Here they are gathered in great quantities. The Banda islands are 80 leagues from Maluco in 4°S latitude. The natives are ready to trade and are great friends of the Spaniards and of the king of Tidore. In the days of our prosperity in Maluco we always traded with them, and at the time when the Portuguese took our fort, there were six or seven junks of Banda which had come to trade with us, and also to molest and rob the Portuguese. While we were in Banda, Quichil Catarabumy came with a fleet to the islands, and Quichil Tidore talked to us with tears in his eyes. He said that if God should give us the good fortune to return home, His Majesty should be informed what good servants to His Majesty the kings of Gilolo and Tidore had been in helping the people of His Majesty whom the Portuguese had destroyed. They prayed that your Majesty would remember your vassals and send a fleet to deliver them from captivity, for the Portuguese treated them very badly in all the islands, besides those whose inhabitants had shown themselves to be servants of your Majesty. Quichil Tidore is a very important chief of Gilolo, and a first cousin of the king, the best friend we found in Gilolo, a man very wise and sagacious. Quichil Catarabumy also conversed with me, with tears in his eyes, although at one time he was our enemy. He said he was anxious to talk to me, but that he had not dared to do so, for fear of the Portuguese, that I knew their intentions well, and that he only asked me, when I reached Spain, to give an account of them to His Majesty.

When I was about to depart from Terrenate, a chief of the king of Tidore came to me, named Baianu. He said that his king had sent him to me, to say how much he wished to write to your Majesty, but that he did not dare because the Portuguese would not like it. He, therefore, entreated me to receive what he wished to say secretly. He prayed His Majesty to remember his vassal who had served His Majesty and helped his people. The Portuguese had desolated his country, and killed the greater part of the inhabitants. Every day they ill treated the survivors, and all this because the king of Tidore had received and helped the ships and people of your Majesty; as well Juan Sebastian del Cano and Espinosa as ourselves. This being the case and His Majesty being so powerful, he entreated him, as a powerful Prince, that he would send out a great fleet to deliver them from their troubles by driving out the Portuguese. If the fleet of His Majesty came, it would find no opposition in any of the islands of Maluco, because all desired to be His Majesty's, and to serve him. The king of Terrenate and his people, on seeing the fleet of His Majesty, would at once rise against the Portuguese, as well as all the people of Maluco and Banda.

We were at the islands of Banda until the month of June, waiting for fine weather; and leaving them in that month, we arrived at the port of Panaruca in Java, where we remained for a few days, taking in provisions. The distance from the isles of Banda to the port of Panaruca is 250 leagues.[1] It is in 7°S more or less. The island of Java is to the south and is very large, yielding many kinds of provisions as well rice as buffaloes, cows, pigs, goats and fowls, and the natives make a very good beverage of rice. They also have much palm wine. There is much sport in hunting deer. There are also horses. In this island of Java there is much gold which is taken to Malacca for sale; and the Portuguese come here from Maluco to trade. There are always Portuguese in this city of Panaruca, because the king is a great friend of theirs.

The people of this island are very warlike and treacherous. They have many bronze guns which they cast themselves, as well as muskets. They have lances like ours, very well

---

[1] See above, pp. 135–6.

made though the iron heads are different, and many other weapons such as bows, azagays, and *zebretanas*.[1] All usually carry daggers in their belts. They use carts a good deal, which are drawn by buffaloes. They have many junks which they navigate to all parts, as well as ships worked by oars, which they call *calaluces*,[2] which go very fast. We also saw that they built many *fustas* like ours, having obtained the plans for them from the Portuguese. The Indians of this kingdom are gentiles.

In Java there are powerful kings, as well heathens as Moors, the greatest of all being the king of Dema who is a Moor, and is continually at war with the Portuguese. This king had the lordship of the pepper of Sunda. The pepper of Sunda goes to China and is better than the pepper of Portuguese India because it is larger. It is much valued in China.

We sailed from the port of Panaruca for Malacca and arrived there in the end of July 1535. The distance is 200 leagues more or less. In this city of Malacca the Portuguese have a fort with a garrison of 500 men. It is a place of great trade, for many junks come here from all parts, as well from Maluco as Timor, Banda with much sandalwood, all Java, Sumatra, India, Ceylon, Paliacati with much cotton cloth of Bengal, where they make the finest in these parts. Vessels also come from Pegu with provisions, gems, and musk, and from many rivers and lands which are near Malacca, bringing gold and tin. From Sumatra they bring more gold than from any other part whatever, and it is very fine gold. While we were at Malacca there was a day when the merchants received seven *quintales* of gold from Sumatra. Much gold and camphor also come to Malacca from Siam, Patani and Burney.

There is also a great trade with China, as well porcelains as silks of all kinds, musks, and other precious things. China, according to what the Portuguese say who have been there, produces the best things there are in these parts.

We were at Malacca until the middle of November, and sailed for Cochín on the 15th of the month in a Portuguese junk called the *Alvaro Oreto*, passing Ceylon where the cinnamon grows that comes to Portugal. We arrived at Cochín in the middle of December, where we found Fernando de la Torre, our Captain, with a few companions. After we arrived, an order came from the Governor, who was at Diu, that Fernando de la Torre and his companions were to be given passages in a ship bound for Portugal. The Captain told me that, when he arrived in India, the Governor received him and his companions well. At the time when the order from the Governor came, the Captain of Cochín told Fernando de la Torre to get ready to depart, but that no more than four or five of his companions could go in the same ship with him. The rest must go in another ship. We were very sorry for this, because we should be safer if we were together. With few of us they might put us into a ship going the other way when at sea, or poison us. I and my friend the pilot embarked in a ship called the *San Roque*. We paid 50 ducats to be allowed space for our provisions which we had bought, but without having a key to lock them up. Since we left Gilolo we had always bought our own food, except rice and a little fish. They gave us some *serapis* at Cochín, a gold coin worth 300 maravedis.

Three other companions embarked with us, but two of them died before we reached the Cape of Good Hope.

---

[1] Assegais and probably blowpipes.
[2] See above, p. xvii.

Four companions remained at Cochín to embark with Fernando de la Torre, who made the fifth. Their ship was called the *Gallega*; and the captain was a relation of the Count of Castañeda. As it might happen that Fernando de la Torre would die during the voyage, or some other disaster prevent his return, it seemed advisable that he should prepare some account for your Majesty, and send it by me. Fernando de la Torre, therefore, wrote a brief account, entrusting further details to me, that I might write a fuller narrative. He also wrote a letter for your Majesty, in which he mentioned the many loyal services I had done for your Majesty in those parts.

On the 12th of January 1536 we sailed from Cochín, which is the port where the spices are shipped for Portugal. There were five ships laden with spices, and two more were being loaded and were to start in eight days. In one of these Fernando de la Torre was to embark. We commenced our voyage, and before we reached San Lorenzo, our Captain, Jordan de Fretes, parted company with the other ships because our ship was the best sailer. We passed the Cape of Good Hope on the 30th of March, and thence proceeded to the island of St Helena to take in water.

This island of St Helena is in 16°S. We were there eight days, where we got many green calabashes to eat, and many oranges and pomegranates, as well as fish, which refreshed the crew. There are also wild pigs and goats on this island. There is a Portuguese hermit there, but no other people whatever. It is a small island, not more than four leagues in circumference.

We left St Helena and proceeded on our voyage to Portugal, arriving at the city of Lisbon on the 26th of June 1536

When I landed in the city of Lisbon the guard examined me very closely, first my person, and then my box, which contained the letter which Fernando de la Torre sent by me to your Majesty, in a letter case. The guard over the ships coming from India took these things, in spite of my remonstrances. They also took the account book of the ship in which we came to Maluco, another large book of mine, and letters written by Spaniards of our company who remained in Portuguese India. We also had charts drawn of the Maluco and Banda Islands on white paper, and sealed up like ordinary letters so as to deceive them. These they also took. They also seized the track charts to Maluco, and from New Spain to Maluco, out of the same box, with other memoirs and writings. The guard seized this property without authority of a writer but merely as their own act.

As the guard seized all these things on their own authority, I determined to go to Evora to complain to the King of Portugal. Arriving there I went direct to the Ambassador Sarmiento, to whom I gave an account of my arrival from Maluco, and how the guard had seized my papers when I landed. Seeing that they would not return my property, I had come to complain to the king. The Ambassador of your Majesty said that he did not care to trouble the King of Portugal about it, but that I should, with all possible despatch, go to your Majesty and give an account of all that had happened, that what would be of service to your Majesty might be done.

I, therefore set out for the court of your Majesty, to give an account of this affair and of everything else, leaving the things I brought from Maluco in Lisbon. While I was at Evora, the King of Portugal heard that we had landed at Lisbon and sent for us. As I was not to be found they brought my companion the pilot to Evora, where the court was. When he arrived he went at once to the inn of the Ambassador of your

Majesty, telling him who he was and that he had come by the king's order. The Ambassador gave him a horse and told him to depart at once, and so he came to this court.

The islands of Maluco which produce clove are Tidore, Ternate, Motil, Maguian, and Bachan. In none of the others, though there are many islands, do they gather clove.

In Ternate, which is in about 1°N, in a good harvest, they gather 3,500 *quintales* of clove. In this island the Portuguese have a fortress.

In Tidore, in about 0°40′ N, 3500 *quintales*. In this island the Spaniards were settled.

In Motil, in about 0° 3′ N, 1,000 *quintales* when there is a good harvest.

In Maguian, which is in 0°15′ N, 3,500 *quintales*.

In Bachan, which is partly on the equator, but mostly to the south of it, 600 *quintales*.

In all the five islands, when there is a good harvest, 11,600 *quintales* a little more or less; at other times they do not gather more than 5,000 or 6,000 *quintales*.

At the time when we arrived in Maluco a *bahar* of clove, which is over four *quintales,* was worth two ducats. When we departed clove was worth 10 ducats the *bahar*. This rise was caused by the numerous Portuguese merchants who go there every year.

To the south of Maluco are the Banda Islands, about 80 leagues, in 10°S. In these islands they gather nutmegs and mace. In one year and another they gather 7,500 *quintales* of nutmegs and a 1,000 of mace.

To the east of the Banda Islands there are many islands whence they bring gold to Banda for sale, though not much. No Portuguese or Spaniards have been to these islands, the natives trading among themselves.

Between Maluco and Banda are the islands of Ambon, or by another name the natives call it Java. In these islands there are many provisions, and one is very large with trees of clove, though few. They had brought the plant from Maluco. In these islands of Ambon they build many junks, and navigate in those parts.

East of Maluco is the island of Batachina, to which the sailors of Magellan's voyage gave the name of Gilolo. It is in 3°N. On this island is the kingdom of Gilolo on the western side. It has a circumference of 150 leagues, for I have been round it, by sea. In this island there are many provisions, such as pigs, goats, fowls, fish, rice, palm wine and coconuts, supplying those of Maluco. This island, on the west side, runs north and south, and is near Maluco. The kings of Maluco subjugated this island of Batachina, and others near it.

To the east of this island of Batachina there are many other islands which they call the Papuas. The inhabitants are all black with woolly hair like those of Guinea, and all use arrows. From these islands they bring gold to Bachan, little but fine. The islands of the Papuas are numerous, according to the natives.[1]

To the NE of Maluco there is an archipelago of islands close together, 200 leagues distant, discovered by a Portuguese vessel. They are between 3 and 9 north latitude.

Talao is to the north of Maluco in 5° N. Off this island we anchored on our way to Maluco, and the natives told us that to the eastward there were two islands, called Galliba and Lalibu, where there was much gold.

---

[1] Urdaneta refers here to the Melanesian indigenous inhabitants of New Guinea.

To the north-east of Maluco in 6° N is Bendenao (Mindanao). In this island there is cinnamon, and much gold. They also fish for pearls and bring up quantities as we were told. Every year two junks come from China to this island to trade.

To the north of Mindanao is Zebu. According to the natives it contains gold, and the Chinese come there every year to trade.

Tristan de Taide, Captain of the fortress of Maluco, received information in 1534 that to the NE of Mindanao there was an island very rich in gold, and he fitted out a ship to discover it.

To the SE of Mindanao is Sanguin within sight of it. Here the caravel *Santa Maria del Parral* was wrecked after the crew had murdered the captain. The natives attacked the crew, killing some and capturing others.

To the west of Maluco there is an archipelago of islands called Célebes, and the natives come every year to Maluco to sell gold, though not in great quantity.

To the SW of Maluco there is a large island called Tubuay, where there is much iron, with which they provide all the other islands of those parts, also taking it to Java, Timor and Borneo. I went to that island with some people of Gilolo. All the iron they sell is worked.

Very near this island to the westward are the islands of Mazacares where there is much gold. In these islands a Portuguese vessel was wrecked, and because some of the islanders went to fight those of another island, they gave the Portuguese a certain quantity of gold, each one more than 300 ducats. They also gave them ten *cates* of gold which are 20 lbs, and the Portuguese did not want to sell their share at any price, and so they went their way.

Near the island of Tubuay, to the eastward, there is a small island called Bangay with a king. The people of this island are very warlike, and hold lordship over other islands, carrying on much trade. I was in that island, and at the time when I arrived the queen had died. During the forty days that I was there they killed more than 150 men and women, saying that it was necessary they should accompany the queen to the other world. They do the same when a king dies. This king of Bangay is very rich and has a large treasure of gold.

To the south of Maluco, about 60 leagues from Tidore, there is a large island called Buru, with other smaller islands round it. There is nothing in this island but provisions, and the natives of it are few and well conducted.

There are many other islands round Maluco, although we had no intercourse with them. They remain to be discovered and subjugated.

Your Majesty should know that although they say that the King of Portugal derives no profit from Maluco asserting that a small amount of clove is received from those parts, it is not correct; for the trade in clove, mace, and nutmegs in. India, besides what come to these parts, is a source of great wealth to the King of Portugal and other persons in Portugal. Though to Portugal they only bring 500 *quintales* of clove and 100 of mace, and 200 of nutmegs each year, the Portuguese also bring to Ormuz, which is at the entrance of the Persian Sea, and sell every year more than 6,000 *quintales* of clove, and there are years when they sell more than 10,000. They also sell there over 6.000 *quintales* of nutmegs and 800 *quintales* of mace. For merchants come to buy, at the island of Ormuz, all this spice. The buyers are Moorish merchants who pass it on, over Persia, Arabia, and all Asia as far as Turkey.

Your Majesty should know that there might be brought from Maluco, if your Majesty were pleased to order commerce to be maintained with Maluco, in every year 6,000 *quintales* of clove, and there are years when there is a harvest of more than 11,000 *quintales,* the trees yielding in some years much more than in others. In the same way there might be obtained from Banda, one year with another, 800 *quintales* of mace, and in some years more, and 6,000 *quintales* of nutmegs, in some years much more. Your Majesty should also know that there is much ginger in Maluco, which might also be brought and prepared as the Portuguese now bring it. The cinnamon of Mindanao can also be obtained in Maluco by trading, and brought to Spain, though I do not know what the quantity would be. A treaty might be made at Maluco with the king of Dema in Java, for a supply of pepper. For this king of Dema has pepper in great quantity and is an enemy of the Portuguese. He has information about the Spaniards, and of the wars we carried on with the Portuguese in Maluco. He will rejoice to be a friend of the Spaniards, and to make a treaty with them. Such a treaty might include the people of Banda and Ambon, who have many junks and would bring the pepper to Maluco.

If your Majesty were pleased to order a treaty to be made with Maluco, for bringing all the clove, mace, and nutmeg harvest to Spain, it would be necessary to buy the spices and drugs in whatever parts your Majesty ordered treaties to be made. For your Majesty should know that in no other part of the discovered universe are there spices, but only in these islands. So that your Majesty would derive much profit from these islands of Maluco and Banda, for only from the spices there would be a yield of more than 600,000 ducats, not counting the ginger and cinnamon. A treaty for the trade in pepper with Java would also ensure a large profit.

Your Majesty will also see, from this report, that there are many rich and valuable conquests to be made round Maluco, and many lands with much trade, including China, which might be communicated with from Maluco.

Dated in Valladolid on the 26th of February 1537.

Andrés de Urdaneta.

APPENDIX 2

Narrative of all that was traversed and discovered by the Captain Alvaro de Sayavedra[1] who sailed from the port of Yacatulo[2] in New Spain on November 1st, 1527: which fleet was despatched by Don Hernan Cortes, Marquis of Valle, Captain General of their Majesties with three ships supplied with all necessary provisions, stores, and brass artillery.[3]

IN the first place the Captain Alvaro de Sayavedra[4] went in a ship called the *Florida* with 38 landsmen and 12 sailors, 50 in all. He took three guns of *fuslera*[5] and 10 of iron. This ship was the *capitana*. In the ship *Santiago* Luis de Cardenas, a native of Cordova, went as captain. She had a crew of 45 men, sailors and landsmen together. She carried one gun of *fuslera* and 8 of iron. The third ship was named the *Espiritu Santo*, and was commanded by Pedro de Fuentes, a native of Xerez de la Frontera. She had a crew of 15 men and carried 6 guns of iron.

On the 1st of November we sailed from the port of Aguatlonejo[6] which is on the coast of New Spain. The winds we experienced were those which are here set down. That day the winds were W and WNW and we steered SSW making good about 10 leagues. Next day, with the same wind, we made 12 leagues. On the third day, with the same wind, we made 15 leagues on the same course; and on the fourth day, another 15 leagues. On the fifth day the wind was NW and our course was SW 20 leagues. In the same weather we made 25 leagues good on the sixth day; and on the seventh 25 leagues. On the eighth day our course was SW 40 leagues. At noon a leak was discovered in the after-part of the *capitana,* at a join in the keel; so we had to give two turns of the glass[7] to the pump, and to rest for half a turn. But we could not find the exact place of the leak; so we shortened sail and closed on the other ships. Captain Alvaro de Sayavedra went below and searched

---

[1] AGI, Patronato 43, N. 2, R. 11, 'Relación de Vícente de Nápoles: navegación armada del Maluco'.

[2] Yacatulo (spelt more correctly Zacatula), on the Río de las Balsas in the State of Guerrero, on the Pacific coast of Mexico.

[3] The original of this manuscript is found in AGI, Patronato 43, N.2, R. 11, and can be read online through the PARES system.

[4] Alvaro de Saavedra Cerón, a cousin of Hernan Cortes. Wright, 'The First American Voyage across the Pacific, 1527–1528', p. 473.

[5] Metal made from the shavings off a brass gun when it is being turned.

[6] Antonio Galvão gives Ciutlanejo. Most likely Zihuatanejo 17°38′36″N, on the Pacific coast north of Acapulco.

[7] *Ampolleta*, an hour-glass. A boy took count of the glasses that ran out during his watch and, after striking the hour on the bell, he ran forward crying – 'One hour passed in two turns, and more will pass if God will. Let us pray to to God to grant us a good voyage and to her, the Mother of God, who is our advocate, to deliver us from pumping our water and other troubles. Forward ahoy!' The watch on the forecastle answered 'What does he say?' and ordered the boy to recite a Lord's Prayer and an Ave Maria.

for the leak, but he could not find it then, nor until we came to an island called Mindanao. The Spaniards call it La Mendana, where we were for two months and a half.

On the eighth day the Captain Sayavedra consulted with the other captains whether they should go back to New Spain on account of the water that the *capitana* was making. They were of the opinion that we should return. The Captain Alvaro de Sayavedra then asked the pilot what he thought of the leak, and he replied that we ought not to give up the voyage on account of it. His advice was taken and owing to the work at the pumps the Captain took the strongest men out of the other ships out of the other ships, and replaced them by the weaker ones in his own ship. The other captains said that Sayavedra should come on board one of the other vessels which were not leaking; he answered that in that ship he had sailed, and in that ship he had to be lost or saved. So he continued the voyage.

On the ninth day we were in 11°S steering to the west, and made good 35 leagues.

On the 10th day we made good 40 leagues on the same course, on the 11th day another 40 leagues, on the 12th the same, on the 13th the same, on the 14th 45 leagues, on the 15th 40, on the 16th 35, on the 17th 45, on the 18th 50, on the 19th 35, on the 20th 60, and on the 21st we Thought we sighted land, and stood to the WNW all night, but in the morning we could see nothing and went back on our course, making 25 leagues. On the 23rd day we went on our course 35 leagues, on the 24th and 25th each 35 leagues, on the 26th 60 leagues, on the 27th 45 leagues, and on the 28th day 40 leagues.

On the 29th day out we discovered another leak in the fore-part of the *capitana,* which filled a compartment of the hold with water, wetting 60 *quintals* of bread, all the oil and vinegar, and other things. Before this leak was found, the ship would not answer her helm, and the Captain asked the master the reason. The master answered that he did not know the cause. The Captain ordered him to go below and ascertain, but he said that it was late, and that he would go down and see in the morning. On the same night the ship would not answer her helm, and as we were between the two other vessels, we could not give way to them nor them to us, so we dropped astern, and encountered a squall. The man at the helm was negligent, and the ship was taken aback and nearly swamped. At last we got the sail down. The other ships passed on ahead with a strong wind, and were soon out of sight. We showed many lights but they never answered, and so we lost them. Our pilot went to bed, and did not care about making sail after them. Next morning we made sail on our course and never more was there any sign of them. This day we made 35 leagues.

On the same course, and with similar weather we sailed for another thirty days, without ever seeing any land.

On the sixtieth day, Saturday night, we altered course and steered WbS. That night it was calm. We made 10 leagues. On Sunday morning we were within a league of land. Captain Alvaro de Sayavedra gave it the name of the Isles of the Kings,[1] as it was the day of the kings. It is an archipelago of islands, numbering ten or twelve, and it is said that they are all inhabited. We were three days among them, turning from one direction to another, but we did not anchor at any of the islands because the sea is so deep that if we were to let go an anchor it would not reach the bottom. The natives came out to us in the small vessels they have, but they would not come near. Seeing that we could not reach

---

[1] Navarrete, *Colección de los Viajes*, vol. V, p. 99, n. 2, notes that this was clearly an error in the transcript of Vicente de Nápoles's report. The islands sighted were the Marianas, known since Magellan's voyage as the Ladrones.

a port by reason of the shoals between us and the land, and considering the length of time we had passed without anchoring anywhere, we continued our voyage on the same course. The people of these islands are well grown, rather brown, with long hair, and no clothes except some matting made of reeds. The mats are so elegantly woven that, at a distance, they look like gold. With these mats they are Clothed. The men have beards like Spaniards. For arms they have staves hardened by fire. We did not see what their food was, as we had no communication with them. These islands are in 11° N.

We went on all night, and next day we sighted other islands of the same kind, with the same sort of people. We went amongst them to see if we could find a watering place, for we were in great straits for drinking water. We found anchorage near one of these islands which was uninhabited, and all the men jumped on shore in search of water. We found a *xaque*[1] an arrow shot from the beach. The island is small. About a league in circumference. We were eight days on this island, getting wood and water on board. At a distance of three leagues there is an inhabited island, and the natives came but would have nothing to do with us and returned. The island is in 11°.

Afterwards the natives came back, and stopped on a low bank half a league from where we were. There were sixteen of them. A Spaniard waded across, only up to his knees, to where they were, and they received him in a most friendly way. The Spaniard asked them by signs to come to where we were, but they did not understand and went back to their island. The Spaniard returned none the worse.

We got 18 barrels of water and made sail with an ENE wind. Course West 30 leagues. Next day we made 25 leagues on the same course, next day 15, then we were becalmed for seven days and the crew began to fall sick. After the calm the wind sprang up again, and we made 30 leagues, next day 35, next day 40, next 45, next 30. The captain then asked the pilot how far we were from our destination, and he replied 150 leagues. Next day we made 25 leagues with the same wind, next 20 leagues. The pilot fell ill, and the next day he was very bad. We took him below, and he made his will. When he finished making it he died. He was a Portuguese named Ortuño de Araujo. We made 15 leagues, and also consigned the blacksmith to the deep. The next day the cooper fell ill, and died at the end of twenty days. Calm for two days.

Next day the wind freshened from ENE three hours before sunset. We made 10 leagues.

The same day we sighted land, and shortened sail. Next morning we came into a very good harbour, anchored the ship, and got the boat in the water. We went to bury a sailor named Cansino, a native of Palos. This island was uninhabited, and, searching for something to eat, we found nothing but shellfish. We were there 28 days, unable to leave the port owing to the bad weather, for it was winter on that coast, being the end of January, 1528. This island, where we took in wood and water, is in 10°.

Thence we made sail before a northerly wind and steered south for 80 leagues along the coast of the great island called Mindanao, for five days. While thus coasting along a king came out in a small vessel, three leagues out to sea, and stopped within a stone's

---

[1] Identified by Markham as meaning a 'sheik or chief'. The wording of the sentence does not suggest an encounter with an individual. If the word is transliterated as 'jaque' it could mean that they found a piece of clothing.

throw from us, where he talked by signs, and we heard him, and replied, and he said by signs that we were to come on shore, where he would give us rice and coconuts. So we followed him, and moored with two anchors, one to the north, the other to the south. We anchored in the afternoon, and called to the natives to come on board, but they would not. Then we threw jars overboard, asking them to bring water, and they took the jars and filled them, and brought them back, and put them in the boat, not consenting that any should get into it, but pushing it with a lance, the boat being secured by a chain, and so we got about ten jars of water.

Next morning a great crowd came on the land, including many women carrying boys who they put down in front of the ship, which was a cross-bow's shot from the beach.

The king is called Catonao in their language, and his son-in-law, who is also a king, came in a small vessel with three persons and his son, a child in arms. They came on board and were very well received by the Captain who took the child in his arms, and gave it some beads. The visitors were given to eat, with wine, but they did not drink it. They remained for half an hour, and then the king said he wished to go on shore as his father-in-law was there. There were about 300 people assembled on the beach.

In the following night three or four men came in a boat, and took the buoy which we had on shore, and plunged it into the water. They tore it from the anchor, which they raised, and got it on board their boat, fastened to the chain. They then hauled on the chain thinking they could go away with the ship. Finding they were unable to do that, they cut the cable and took the anchor on shore. Then they took reeds, as thick as a man's thumb, twisted into a length of 300 fathoms, and went back to where they had cut the cable. They then fastened their cable to ours and returned on shore, where all the people began to haul with the object of wrecking the ship. They did this under the direction of three captive Spaniards who had been wrecked in one of the ships of the fleet of the Comendador Loaysa. Seeing that they could not drag the ship on shore they asked the Spaniards the reason. They were told that there must be another anchor down which prevented it. They then went under the ship's bows in their boat. The watch on the forecastle saw them come close under the bows, but the Captain had ordered that even if the natives came quite close, no harm was to be done to them. The watch, therefore, let them come quite close without saying anything. Being there they raised a hatchet to cut the other cable. Seeing this the watch cried out and they, seeing that they were found out, went away laughing and pretending it was a joke. So they went on shore, and by that time it was dawn.

Next day the wind blew from the sea, and the anchor dragged. Then we began to haul on the cable and found it cut, and the end fastened to the shore cable. Then we saw the damage that had been done, and the intended treachery. On this day, in the morning, one of the Spaniards who were in captivity, fled into the forest. When the natives missed him, thinking that he had gone on board the ship, they went away without saying a word, taking the other two Spaniards with them.

The fugitive came down to the beach near the ship, hiding behind some stones, and made signals to us with his hand. The Captain ordered the boat to go and see who it was. On seeing this the man swam out and was taken into the boat, and brought to the ship. From him we learnt all that had been done, and many things concerning the land and its people. His name was Sebastian, a native of Oporto and married in Coruña. We gave him refreshment and the Captain gave him clothes.

This Spaniard was asked whether he knew in what latitude that land was. He said that the Bachiller Tarragona, who came in the fleet of the Comendador Loaysa, told him that a bay that was near was in 8°. These natives are called Celebe, and they are very treacherous. They obtain much gold from mines. They dress in cloths of good cotton. They are handsome, the women beautiful, and both sexes let their hair go loose. For arms they have swords which they call *alfanjes*,[1] lances, and arrows with blowpipes, blown from the mouth, the dart a *palmo*[2] in length. For defensive arms they have very good cuirasses of cotton. They have bronze guns, and can make gunpowder. They are a warlike people and fight among themselves. They have kings adorned with crowns of gold and stones of great value. They have many pigs and fowls, much rice, and other provisions.

We made sail with a northerly wind and arrived off a cape called Tacabalua, which is in 5°N and 50 leagues from our anchorage. This had taken us three days, when we passed the cape. When we were two leagues south of the cape it blew hard from the north and we shortened sail. Then the wind veered to ENE and we were driven into a bay formed by an island three leagues in circumference. It was inhabited and three leagues from the large island. We wanted to anchor but, on sounding, found no bottom. We shortened sail and went on shore in the boat, the Captain with twelve other men and the fugitive Spaniard as interpreter. We had scarcely landed when about 50 armed men approached us. The interpreter declared to them that we did not come to do them any harm, but only to buy provisions for which we would pay. They were surprised to hear any stranger speak in their language, and said they would go for orders to their king who was about half a league away, and bring back the answer. They came back and said that the king was gouty, but that he was coming though his illness prevented him from moving faster. He arrived with his wives, two daughters and two sons. One of the sons carried arms, a helmet of plumes in one hand, sword and shield in the other. The king sat on some cloths, and the interpreter said to him that a captain from the Emperor of Spain had come, to be their friend and to make peace, without doing them any harm or injury. The king enquired what they wanted. The interpreter replied that the Captain needed provisions and would pay for them. The king said he would give nothing until peace had been made with him but when made he would give what he had. The Captain asked the interpreter what was the custom in making peace. The answer was that blood must be taken from the arm of each, and that they must mutually drink each other's blood.[3] The Captain asked the king to come into the boat as there was no cause for fear. The king said he did not wish to get into the boat, and asked the Captain to come on shore, pointing out that it was quite safe as he had his wife and children with him. The Captain was about to land when he saw that the natives were coming armed, in warlike array. He said that they should not come with arms but without them, as he feared they might kill him or do him some injury. The king said that the Spaniards must not land with arms, as he was ill and could not defend himself. He told them to return to their ships, and that he would send them all the provisions they needed. To this the Captain agreed, and returned to the ship. As the depth of water was so great the ship could not be anchored, and as the wind began to blow from the NW we were forced to make sail and proceed on our voyage without being able to have any further communication with

[1] A curved sword like a scimitar.
[2] A handspan.
[3] See above, pp. 133–4.

the king who was on shore. This day we made good ten leagues. Leaving the bay we passed two islands called Candigar and Sarragana,[1] both inhabited, about half a league apart. Candigar is a high wooded island about three leagues in circumference. The other is low, having some hills of moderate height, and is about four leagues round. They are three leagues from Mindanao, in 4°N.

We reached a port[2] at noon and before anchoring the natives came out to us in a large boat containing twenty persons. They brought with them the two captive Spaniards with their hands tied behind their backs and naked except for a kind of shoes on their feet. These had been in the fleet of the Comendador Loaysa. The boat came alongside and the Spaniards saluted us in our language. They said that they belonged to the fleet of the Comendador, and had been captives for five months. They entreated the Captain, for the love of God, to ransom them and not to leave them in slavery. The Captain answered 'Be assured that though they ask for all I bring, not including the ship, I will not abandon you. Speak to the natives and tell them that I come in the name of the Emperor to establish peace with them, and that I need provisions for which I will pay to their satisfaction.' They returned to the shore, and the ship came to an anchor. Presently the natives came back, bringing the Spaniards with them, and said that, before anything else, to make peace we must drink blood with them. The Captain said that one native must come on board, and one Spaniard would go on shore. This was done, and next day the king came on board and made peace. They then brought us plenty of provisions, fowls, rice, wine of the country, clove and cinnamon, for which we exchanged cloths, and rich garments of New Spain. We were three days at this island, during which we ransomed the two Spaniards for gold of the bulk of 70$ which the Captain paid. The two Spaniards were received on board. They told us that the Spaniards were at an island called Tidore and that they were at war with the Portuguese.

We made sail with a southerly course, the wind North, and proceeded for four days, always seeing inhabited islands, until we came to the to the island of Terrenate where the Portuguese have a fortress. At noon we saw three native row boats bringing five or six Portuguese. One came alongside and saluted us us, asking whence the ship came. We told him we were Spaniards and that we came from New Spain. Without another word they returned to their fortress which was distant ten leagues. In the afternoon of the same day three boats came to us from the city of Gilolo, where the Spaniards of the Comendador Loaysa had a fortress. They came alongside and in each boat there was a Spaniard. They asked us whence the ship came and we replied from New Spain. They did not believe us, saying that we were joking and that we were Portuguese. We told them to look at our flag which bore the Emperor's arms. We assured them that we were Spaniards, and that they should come on board, and have no fear. Having sworn all the oaths that we could think of that we were Spaniards, they still could not believe it. At last one came aboard full of suspicion, and when he was satisfied that we were Spaniards, he called up the other two, who also came on board. The Captain was informed by them that, ten leagues away, the Captain Fernando de la Torre was established with 80 men of the fleet of the Comendador Loaysa. Then one of the Spaniards departed, to announce our arrival to the

---

[1] Lach, *Asia in the Making*, vol. 1, bk II, suggests that C/Sandigar may have been Sampantangu, a point on the southern coast of Mindanao, 7°7′S, 127°55′E. Pulau Serangan, lies 8°43′44″S, 115°13′59″E.

[2] Presumably on Mindanao.

said captain, the other two remaining on board; while the two native boats went to take the news to the king of Gilolo, who was three leagues away from where the ship was.

Next morning a *fusta*[1] and 10 or 12 *coracoras* arrived, which were rowing boats, and they were propelled with oars because it was calm. They came from the island of Terrenate where the Portuguese are, and arrived at our ship. Seeing them coming, the two Spaniards who were aboard told the Captain that they came to seize the ship or else to sink her. They knew them, and these Portuguese had declared that they would not let Spanish ships remain, but would destroy them with their guns, on coming near. They intended to be lord over him, not he over them. The Captain answered that he did not come to fight with anybody, nor to do any harm so long as they did not attack him. Arrived within hail, the Portuguese saluted and asked where the ship came from. We replied that she was from New Spain. The Captain, named Hernando de Vanday, who was in the *fusta*, ordered our captain to come on board his vessel. Our Captain said that the Portuguese might come on board our ship while he went on board the *fusta*, and that they could then talk. The Portuguese insisted that our Captain must come on board the *fusta*, and he answered he would not leave his ship. Our Captain then asked the Portuguese whether there were any Spaniards in that country. The answer was that a Spanish ship arrived about seven or eight months ago, and that she came to the Portuguese fortress, where the Spaniards were given provisions and a cargo of spices, and sent on to Spain. The same would be done now if our Captain would come to the fortress. The Captain told them to go, and that he would follow later. They replied that they would not go unless they brought him with them. Seeing that we did not intend to do what they wanted, they again ordered us to come with them, and declared that our Captain would be responsible for any consequences that might ensue from a refusal. Our Captain answered that if there were no Spaniards in the land he would go with them, but if there were he desired to join his countrymen. The Portuguese answered that there were no Spaniards in all the country. Then one of the two Spaniards on board, named Simon de Vera, cried out 'Why cannot you speak the truth?' When the Portuguese heard that they turned their faces, and ordered the gunner to fire off a cannon that was in the bows. He fired, but it pleased God that nothing should come of it, and the same happened twice.

Seeing what they were trying to do, our Captain ordered our guns to be fired, but, as the *fusta* was small and very close to us, the guns could not be trained on her and no harm was done. At this time a breeze sprang up from the SE and we shaped a course to the port of the city of Gilolo where the Spaniards were, leaving the Portuguese astern. They followed but could not overtake us, and so they continued, firing shots until we reached the port. After we had arrived, the Portuguese returned to their fortress. On their way back they met a vessel with another Portuguese captain on board bringing more help and much artillery. So they again turned upon us, and began to open fire which we returned. It pleased God that they should hit our mainmast more than once, and one ball fell on the deck without hurting any one. They were firing upon us for three or four hours, when a *fusta* came to our help, which had been sent by the Captain Fernando de la Torre. Seeing this the Portuguese fled, returning to their fortress. We had arrived at the port occupied by the people of the Comendador Loaysa, who were under the command of the Captain Fernando de la Torre, a native of Burgos, who had with him 120 men and 24 pieces of

---

[1] A cargo vessel with lateen sails. See above, p. xvii.

artillery, besides the *fusta* which had come to our help.[1] Our Captain and all the crew, numbering about thirty, went on shore and were well received by the Captain and his people, who had been there eight months. They had arrived only with the *capitana*, and the king of Tidore had welcomed them, supplying them with provisions in exchange for their money. This king of Tidore, named Rajamir, received them and helped them in their war with the Portuguese, for he had been ill treated by them because he had favoured the affairs of the Emperor. This was long ago when the Captain Espinosa, with one of the ships of Magellan's fleet, came, and the king of Tidore became favourable to Spanish interests. The Captain Fernando de la Torre lodged us all and treated us very well. We were there two months, careening our ship, and refitting her. On the second day after our arrival the Portuguese came back with their armed vessel and *fusta* to bombard us, but they did us no harm.

At the end of fifteen days they came back again with their *fusta*, intending to bombard our ship when she was hauled up ready to be careened, and believing that the *fusta* of the Captain Fernando de la Torre was not there. They had been told so by a spy they had sent. They came along close to the shore so as to be concealed from us, and to take us by surprise. But our *fusta* had been got ready by one de los Rios, a native of Toledo. He was told that he could not engage them owing to their superiority in artillery, but that he should board them. This he did, killing many of them, including their Captain, named Hernando de Vanday. The rest surrendered, and the *fusta* was brought to our fortress with the crew as prisoners.

The refitting of our ship was completed in the end of May 1528 and, being ready for sea, a Portuguese came from their fortress with a letter to our Captain Alvaro de Sayavedra. It was from Gonzalo Gomez de Acevedo,[2] the captain who had recently arrived with 200 men and 5 ships. On his arrival the Captain Don Jorge de Meneses wanted to attack and destroy us, to which Gonzalo Gomez de Acevedo was opposed. He said that he had his mandate from the King of Portugal, and that he would do all that he was ordered to do, but not what he was not ordered to do. He said, in the letter to Captain Alvaro de Sayavedra, that he wished to arrange an interview, but it did not take effect for many reasons urged by Fernando de la Torre, which hindered it. Seeing that the ship was ready for sea, our Captain determined to embark, and the Captain Fernando de la Torre gave him 60 *quintals* of clove as a cargo, out of what belonged to the Emperor. Being ready to sail, one Simon de Brito, a Portuguese who was there with Fernando de la Torre, of his own free will, said to our Captain that he wished to go with him. As our pilot was dead, and this man said that he was one, and at the request of Fernando de la Torre, our Captain consented. Four other Portuguese, of those who were made prisoners, also joined, and thus we embarked 30 men. We made sail on the 3rd of June 1528.

Our course was ENE for three days with a SW wind, but then we met with calms which continued for 25 or 30 days. We then arrived at an island called 'del Oro' and anchored. This is a large island, well peopled by a black race with woolly hair, who go naked.[3] They have arms of iron and swords. They supplied us with fowls, pigs, rice, and beans. We were there 32 days, owing to the weather not being favourable.

[1] Saavedra's ship arrived at the Spanish fort on Tidore on 30 March 1528.
[2] See above, p. 21.
[3] See above, p. 152, n. 1.

When we were ready to get under way this Simon de Brito, and the four other Portuguese, while our Captain was on shore, took the boat saying they were going to the island. But they stood out to sea, by the way we had come. Deprived of our boat, both those of us who were on board, and those who were on shore were hindered.

When the Captain saw that our boat was gone, he constructed a raft, and reached the ship with those who were with him. He then ordered sail to be made and steered SE 14 leagues when we came to an island. Thence we passed many islands. The inhabitants of one came out for two leagues to shoot arrows at us. They were black, ugly, and naked. We were there for three days and captured three natives, bringing them on board. We passed on to another island where the people were white and bearded. They came out in their canoes with slings and stones, threatening to attack us, and then returned to their island which is in 7°.

Thence we stood to the N and NNW until we were in 14°, where we met with strong contrary winds which forced us to steer a course in the direction whence we came. This brought us to an island which is 380 leagues from Maluco. It is one of the Ladrone Islands. Thence we steered a course which brought us to the island of Mindanao. The part where we reached it is called Bizaya, the name of the inhabitants. Thence we came to Sarragana, where we had left a Spaniard who was ill, when we were there before. Here we anchored and remained for two days, waiting for the natives to come, to give us water and tell us about the Spaniard. They came and told us that the king was not there, and that the Spaniard was with him. They lied for they had sold him. We heard this at Malacca afterwards, from the same Spaniard who was there. His name was Grijalva. As we had no boat, or any means of getting water, and as the natives would not help us, we took a route for the islands of Mehao, twenty leagues from Maluco. Thence we went back to Tidore, whence we had sailed the first time.

There we found Fernando de la Torre with the people he had with him before, and there we anchored again. This was in October 1528. We once more careened the ship, and were employed in this way for six months. Here we found Simon de Brito, and one of the other Portuguese who stole the boat. They had stated that our ship and all her crew had been lost, and that they alone had escaped in the boat. The Captain Fernando de la Torre proceeded against them, and sentenced one to be beheaded and quartered, and the other to be hung. So it was done.

We got underway and left Tidore on the 8th of May 1529, steering ENE, taking the same route as on the former occasion, passing the same islands, and reaching the place where we had seized the three natives. Two of them jumped into the sea. The third remained, and we landed him on the same island whence we had taken him. He had become a Christian and had acquired our language. He had been taught that he might tell the natives what people we were, and that if they would bring us provisions we would pay for them. That we might not have to get the boat out, and as he was ready to swim, the Captain let him swim of his own accord. But the natives of the island killed him in the water, and he cried out to us, but nevertheless they killed him. So we made sail on an ENE course, and, after 250 leagues, we came to some other small islands, all inhabited by brown people, bearded, and naked except for some palm matting.

Four or five natives pulled off in a canoe, and came so near that we could have spoken to them. They made threatening signs and one of them threw a large stone which struck the stern of the ship, splitting the plank. The Captain ordered a musket to be loaded and fired at him, but he was not hit, so they went back to their island[1] and we proceeded on our voyage. These islands are in 7°, a thousand leagues from where we started, and to New Spain another thousand.

Thence we steered NE 18 leagues, and came to some low islands,[2] anchoring near one of them. We then hoisted a flag and six or seven canoes came out and made fast to our bows. The Captain gave them a cloak and a comb, and they, in taking the presents, came on board. There were twenty men and one woman who appeared to be a witch. They brought her to tell them what people we were according to what she could make out from our hands. The Captain treated them well and gave them presents. We made friends insomuch that a Spaniard undertook to go on shore with them, and did so. On landing the chiefs of the land met him, and took him to their houses, which are large and roofed with palm leaves. These people are white, and painted on their arms and bodies. The women are beautiful with long black hair, very graceful and well made. They go barefoot. The men have for arms, staves hardened in the fire, and their food is coconuts and fish. The length of the island is one league. The captain and most of the crew landed, and the men and women came forward to receive them, singing and playing on drums. The Captain sat down with the chief, and among other questions the chief asked what a musket was which he saw. By signs the Captain gave him to understand what it was. The chief asked him to fire it off, and to please him he did so. It caused such terror that all the people fell down, and then to run for shelter of the palm trees. The chief and some others remained, though they were much startled. The chief, and all his people to the number of a thousand souls, got into their canoes and went to an island three leagues off. We remained there without receiving any injury from them. We were eight days at this island owing to the illness of the Captain, during which time the natives came back, and helped us to get 18 barrels of water on board. They gave us 2,000 coconuts, and did everything we asked them. These islands are in 11°N. Thence we continued our voyage, steering north until we reached 26, and here our Captain died. At the time of his end and death he called all the crew, and asked them to navigate as far as 30°N. When there, if the weather was not favourable for returning to New Spain, they were to go back to Tidore, and give up the ship, with everything in it to the Captain Fernando de la Torre that he might do with it what would be best for the service of our Lord the Emperor. He appointed Captain Pedro Laso to succeed him, a native of Toledo, who died at the end of eight days. The master and pilot remained the principal persons on board. We went on until we reached 20°N, always with contrary winds, and as we did not find any weather that would help is there, we were forced to return whence we had come.

From 31° N we shaped a westerly course until we came to an island of the Ladrones, where we anchored. We calculated the distance to the Maluco Islands to be 1,200 leagues, and to New Spain another 1,000 leagues. We were one day at this island getting refreshment, and here we lost an anchor.

Thence we made sail back to Maluco, making for Bisaya which we could not fetch. Passing on we came to the island of Tarao, 120 leagues from Maluco, but we could not

[1] Isla de los Pintadas.
[2] Los Jardines.

176

find bottom, and were obliged to go on to the port of Zamafo, in the island of Gilolo, where we anchored.

We reached this port in the end of October, and found the Captain Fernando de la Torre here who had lost the fortress of Tidore, which had been taken by the Portuguese. We delivered up the ship to him, with all that was on board. The Captain took charge as well of the ship, as of the property of our late Captain.

All the crew of the ship, numbering about 18 men, went on shore. The ship was seen to be destroyed by barnacles. Those Spaniards who were there, had to suffer much owing to the disorder that prevailed. Some made their way to Malacca, others remained at Gilolo. Those who went to Malacca were arrested by the Captain Don Jorge de Castro, who ordered that we should not be allowed to depart from there until two years and a half. Of twenty of our men who arrived there, no more than nine escaped, when at last the king of Portugal ordered that we should be allowed to go. The author of this narrative is Vicencio of Naples, who left New Spain in the said fleet, went through all that has been described, reached Lisbon, and from thence came to. Spain. He was at the Court of His Majesty, and gave an account of the whole voyage. He asked for help in his work, and they ordered him to receive 14 ducats. These were the mercies of the Council. All the accounts, reports, and charts of this navigation were seized by Nuño de Acuna, Governor of India, because Fernando de la Torre had remained in his power.[1]

The man named Grijalva, already mentioned, who had been left on an island and forgotten, met with the following destiny.

At the time when we were making our voyage to the islands of Maluco, we arrived at the island of Sarragan, which is in the archipelago, and some 120 leagues from Maluco. Off this island we anchored, and were bargaining with the natives for three days, buying fowls, pigs, and rice, which were plentiful. This Grijalva was then so ill that it was thought he could not recover. He requested the Captain that, as he was about to die, he might be allowed to remain on that island. Seeing that he was very ill, the Captain left him in charge the governor of that island, requesting that he might be well treated and cured. The natives promised that they would do so, and the ship sailed without him.

This Spaniard was on the island for eight months, when the governor of it sold him to the king of the island of Mindanao. There were two other Spaniards at Mindanao, of those who had been lost in the fleet of the Comendador Loaysa. This became known in Malacca, and the Governor, Garcia de Sá, wrote to the king of Borneo that three Spaniards who were in his power, on that island, were to be sent to Malacca. The king spoke to the Spaniards, saying that they had been sent for from Malacca. If they feared to go there he said that he would not send them, but if they wished to go, he would give them the means of doing so. The distance from that island to Malacca is 200 leagues. The Spaniards chose to be taken there and we saw them in Malacca, and received this account from them.

This island of Borneo is more than 120 leagues in circumference. In it there are Moors and Gentiles who, make war with each other. They are friends with the Portuguese, but do not contribute anything beyond the trade with them in camphor, of which they have quantities, and slaves whom they sell.

---

[1] A different version of the author's report presented at the court in Madrid in 1534, likely to the Consejo de Indias, can be found in Navarrete, *Colección de los Viajes*, vol. V, pp. 476–86. The report translated here by Clements Markham clearly postdates it, since Nápoli refers to his previous presentation at the royal court.

BIBLIOGRAPHY

PRIMARY SOURCES

Manuscript Sources

Sevilla, Archivo General de las Indias
Indiferente General 422, L. 15, F, 121v (2)
                 L. 16, ff. 123r–125v
Patronato, L. 37, Ramo 3
               Ramo 27
        L. 38, Ramo 7
        L. 43, N 2, Ramo 11

Printed Primary Sources

Blair, E. H. and Robertson, J. A., trans. and eds, *The Philippine Islands, 1493–1898*, vol. XXXIV, Cleveland, OH, 1903–9.

Campbell, Richard J., Bradley, Peter T., and Lorimer, Joyce, *The Voyage of Captain John Narbrough, to the Strait of Magellan, and the South Sea in His Majesty's Ship* Sweepstakes, *1669–1671*, Hakluyt Society, 3rd ser., 33, London, 2018.

Isidore of Seville, *Etymologies* (*c*.616 CE), trans. and ed. Stephen A. Barney, W. J. Lewis, J. A. Beach, and Oliver Berghof, Cambridge, 2006.

Herrara y Tordesillas, Antonio de, *Historia general de los hechos de los castellanos en las islas, y tierra firme de el Mar Océano*, eight decades in five volumes, Madrid, Imprenta Real de N. Rodríguez Franco, 1726–28.

Markham, Sir Clements, ed., *Early Spanish Voyages to the Strait of Magellan*, Hakluyt Society, 2nd ser., 28, London, 1911.

Mártir de Anglería, Pedro, *Décadas del Nuevo Mundo*, Madrid, 1989.

Navarrete, Martín Fernández de, ed., *Expediciones al Maluco*, in *Colección de los viages y descubrimientos, que Hicieron por Mar los Españoles desde el fines del siglo XV*, vol. V, Madrid, 1837.

Oviedo y Valdés, Gonzalo Fernández de, *Historia General y Natural de las Indias*, Part II, Bk XX, Valladolid, 1557.

—, ed. J. Pérez de Tudela y Bueso, in *Biblioteca de Autores Españoles*, vols 117, 118, Madrid, 1959.

—, *Misfortunes and Shipwrecks in the Seas of the Indies, Islands, and Mainland of the Ocean Sea* (*1513–1548*): *Book Fifty of the General and Natural History of the Indies*, trans. and ed. Glen F. Dille, Gainesville, FL, 2011.

Pigafetta, Antonio, *The First Voyage Around the World* (*1519–1522*): *An Account of Magellan's Expedition*, ed. Theodore J. Cachey Jr, Toronto, 2007.

—, *The First Voyage Around the World by Magellan: Translated from the Accounts of Pigafetta and Other Contemporary Writers*, ed. Henry Edward John Stanley, Cambridge, 2010.

—, *Magellan's Voyage: A Narrative Account of the First Circumnavigation*, trans. and ed. R. A. Skelton, New Haven, CT, 1969.

Pliny the Elder, *Natural History*, Bks XXI–XXIV, trans. and ed. W. H. S. Jones, in Loeb Classical Library, vol. VI, Cambridge, MA, 1951.

Seixas y Lovera, Francisco de, *Descripcion geographica y derrotero de la Region austral Magallanica*, Madrid, 1690.

SECONDARY SOURCES

Abdurachman, Parmita R., 'Niachile Pokaraga: A Sad Story of a Moluccan Queen', *Asian Studies in Honour of Professor Charles Boxer*, special issue, *Modern Asian Studies*, 22.3, 1988, pp. 571–92.

Amich, Julián, *Diccionario marítimo*, Barcelona, 2003.

Andaya, Leonard Y, 'Los primeros contactos de los españoles con el mundo de las Molucas en las Islas de las Especias', *Revista Española del Pacífico*, 2, 1992, pp. 61–85.

—, *The World of Maluku*, Honolulu, 1993.

Argensola, Bartolome Leonardo de, *Conquista de las islas Malucas: al Rey Felipe Tercero, Nuestro Señor*, Zaragoza, 1891. Facsimile reprint.

Arteche, José de, *Urdaneta: El domador de los espacios del Océano Pacífico*, Madrid, 1943.

Ballantyne, Tony, ed., *Science, Empire and the European Exploration of the Pacific*, London, 2004.

Barros, João de, *Da Asia de João de Barros e de Diogo de Couto*, Lisbon, 1778.

Bergreen, Laurence, *Magellan: Over the Edge of the World*, New York, 2003.

—, *Columbus: The Four Voyages 1492–1504*, New York, 2012.

Black, Jeremy, *Maps and History: Constructing Images of the Past*, New Haven, CT, 1997.

Blackmore, Josiah, *Manifest Perdition: Shipwreck Narrative and the Disruption of Empire*, Minneapolis, 2002.

Bolaños, Alvaro Félix, 'The Historian and the Hesperides: Fernández de Oviedo and the Limitations of Imitation', *Bulletin of Hispanic Studies*, 72.3, 1995, pp. 273–88.

—, 'Panegírico y libelo del primer cronista de Indias: Gonzalo Fernández de Oviedo', *Thesarus: Boletín del Instituto Caro y Cuervo*, 45.3, 1990, pp. 577–649.

Boorstin, Daniel J., *The Discoverers: A History of Man's Search to Know His World and Himself*, New York, 1985.

Borrero, Luis, 'The Origins of Ethnographic Subsistence Patterns in Fuego-Patagonia', in Colin McEwan, Luis A. Borrero, and Alfredo Prieto, eds, *Patagonia*, pp. 60–81.

Boyajian, James C., *Portuguese Trade in Asia under the Habsburgs, 1580–1640*, Baltimore, MD, 1993.

Boxer, C.R. *The Portuguese Seaborn Empire: 1415–1825*, New York, 1969.

—, 'Some Portuguese Sources for Indonesian Historiography', in Soedjatmoko, ed., *An introduction to Indonesian Historiography*, Ithaca, NY, 2007, pp. 217–33.

Braudel, Fernand, *The Mediterranean and the Mediterranean World in the Age of Philip II*, New York, 1972.

Brokaw, Galen, 'Ambivalence, Mimicry, and Stereotype in Fernández de Oviedo's *Historia General y Natural de las Indias*: Colonial Discourse and the Caribbean *Areíto*', *New Centennial Review*, 5.3, 2005, pp. 143–65.

Brown, Lloyd A., *The Story of Maps*, Boston, 1949.

Brown, Stephen R., *1494: How a Family Feud in Medieval Spain Divided the World in Half*, New York, 2011.

Brotton, Jerry, *A History of the World in 12 Maps*, New York, 2013.

Cambridge History of Islam: The Indian Sub-Continent, South-East Asia, Africa and the Muslim West, vol. 2A, ed. P. M. Holt, A. K. S. Lambton, and B. Lewis, Cambridge, 1980.

Carillo, Jesús, 'The *Historia General y Natural de las Indias* by Gonzalo Fernández de Oviedo', *Huntington Library Quarterly*, 65, 2002, pp. 321–44.

—, 'Oviedo on Columbus', *Repertorium Columbianum*, vol. IX, 2000, pp. 9–35.

Casaban, Jose Luis, 'Outfitting and Sailing of Early Sixteenth-Century Vessels in the Pacific: The Loaysa and Saavedra expeditions (1525–36)'. Paper presented at the Asia Pacific Regional Conference on Underwater Cultural Heritage, Honolulu, May 2014.

Chaplin, Joyce E., *Round about the Earth: Circumnavigation from Magellan to Orbit*, New York, 2012.

Clayton, Lawrence A., *Bartolomé de las Casas: A Biography*, Cambridge, 2012.

Cliff, Nigel, *Holy War: How Vasco da Gama's Epic Voyages Turned the Tide in a Centuries-Old Clash of Civilizations*, New York, 2011.

Coello de la Rosa, Alexandre, 'Héroes y villanos del Nuevo Mundo en la *Historia General y natural de las Indias* de Gonzalo Fernández de Oviedo y Valdés', *Anuario de Estudios Americanos*, 61.2, 2004, pp. 599–618.

Columbus, Ferdinand, *The Life of the Admiral Christopher Columbus by his Son Ferdinand*, trans. and ed. Benjamin Keen, New Brunswick, NJ, 1959.

Corn, Charles, *The Scents of Eden: A Narrative of the Spice Trade*, New York, 1998.

Crofton, Richard Hayes, *A Pageant of the Spice Islands*, London, 1936.

Crowley, Roger, *Conquerors: How Portugal Forged the First Global Empire*, New York, 2015.

Cuevas, P. Mariano, SJ, *Monje y marino: La vida y los tiempos de Fray Andrés de Urdaneta*, Mexico, 1943.

Davies, Arthur, 'Columbus Divides the World', *Geographical Journal*, 133.3, 1967, pp. 337–44.

Detienne, Marcel, *The Gardens of Adonis: Spices in Greek Mythology*, Princeton, NJ, 1977.

Dille, Glen F., trans and ed., *Writing from the Edge of the World: The Memoirs of Darién, 1514–1527*, Tuscaloosa, 2006.

Disney, A. R., *Portuguese Empire*, vol. I, *From Beginnings to 1807*, Cambridge, 2012.

Donkin, R. A., *Between East and West*, Philadelphia, 2003.

Dunn, Oliver and James E. Keller, Jr, transcr, and trans., *The* Diario *of Christopher Columbus's First Voyage to America 1492–1493 Abstracted by Fray Bartolomé de las Casas*, Norman, OK, 1988.

Duviols Jean-Paul, 'The Patagonian "Giants"', in Colin McEwan, Luis A. Borrero, and Alfredo Prieto, eds, *Patagonia*, pp. 127–39.

Ellen, R. F., 'Conundrums about Panjandrums: On the Use of Titles in the Relations of Political Subordination in the Moluccas and along the Papuan Coast', *Indonesia*, 41, 1986, pp. 46–62.

Fernández-Armesto, Felipe, *Columbus*, Oxford, 1991.

—, *The Times Atlas of World Exploration*, New York, 1991.

—, *Columbus and the Conquest of the Impossible*, London, 2000.

—, *Civilization: Culture, Ambition, and the Transformation of Nature*, New York, 2001.

—, *Amerigo: The Man Who Gave his Name to America*, New York, 2007.

—, *1492: The Year the World Began*, New York, 2009.

Gerbi, Antonello, *Nature in the New World: From Chistopher Columbus to Gonzalo Fernández de Oviedo*, trans. Jeremy Moyle, Pittsburgh, 1985.

Goodwin, Robert, *Spain: The Centre of the World 1519–1682*, New York, 2015.

Haddon, A. C., 'The Outriggers of Indonesian Canoes', *Journal of the Royal Anthropological Institute of Great Britain and Ireland*, 50, 1920, pp. 69–134.

Hall, Kenneth R., 'Local and International Trade and Traders in the Straits of Melaka Region: 600–1500', *Journal of the Economic and Social History of the Orient*, 47, 2004, pp. 213–60.

Hernandez, M., Garcia-Moro, C., and Lalueza-Fox, C., 'Brief Communication: Stature Estimation in Extinct Aónikenk and the Myth of Patagonian Gigantism', *American Journal of Physical Anthropology*, 10, 1998, pp. 545–51.

Homenaje a Gonzalo Fernández de Oviedo en el IV centenaio de su muerte, Madrid, 1957.

Hourani, George F. and Carswell, John, *Arab Seafaring in the Indian Ocean in Ancient and Early Medieval Times*, Princeton, NJ, 1995.

Joyner, Tim, *Magellan*, Camden, ME, 1992.

Kathirithamby-Wells, J. and Villiers, John, *The Southeast Asian Port and Polity: Rise and Demise*, Singapore, 1990.

Keay, John, *The Spice Route: A History*, Berkeley, CA, 2006.

Kelsey, Harry. 'Finding the Way Home: Spanish Exploration of the Round-Trip Route across the Pacific Ocean', *Western Historical Quarterly*, 17.2, 1986, pp. 145–64.

—, *The First Circumnavigators: Unsung Heroes of the Age of Discovery*, New Haven, CT, 2016.

Lach, Donald F., *Southeast Asia in the Eyes of Europe: The Sixteenth Century*, Chicago, 1968.

Lach, Donald F. and Van Kley, Edwin J., *Asia in the Making of Europe*, vol. III, *A Century of Advance*, Chicago and London, 1993.

Lester, Toby, *The Fourth Part of the World*, New York, 2010.

Levathes, Louise, *When China Ruled the Seas: The Treasure Fleet of the Dragon Throne, 1405–1433*, New York, 1994.

Levesque, Rodrigue, *A History of Micronesia*, vol. I, Honolulu, 1994.

Manning, Patrick and Owen, Abigail, eds, *Knowledge in Translation: Global Patterns of Scientific Exchange 1000–1800 CE*, Pittsburgh, 2018.

Mariano Cuevas, P. *Monje y marino: La vida y los tiempos de Fray Andrés de Urdaneta*, Mexico, 1943.

Martinic Berros, Mateo, 'The Meeting of Two Cultures: Indians and Colonists in the Magellan Region', in Colin McEwan, Luis A. Borrero, and Alfredo Prieto, eds, *Patagonia*, pp. 110–26.

McEwan, Colin, Borrero, Luis A., and Prieto, Alfredo, eds, *Patagonia: Natural History, Prehistory and Ethnography at the Uttermost End of the Earth*, Princeton, NJ, 1997.

Mena García, María del Carmen, *Sevilla y las flotas de Indias: la gran armada de Castilla del Oro (1513–1514)*, Seville, 1998.

Miguel Bosch, José Ramón de, 'Andrés de Urdaneta y el tornaviaje', at http://www.euskonews.com.

Miller, J. Innes, *The Spice Trade of the Roman Empire: 29 B.C. to A.D. 641*, Oxford: 1969.

Mitchell, Mairin, *Friar Andrés de Urdaneta, OSA*, London 1964.

Morison, Samuel Eliot, *Admiral of the Ocean Sea: A Life of Christopher Columbus*, 2 vols, Boston, 1942.

—, *The European Discovery of America: Southern Voyages 1496–1616*, New York, 1974.

Myers, Kathleen Ann, *Fernández de Oviedo's Chronicle of America: A New history for a new World*, Austin, TX, 2007.

Nowell, Charles E., 'The Loaisa Expedition and the Ownership of the Moluccas', *Pacific Historical Review*, 5.4, 1936, pp.325–36.

—, 'The Discovery of the Pacific: A Suggested Change of Approach', *Pacific Historical Review*, 16.1, 1947, pp. 1–10.

—, 'Arrellano versus Urdaneta', *Pacific Historical Review*, 31.2, 1962, pp. 111–20.

Nunn, George E., 'Magellan's Route in the Pacific.' *Geographical Review*, 2.44, 1934, pp. 615–33.

Oxford Companion to Ships and the Sea, ed. I. C. B. Dear and Peter Kemp, eds, New York, 2016.

Oyarzun Iñarra, Javier. *Expediciones españoles al estrecho de Magallanes y Tierra del Fuego*, Madrid, 1999.

Parr, Charles McKew, *So Noble a Captain: The Life and Times of Ferdinand Magellan*, New York, 1953.

Parry, J. H., *The Discovery of America*, New York, 1979.

Pepperell, Julian, *Fishes of the Open Sea: A Natural History and Illustrated Guide*, Chicago and London, 2010.

Pérez de Tudela Bueso, Juan, 'Vida y escritos de Gonzalo Fernández de Oviedo', in *Historia general y natural de las Indias, Biblioteca de autores españoles [BAE]*, vol. 117, pp. vii–clxxv, Madrid, 1959.

Pérez-Mallaína, Pablo E., *Spain's Men of the Sea: Daily Life on the Indies Fleets in the Sixteenth Century*, trans. Carla Rahn Phillips, Baltimore, MD, 1998.

Phillips, Carla Rahn. 'The Growth and Composition of Trade in the Iberian Empires, 1450–1750', in James D. Tracy, ed., *The Rise of Merchant Empires, Long Distance Trade in the Early Modern World, 1350–1750*, Cambridge, 1990, pp. 24–101.

—, *Six Galleons for the King of Spain: Imperial Defense in the Early Seventeenth Century*, Baltimore, MD, 1992.

Preus, Antony, *Historical Dictionary of Ancient Greek Philosophy*, Lanham, MD, 2015.

Quimby, Frank, 'The Hierro Commerce: Culture Contact, Appropriation and Colonial Entanglement in the Marianas 1521–68', *Journal of Pacific History*, 46.1, 2011, pp. 1–26.

Russell, Peter, *Prince Henry 'the Navigator': A Life*, New Haven, CT, 2000.

Schurz, William Lytle, *The Manila Galleon*, New York, 1959.

Sobel, Dava and Andrewes, William J. H., *The Illustrated Longitude: The True Story of a Lone Genius Who Solved the Greatest Scientific Problem of His Time*, New York, 1998.

Sollewijn Gelpke, J. H. F., 'On the Origin of the Name Papua', *Bijdragen tot de Taal-, Land- en Volkenkunde*, 149.2, 1993, pp. 318–32.

Spate, O. H. K., *The Spanish Lake; The Pacific since Magellan*, vol. I, Canberra, e-book, 2004.

Subrahmanyam, Sanjay. *The Career and Legend of Vasco da Gama*, Cambridge, 1997.

—, *The Portuguese Empire in Asia 1500–1700: A Political and Economic History*, New York, 1993.

Thomas, Hugh, *Rivers of Gold: The Rise of the Spanish Empire, from Columbus to Magellan*, New York, 2003.

—, *Who's Who of the Conquistadors*, London, 2000.

Torodash, Martin, 'Magellan Historiography' *Hispanic American Historical Review*, 51.2, 1971, pp. 313–35.

Tracey, James D., *The Rise of Merchant Empires: Long-Distance Trade in the Early Modern World, 1350–1750*, Cambridge, 1990.

Turner, Daymond. 'The Aborted First Printing of the Second Part of Oviedo's *General and Natural History of the Indies*', *Huntington Library Quarterly*, 46, 1983, pp. 105–25.

—, 'Forgotten Treasure from the Indies: The Illustrations and Drawings of Fernández de Oviedo', *Huntington Library Quarterly*, 48, 1985, pp. 1–46.

—, '*Gonzalo Fernández de Oviedo y Valdés: An Annotated Bibliography*', University of North Carolina Studies in the Romance Languages and Literatures, no. 66, Chapel Hill, 1966.

Villiers, John. 'Trade and Society in the Banda Islands in the Sixteenth Century', *Modern Asian Studies*, 15.4, 1981, pp. 723–50.

Volo, Dorothy D. and Volo, James M., *Daily Life in the Age of Sail*, Westport, CT, 2002.

Wey Gómez, Nicolás, *The Tropics of Empire: Why Columbus Sailed South to the Indies*, Cambridge, MA, 2008.

Wright, Ione Stuessy, 'The First American Voyage across the Pacific, 1527–1528: The Voyage of Alvaro de Saavedra Cerón', *Geographical Review*, 29.3, 1939, pp. 472–82.

INDEX